Who Travels with the Doctor?

Who Travels with the Doctor?

Essays on the Companions *of* Doctor Who

Edited by GILLIAN I. LEITCH *and* SHERRY GINN

McFarland & Company, Inc., Publishers
Jefferson, North Carolina

ALSO OF INTEREST AND FROM MCFARLAND

Doctor Who in Time and Space: Essays on Themes, Characters, History and Fandom, 1963–2012 (2013), edited by Gillian I. Leitch

The Multiple Worlds of Fringe: *Essays on the J.J. Abrams Science Fiction Series* (2014), edited by Tanya R. Cochran, Sherry Ginn and Paul Zinder

The essay by Sherry Ginn uses portions of her essay from *Doctor Who in Time and Space* by permission of McFarland & Company, Inc., Publishers.

LIBRARY OF CONGRESS CATALOGUING-IN-PUBLICATION DATA

Names: Leitch, Gillian I., 1967– editor. | Ginn, Sherry editor.
Title: Who travels with the doctor? : essays on the companions of Doctor Who / edited by Gillian I. Leitch and Sherry Ginn.
Description: Jefferson, North Carolina : McFarland & Company, Inc., Publishers, 2016. | Includes filmography. | Includes bibliographical references and index.
Identifiers: LCCN 2016011763 | ISBN 9780786495252 (softcover : acid free paper) ∞
Subjects: LCSH: Doctor Who (Television program : 1963–1989) | Doctor Who (Television program : 2005–) | Characters and characteristics on television.
Classification: LCC PN1992.77.D6273 W57 2016 | DDC 791.45/72—dc23
LC record available at https://lccn.loc.gov/2016011763

BRITISH LIBRARY CATALOGUING DATA ARE AVAILABLE

ISBN (print) 978-0-7864-9525-2
ISBN (ebook)978-1-4766-2412-9

© 2016 Gillian I. Leitch and Sherry Ginn. All rights reserved

No part of this book may be reproduced or transmitted in any form or by any means, electronic or mechanical, including photocopying or recording, or by any information storage and retrieval system, without permission in writing from the publisher.

Front cover: Amy Pond (Karen Gillan), companion of the eleventh Doctor (Matt Smith) from the 2010 series of *Doctor Who* (BBC/Photofest)

Printed in the United States of America

McFarland & Company, Inc., Publishers
  Box 611, Jefferson, North Carolina 28640
  www.mcfarlandpub.com

This book is dedicated to Sherry's brother,
Neal (Freddie C. Ginn, 1956–2015),
who did not live to see it completed.

Acknowledgments

Having the opportunity to write about *Doctor Who* is perhaps the fan's ultimate dream, aside from actually being a companion on the series itself. I want to thank everyone who has made this book possible, most of all my co-editor Sherry. To our contributors, I am sincerely grateful for their hard work and patience. I am living the dream, really. Now, if they need a new companion....—Gillian I. Leitch

I believe my dedication says it all—this has been a very distressing year. I really appreciate the support I have received from my friends during this difficult time. Thanks to all of our contributors for being so understanding about the delays. Thanks to Gillian for co-editing another book with me and for our ultimate fan experience at this year's Ottawa Comiccon: Rose Tyler and Lt. Commander Uhura. This book is for all Whovians out there—whether from the classic era or the new. There are so many companions who need study—why not take on the job? By the way, my favorite companions are Donna Noble, Sarah Jane Smith, and River Song.—Sherry Ginn

Table of Contents

Acknowledgments vi

Introduction—Comrade, Confidante, Companion, Chum: A Friend by Any Other Name
    SHERRY GINN AND GILLIAN I. LEITCH 1

With Whom He Travels: The Companions of the Doctor
    GILLIAN I. LEITCH 9

"It's bigger on the inside": Verisimilitude and Companion Reactions to the TARDIS
    CRAIG OWEN JONES 26

"The battle-scarred, the insane, the ones even you can't control": Disability and the Female Bodies of the Doctor's Companions
    KIMBERLEY MCMAHON-COLEMAN 37

"There's nothing *only* about being a girl": Learning to "Play" the Doctor's Companion
    DAVID BOARDER GILES *and* AMY PELOFF 52

Life Post–TARDIS? The Case for Jo Grant and Sarah Jane Smith
    SHERRY GINN 69

Rose *Is* England: Nationhood, British Invasion Anxiety and Why the Doctor Will (Almost) Always Rescue His Companions
    TANJA NATHANAEL 79

Rory Williams: The Boy Who Waited
    Teresa Forde   91

A Muted Melody: The (Dis)Empowerment of River Song
    Tom Powers   106

Companions Who Weren't: The Pompadour and the Pauper
    Pamela Achenbach   123

When No One Can Hear You Scream: *Doctor Who*
    Companions on the Printed Page
    Aaron John Gulyas   135

Selected Filmography   151

Selected Bibliography   157

About the Contributors   165

Index   167

Introduction—Comrade, Confidante, Companion, Chum
A Friend by Any Other Name

SHERRY GINN *and* GILLIAN I. LEITCH

> *In 900 years of time and space, I've never met anyone who wasn't important.*—The Doctor, "A Christmas Carol," 2010

When reading a novel or short story, one is privy to the thoughts, emotions, and motives of the characters therein. Along with the plot elements, the author—either as a third-person observer or as the first-person narrator—provides the reader with the information necessary to understand what is happening and why. A good author plays fair with the reader; in detective fiction the reader is provided with the clues necessary to solve the mystery. Similarly, enough information is provided in other genres for the reader to participate in the events in question.

However, drama is entirely different. In a live performance the audience is not privy to the characters' inner-workings. In order to provide such information to the audience, characters engage in exposition about events that have occurred prior to the present story-time. In this way the audience is aware of events that have occurred beyond its immediate awareness and is informed of what is happening along with the characters in the drama. They can passively observe the events as they unfold, or they can participate actively and perhaps solve the mystery before those on screen do. Television has used these narrative forms in many series with recurring characters, at least one of whom is considered the "main" character and another who is the "sidekick." Famous couples of this type include Starsky and Hutch, Cagney and Lacey, Crockett and Tubbs, and McGarrett and Danno. Within the science fiction and fantasy universe these include Batman and Robin, Kirk and Spock, Buffy and the Scoobies.

2   Introduction

Perhaps the most developed of the sidekicks is Dr. John Watson, who in literature and in film and television adaptations of Sherlock Holmes, is used to forward both the mystery in play and the understanding of the character Sherlock Holmes. As P. D. James stated, "writers obviously felt the need to have a character to whom the detective could communicate, however slightly, the progress of his investigation, as much for the reader's benefit as for his own."[1] Watson was the ultimate sidekick, acting as narrator in the written works, and gateway character in the performed adaptations. Sherlock Holmes, the enigmatic detective, is viewed through the eyes of Watson, and the clues to the evitable mystery are presented to him and the audience to interpret.

Doctor Who is a great deal like a detective mystery and the companion much like Watson. Each adventure is a bit of a mystery: Where are they? What is going on? How can this be resolved? Each episode takes place in a different time and place. The story then requires a narrative trick for the audience to understand the circumstances, and the source of dramatic tension in the adventure. The Doctor is expected to fix things, but it is through the companion that scene is set, and a great deal of the answers are generated. The companion gets into the situation and interprets the events much as the audience does, and the Doctor—enigmatic like Sherlock Holmes—solves the problems as they arrive. This can vary from saving the companion from certain death (preceded by a great deal of screaming) or having the companion assist them as they find a solution, usually scientific, to defeat an enemy or save a people.

For *Doctor Who*, the sidekicks are essential to the story, and include the numerous companions who have traveled with the Doctor for the past 50 years. As Malcolm Hulke and Terrance Dicks wrote in 1972:

> [H]eroes on television must have someone to talk to. This is known as "the confidant," a person to whom things can be explained. In this way, the audience can be told what is going on. So the Doctor had to have companions. The creators of the idea, [Sydney] Newman and [Donald] Wilson, decided that by various means the Doctor should pick up young companions on his journeys, but that of course later he should always try to get them back to the place and the time where he first met them.[2]

The companions' job was to serve as a stand-in for the audience, to query the Doctor as to what was happening, and to be suitably impressed by the wonders of the universe and the Doctor's brilliance (not necessarily in that order). Nevertheless the companions' job has changed over the years, and it can be argued that the companions of new *Who* have a much more difficult job than those of classic *Who*. Russell T. Davies believes that the companions make the show more accessible to the public. Companions in the New *Who* are far more developed than those in the classic series: they have real lives, jobs, friends and families; they come from a world with which we can all identify.[3]

While the Doctor is a permanent fixture of the narrative, the companions change. Over the run of the series, the Doctor has been joined by more than 43 different companions. They stay for a while, and then they leave. Katy Manning, who played companion Jo Grant (1971–1973) for the third Doctor, thinks that a companion should change after 3 seasons, as a new companion keeps the show fresh and changes the dynamics of the relationship between the companion and the Doctor.[4] David Tennant (who played the 10th Doctor from 2005–2010) believes that the Doctor cannot be seen to change too much, so the possibility of a different companion offers a way to show different aspects of his personality.[5] Executive Producer Davies thinks switching companions causes the Doctor to change and to grow.[6]

Doctor Who broadcast its first episode in November 1963 and enjoyed a continuous run in the UK until 1989. Soon after its first appearance it was sent to other Commonwealth countries, airing in New Zealand in 1964 on NZBC and Australia in 1965 (ABC). Canadian audiences first saw it on CBC in 1965, but it aired only for one year, to return in 1976 on TVOntario. American audiences first gained access to the series in the 1970s when the series broadcast on Public Television rather than the various network stations. After a 16-year hiatus Russell T. Davies re-booted the series in 2005 to much critical acclaim. It boasts a huge worldwide audience.

During its hiatus, the Doctor continued to have various adventures (one of which was the "Time War"), of which we do not learn the details until 2014. Prior to 1989, the men and women who traveled with the Doctor could be termed as assistants as well as companions because many of them were apparently not welcomed or even liked by the Doctor. Some, such as Liz Shaw or Romana, were assigned to him to assist. Some traveled with him under a pretext, such as Turlough or Kamelion. Others actually liked him and considered him a friend, as he did them. However, after the reboot in 2005, many of the companions seem to be less a comrade and confidante and more a caregiver, someone who must keep an increasingly dangerous Doctor from harming himself and others.

Exactly Who Can Be a Companion?

As noted by many others (such as Frankham-Allen) over the past 50 years it has not been easy to define a companion. Should anyone who has traveled with the Doctor be considered a companion? What about those men and women whose travels are not recorded on television, but rather in the novels and audio-books? What makes a companion or an assistant, as these beings were once called? Prior to the beginning of the eighth season of the new series, Peter Davison, the fifth Doctor, asked, "What makes the Perfect Companion?" in a study of the "Ultimate Companion," but he failed to ask what made a companion in the first place. Every adventure features the Doctor working with others to achieve some goal, or to work through some problem. What signals that character as different from the rest, and one who is a companion?

The Doctor never works alone, even when he does not travel with a companion in the TARDIS—as did the fourth Doctor in "The Deadly Assassin" or the tenth Doctor during the specials that aired between 2008 and 2010. Though technically alone, he has someone who acts as an assistant, helping him as he navigates new places and circumstances. These characters, whether temporary or more permanent within the series, are essential to the *Doctor Who* narrative.

Is there a particular reason why the companions are primarily female? Of the 40-odd companions who have traveled with the Doctor, only 7 have been male. Notwithstanding the long tradition of "buddy" films and television series, the Doctor rarely has a buddy, although one could argue that role for Jamie McCrimmon and Brigadier Lethbridge-Stewart. Instead, the Doctor travels most often with female companions, usually human, who occasionally bring along a male (boy)friend (e.g., Mickey Smith, Rory Williams) and that occurs mostly in the new series.

If one believes the mythology of the series' production, it was not really created for children but rather to appeal to a younger audience while slipping in material adults would "get." Because children watched with their parents—typically their fathers—the series' producers added things that would appeal to the dads: young, good-looking women in short skirts. Children would hide behind the sofa whenever scary monsters appeared on screen. Such notions reinforced the stereotype that boys were interested in science fiction and girls were not. However, by 2005 the writers and producers of new *Who* had learned that girls (and women) did enjoy science fiction. Unfortunately, they also assumed that those of the female persuasion liked romance and story lines in the rebooted series played on that stereotype. Thus early companions like Rose Tyler and Martha Jones harbored serious romantic feelings for the Doctor, while later ones, such as Amy Pond and Clara Oswin Oswald, were torn between their feelings for the Doctor and the men in their lives.

Although these types of stories appealed to some of the audience, many others were disappointed, especially when the female companions were stripped of their agency by all of that romance.[7] For example, Martha Jones was a medical doctor in her residency when she met the Doctor. But her intelligence and status as an MD was undermined throughout her tenure with the Doctor because she was continually played as lovelorn and depressed, knowing the Doctor loved someone else and could never love her. Donna Noble, who had no romantic feelings for the Doctor, was nevertheless stripped of everything she learned during her travels with the Doctor and returned to Earth with no memory of how she had grown as a human being and a woman. And, Amy and Clara are so enamored of the Doctor that they have difficulty seeing the men who love them and who can never compete against the brilliant Doctor and his TARDIS.

"The universe is big. It's vast and complicated and ridiculous."[8]

One important question one must also ask about the companion is, what does the Companion get from travel with the Doctor? Oh, not just adventure and time and space, but something beyond the Doctor? Some[9] have argued that travel with the Doctor actually harms the companion, and he or she is never the same again—some of them even die (see, e.g., Britton, Porter). Others have argued that traveling with the Doctor teaches the companion about the wonders of the universe of course, but also about their own strengths as human individuals (see, e.g., Chapman). And, the companions help the Doctor. This is especially true in the new *Who*, where we have various incarnations of the Doctor who are experiencing what can only be regarded as Post-Traumatic Stress Disorder (PTSD). Essays in this collection will argue for these points. Although the majority of essays are about the new series, the classic series is also represented.

The collection begins with an essay by Gillian I. Leitch entitled "With Whom He Travels: The Companions of the Doctor." Leitch explores the various companions who have traveled with the Doctor throughout the series. She examines each in terms of his or her characteristics to determine what works and what does not work with respect to such travel. In addition, she compares results of a survey she conducted concerning fans' ratings of the various companions and contrasts this to surveys conducted by others.

Craig Owen Jones explores how the new series' change to an episodic rather than a serial format leaves little time for the traditional role of the companion: someone to ask the Doctor what is happening and then have him explain. Jones' essay, "'It's bigger on the inside': Verisimilitude and Companion Reactions to the TARDIS," explores the increasingly frenetic pace of new *Who*, noting that it is not only the audience who is caught up in this pace but the companion as well. No longer given the time to comprehend the wonder of the Doctor's alienness or his mysterious blue box, there is but a "moment" to figure out what is happening.[10]

Kimberley McMahon-Coleman's essay entitled "'The battle-scarred, the insane, the ones even you can't control': Disability and the Female Bodies of the Doctor's Companions" examines companions in new *Who*, particularly in the Moffat era. McMahon-Coleman notes that problems of disability are conflated with gender: female companions suffer disproportionately from maladies ranging from infertility to mental illness and instability. Like Lynnette Porter, McMahon-Coleman proposes that the companion is often worse off for travelling with the Doctor.

In one essay about the classic series, David Boarder Giles and Amy Peloff explore Sarah Jane Smith's tenure with the Doctor in "'There's nothing *only* about being a girl': Learning to 'Play' the Doctor's Companion." Relying upon episodes featuring Sarah Jane along with Elisabeth Sladen's memories of her time in the series, Giles and Peloff explore how Sladen's portrayal of Sarah Jane re-invented the companion into a woman with more character than a simple sounding board. Nevertheless Sladen and other female actors who played the Doctor's companion after her were hindered by the production team's resistance to affording the companion any agency within the series.

Following Sherry Ginn's previous work[11] examining the life of Sarah Jane beyond her tenure with the Doctor, her essay in this collection "Life Post–TARDIS? The Case for Jo Grant and Sarah Jane Smith" investigates Jo Grant's life during and after her travels with the third Doctor and compares it to Sarah Jane's. Jo was about 19 when she first became the Doctor's assistant and her tenure lasted about three years (in our time). She left the Doctor to marry a man who appeared to be a younger version of the Doctor, and they were apparently happy together. Two theories from developmental psychology are used to provide a lens through which to study Jo's life and determine how her life-course developed beyond the Doctor. This is meant to address a question that others, such as Lynnette Porter, have asked: Is the companion better off for having traveled with the Doctor, or worse?

No collection on the Doctor's companions would be complete without an essay on Rose Tyler, whom some have voted as the best companion in the history of the series. In her essay, "Rose *Is* England: Nationhood, British Invasion Anxiety and Why the Doctor Will (Almost) Always Rescue His Companions," Tanja Nathanael speculates about the name given to this character and how it fits into the mythology of the series and the Doctor's obvious love of England. Furthermore, Nathanael argues that the Doctor's choice of Rose as a companion begins the process of healing he needs following the events of the Time War. Rose refuses to support him unilaterally, questions decisions he makes, and gradually brings him back from the brink of destruction. Nathanael thus argues that the Doctor is better off because of his companions.

Teresa Forde celebrates "Rory Williams: The Boy Who Waited," noting that Rory starts his tenure with the Doctor as more of a companion's companion to Amy Pond than as an assistant to the Doctor. One gets the idea in early episodes showcasing the eleventh Doctor and Amy that Rory is an after-thought, much as were Mickey Smith and even Danny Pink, boyfriends who paled in comparison to the Doctor. However, Rory refuses to accept that he cannot win in a contest for Amy's affections and he is indeed correct. The Doctor values Rory as both Amy's companion and eventually his own.

An essay by Tom Powers entitled "A Muted Melody: The (Dis)Empowerment of River Song" also argues that companions are not enriched by their travel with the Doctor, and this includes his wife. Fans celebrated the character of River Song when she was first introduced and were then dismayed as the character was increasingly disempowered. Beginning as an equal of the Doctor—one whom he fell in love with and married—plot points had her brainwashed into trying to kill the Doctor and giving up her regenerations in order to save his life. Although the latter can be read as indicative of her love for him, it also indicates a general tendency on the part of the *Doctor Who* production staff to not write female characters who maintain their agency with respect to the Doctor.

Whereas many people argue about who is and who is not a companion, Pamela Achenbach's essay explores "Companions Who Weren't: The Pompadour and the Pauper." In this essay Achenbach discusses two new *Who* episodes in which the Doctor encounters women who would have been perfect traveling companions for him. One woman was a self-educated intellectual, a woman who rose above her station in life, created by a King, but who became so much more than a mere King's companion. The other was a woman who wanted more, who yearned for a life beyond what she had, and when offered a glimpse of that life, was truly happy with just that glimpse. The Doctor was unable to take either woman with him on his travels and that loss left him a sadder and lonelier man.

Finally, Aaron John Gulyas' essay "When No One Can Hear You Scream: *Doctor Who* Companions on the Printed Page" explores the rich history of companions who have appeared in novels and audio dramas. Some of these continue to explore the story of a companion introduced in the televised series, filling in gaps in the characters' history or exploring what happened to the companion following the end of his or her travels with the Doctor. Others introduce companions who only have existed within the printed page. Given that these stories were published with the consent of the BBC, information in them can be taken as "canon," although that has not stopped them from contradicting previously televised serials or other novels and dramas, sometimes by the same author. Some of these stories tell of disturbing futures for the companions and some have more optimistic plots.

It is obvious that the Doctor loves humans and chooses to visit contemporary Earth and involve himself in the affairs of its inhabitants more than any other time or place in the universe. And, the majority of his companions have been humans, especially human women. The Doctor tells "Victorian" Clara in "The Snowmen" (Christmas, 2012) that he always knows whom he should choose:

> CLARA: Why are you showing me all this?
> THE DOCTOR: You followed me, remember? I didn't invite you.
> CLARA: You're nearly a foot taller than I am. You could have reached the ladder without this. You took it. For me. Why?
> THE DOCTOR: I never know why. I only know who.

And it does seem as if he also knows when a particular companion should leave, although this is not always true.

During "The Death of the Doctor," Sarah Jane and Jo compare notes about their experiences in the TARDIS. Sarah Jane tells Jo that she has spent some time looking for others who traveled with the Doctor, although she admits she will never know for sure. She says Tegan works for aboriginal rights in Australia. Ben and Polly run an orphanage in India. Ian and Barbara are professors at Cambridge. Dorothy runs an organization called "A Charitable Earth." And Harry was a doctor, noting the past tense. Although the Doctor's companions had amazing adventures in time and space, they also learned about themselves during their travels. They witnessed the Doctor's drive to help others, his curiosity, his delight in the wonders of the universe as well as his anger and his wrath: lessons he imparted to each and every companion and which they returned in kind.

NOTES

1. James, *Talking about Detective Fiction*, 57.
2. Hulke and Dicks, *The Making of Doctor Who*, 4.
3. *Life on Earth* Special Feature, "Terror of the Autons."
4. Commentary by Katy Manning, "Frontier in Space."
5. "The Ultimate Companion."
6. Commentary by Russell T. Davies, "The Green Death."
7. See Lorna Jowett's essay on female companions and gender for a recent review of this issue. Jowett notes that many female fans have "fought back" against the ways in which women are depicted in the series, especially in the new *Who*, by composing their own stories about the characters.
8. "The Pandorica Opens."
9. Porter, *Tarnished Heroes*.
10. Hills, "The dispersible television text," 26.
11. Ginn, "Spoiled for Another Life."

With Whom He Travels
The Companions of the Doctor

Gillian I. Leitch

In the final two episodes of the fourth season of new *Doctor Who*, "Stolen Earth" (4.12) and "Journey's End" (4.13), some of the Doctor's companions, past and present, are brought together to help him defeat the evil Davros and the Daleks and to save the universe. This reunion of the Doctor and some of his more popular companions brought home the point that the Doctor was, in a manner, powerless without his companions.

And perhaps that is the case as—with the exception of "The Deadly Assassin" (#88) in the original series and the first two specials of the 2009 season in the new series—the Doctor has always travelled with a companion. Even when there are moments without companions present, there are still characters who act *in loco comitis*.[1] The character of the Doctor only works when juxtaposed against a companion, and in fact the companion's presence is integral to the ways in which the stories are structured.

This essay will focus on the role of the companion in *Doctor Who*, taking a historical and analytical look at the Doctor's companions over the run of the series, what kind of companions the Doctor had, what kind of characteristics they displayed, and asking the questions: was there a typical companion, and what kind of companion worked the best with the Doctor, especially for the fans.

When the series was conceived in 1963 by Sydney Newman at the BBC, the Doctor was always seen as travelling with "everyday" companions. The Doctor, as portrayed by William Hartnell, was crotchety, cocky and old, so his character was balanced out by his companions, who had none of these characteristics. Hartnell's Doctor was paired with three companions. Each served a specific function in the story lines. Susan Foreman, his teenaged granddaughter, was created specifically to appeal to the younger audience, as a not-so-typical teenager. She was given a familial relationship because the producers wanted to explain why a young girl would be travelling with a much older man.[2] Ian Chesterton and Barbara Wright were two of her teachers, who joined the TARDIS crew, unwillingly, at first. They were younger and more personable than the Doctor. They served a pedagogical purpose, as both were teachers. They were also more active, and they were used often in the 'action' sequences, particularly Ian.[3] And so the stage was set for the companion in the long history of the series.

Defining the "Companion"

In the 2008 Christmas special "The Next Doctor" Jackson Lake (who believes he is the Doctor) tells Rosita that the companions must always do what the Doctor says. An interesting perspective, but it is mostly an illusion (and wishful thinking on the part of the Doctor). But what role does a companion really play in the stories of *Doctor Who*? The companions are a foil to the Doctor. He or she often is the one who will ask the questions: 'what is it?'; 'who are they?'; and 'what should we do?.' They pronounce the questions that the viewer might also have. John Nathan-Turner went as far as to say that the "companion represents the younger viewer and he/she hopefully asks the questions that all viewers would like to ask."[4]

In the earlier years of the series, the companions were also used to generate action and tension. A much-used device was when the Doctor and the companions were separated or got lost. Such separations were ways to ramp up the tension in the episode. The Doctor would then save the day using his knowledge and expertise. Companions were also able to scream most effectively, and many episodes ended in a cliffhanger, with a view of the female companion du jour in mortal danger screaming in panic. Fade to black. The Doctor was then compelled to rescue him or her in the next episode. Companions were essential to the furthering of the narrative.

In each episode the viewer is introduced to a number of interesting characters who become friendly with and assist the Doctor's passage through the adventure. They could be considered companions of a sort or, as stated previously, *in locus comitis*, but most do not last longer than one story arc and are never invited into the Doctor's ship, the TARDIS. In order to analyze the various companions, they must be identified separately from these temporary characters.

So what differentiates a companion from a recurring character who greatly assists the Doctor and crew throughout a story? This is not an easy call to make. Should characters such as Brigadier Lethbridge-Stewart, Sgt. Benton, or Rose's mother Jackie Tyler be considered? Andrew Cartmel says it best when he states that to be a "full-blown companion," "you have to renounce your ordinary life and make him and his erratic odyssey your first loyalty."[5] The companion is someone who totally embraces the TARDIS lifestyle, and in some way defers to the Doctor as his or her leader.

The BBC's official website provides a list of companions[6] but there is some debate about whom to include. For example, fans contest whether the character of Sara Kingdom (played by Jean Marsh) was a companion, as she did travel with the Doctor for several episodes of the "Dalek Master Plan" in 1965, before her character was killed off. However, the official BBC Website does not list her as such, and actress Jean Marsh steadfastly states that the character was not one. Most fans disagree, however, and her character was furthered in Target novelizations and Big Finish audio productions.[7] For the purposes of this chapter, Sara Kingdom will be considered a companion, despite her limited time in the TARDIS.

Here, companions will include those who travelled with the Doctor in the TARDIS, were invited to accompany the Doctor, and those recurring characters who may or may not have been on board the ship, but who appeared in a number of story arcs and assisted the Doctor in significant ways to further the story arc. With this in mind, Sara Kingdom, the Brigadier, and Rose's mother were companions, because they did travel with the Doctor in the TARDIS. I won't, however, treat Sgt. Benton, Capt. Yates, Rose's father, or Martha and Donna's families as companions. They were not travelers with the Doctor, just recurring characters. Also for the sake of precision, I will count Romana as one character, although she was played by two actresses: Mary Tamm and Lalla Ward.

In "The Doctor's Wife" (6.4), the TARDIS takes on a human form and becomes the embodiment of a companion. As Kimberley McMahon-Coleman discusses in Chapter 4, the TARDIS is at its heart the Doctor's ultimate companion. However, apart from this episode, its actions, emotions, and relationship with the Doctor are muted, or merely seen through the actions or words of the Doctor—speaking to it as an inanimate object, or about it, as a beloved machine. It exists outside of the narrative, and so will be left out of the analysis.

Personal Characteristics of the Companions

In a general way, the companions have been analyzed by their various personal characteristics and then sorted into different categories to further the analysis. Characters have been placed into various categories based on the ways in which they situated their relationship with the Doctor (in whichever incarnation) and their back-stories. Many companions appear in more than one category. These are the categories that will be used to further the discussion of their role in *Doctor Who*: species, gender, age, technical knowledge, action, eye candy, romance, and familial. I have tried to classify the kind of characteristics that each companion exhibited in relation to the different Doctors and other companions, and the type of stories and situations in which they were placed.

For the purposes of comparison and study, a list of all the companions has been compiled, outlining some of their more essential characteristics. This includes those attributes based on their back-stories, where known, the way they related to the Doctor, and how they were presented to the audiences, including costume, and to some extent the media promotion. Such categorization is often simplistic, but is offset by the fact that many of the companions are represented in a number of categories.

Up to and including the 2014 Christmas special, "The Day of the Doctor," the Doctor has had 45 companions. The majority of the companions, 30 in total, were women. He also travelled with 13 men, and two mechanical companions who were played as masculine. The categories of species (and nationality), gender, age, technical knowledge, action, eye candy, romance and family will be used to discuss further the role of the companion within the story/narrative.

Species

By far, the majority of the Doctor's companions were human, and most of them originated from the era and region in which the episode was aired—contemporary Britain. As stated previously by producer John Nathan-Turner, the companion was envisioned as a character relatable to the viewing audience. The use of characters with similar cultural references, and who fit within the target audience, could instantly relate to the viewing audience. These companions served as gateway characters. Through them one could understand the central character of the Doctor, who is a bit of an enigma, through a person who is more easily recognized.

Age

The Doctor's companions are never older than he is. Considering that the Doctor's age through the run of the series ranges from that of an old man (played by William Hartnell) to stated ages of about 500 (Patrick Troughton) to the present Doctor (Peter Capaldi) being described as about 1,200, it seems unlikely that he could find a person of similar age. Notwithstanding, even when he was paired with Romana, another Time Lord, he was still considerably older than her 125 odd years. The Doctor is played as an older and wiser man to companions who essentially are children to him.

Of course, age can be viewed through the actual ages of the actors who play the Doctor or the companion—the age most evident to the viewer. Companions are rarely played by those of the same age as the Doctor. This was most obvious when the Doctor was played as an old man in the form of William Hartnell, who looked much older than his 55 years (in 1963). Ian and Barbara (William Russell and Jacqueline Hill) were in their thirties, and Susan (Carol Ann Ford) was in her early twenties, but playing younger. And while the character of the Doctor was subsequently played by younger men, the difference in ages between companion and Doctor remained in place. It was only when the Doctor was played by Peter Davison (b. 1951) that one of his companions was close to him in age—Tegan Jovanka (Janet Fielding b. 1953). In the new series, Capt. Jack Harkness (John Barrowman b. 1967) and Donna Noble (Catherine Tate b. 1968) were close in age to their Doctor (David Tennant b. 1970).

Most companions are played by actors in their twenties. It is only when Matt Smith was cast as the youngest actor to play the Doctor does he have a generational equivalency[8] with all of his companions (with the exception of River Song played by Alex Kingston [b. 1963] who was cast originally alongside David Tennant). However throughout his tenure, Smith's Doctor's age was emphasized, and he was shown to age from about 900 years at the beginning of his tenure, to 1,200 at the end. In his final episode, "The Day of the Doctor," he is shown to age about 300 years. The Doctor is incredibly old. The companion is played as a junior, less experienced person, emphasized through casting and by playing up the vast amount of time and experience the Doctor has lived within the text. Such vast age differences demonstrate an unequal relationship.

Gender

The relationship of gender is a very important marker among the companions. Most of the Doctor's fellow travelers have been women. In the earlier years of *Doctor Who*, there were usually two, sometimes three companions, and there was a habit of having at least one male companion within the group. This mirrors the original configuration of the series with Susan, Ian and Barbara. What this meant was that men were usually a part of the group. Following "The War Games" and the introduction of the third Doctor, he began to travel with just one steady female companion. Characters like the Brigadier and other members of UNIT would appear regularly and often served as companions, but the relationship with the female companion remained central to the narrative. The character of Harry Sullivan as a companion with

Sarah Jane Smith lasted only one season, and the series continued with the pairing of a female companion. Producer John Nathan-Turner returned the companion relationships to a group dynamic with the introduction of Adric, who was then joined by Nyssa and Tegan. When Adric left he was replaced by Turlough. The series then returned to the single female companion dynamic with Colin Baker's Doctor. When the series was rebooted, it began again with the single female. Male companions have travelled with the Doctor since: Mickey, Rose's erstwhile boyfriend, Captain Jack, Adam and Rory, Amy's boyfriend/husband. These men never appear as long as the female companions and two of them are there only because their girlfriend joined the Doctor on his travels. The Doctor never travels with a single male companion.

Women are the preferred companions on the TARDIS. Some were played as subordinates, working for the Doctor rather than with him. Tulloch and Alvarado observed that the female companion "oscillated between two limitations—passive/screamer and active/initiator."[9] She may have joined for her own reasons, but it is clear that she follows the Doctor's direction: he is the leader, and she is the follower. This is a patriarchal pattern. The Doctor is a man (a casting choice re-affirmed when Moffat was casting the twelfth Doctor and chose, despite fan and media speculation, another male—Peter Capaldi).[10] This plays into the gender stereotype in many ways, with the woman acting as a helper, but under the direction of a man.

Technical Knowledge

While the Doctor is clearly portrayed as having an astronomical body of knowledge and experience, a number of his companions have had some kind of technical or scientific knowledge allowing them to converse more intellectually with the Doctor or perform some task of assistance. They are able to at least comprehend some of the things going in on a particular story, understand the principles of time travel or even able to operate the TARDIS. This should not be confused with intelligence, as there were companions who were smart, just lacking the tools to operate within the Doctor's world.

Eleven assistants had some kind of technical expertise, be it from superior education or that they came from a future time where they were exposed to different kinds of technology. Romana, of course, was the most able in this category. She was a Time Lord, like the Doctor, although only about 125 years old.[11] She understood the workings of the TARDIS, time travel and other scientific matters. She lacked the Doctor's vast experience, which still put her at a bit of a disadvantage in terms of the adventures they shared, but she did not have to have every scientific principle explained to her and could provide technical assistance when required. John Nathan-Turner though, felt that her intelligence put her character at a disadvantage. "This array of characters possessed such wide-reaching and all encompassing knowledge and intelligence, we felt the 'baddies' of the stories were complete idiots, or at least they should pack up the minute the Tardis crew reveal themselves."[12]

Another kind of expertise was the math genius, of which Zoe and Adric are the best examples. They could assist the Doctor with some problems. In "The Krotons" (#47) Zoe and the Doctor are trying to gain access to the Kroton ship; it is Zoe who first passes the intelligence test that opens the door, she has to assist the Doctor in his attempts. Rarely were the technically gifted companions contemporary humans. Zoe was a genius from the late 21st century, Adric from a distant planet in E-Space. Most of the technically gifted were from the future, and many of them were not human at all. Ace and Dr. Liz Shaw were the exceptions. Ace was a math wiz from contemporary Perivale; however, her skills were influenced by the alien Fenric, which was explained in the episode "The Curse of Fenric" (#154). Liz Shaw was a scientist from contemporary England, who was clearly gifted, but her scientific knowledge always played second fiddle to the Doctor's, and many scenes were shown of her assisting the Doctor.

K-9 was perhaps the closest to the Doctor in technical knowledge, as the Doctor programmed him. But he was also programmed to behave like a dog, i.e., obey his "Master" as he called the Doctor. He was limited by his programming, wheels, and his battery power, so in the end the Doctor still had the advantage.

Action

I like to think of this category as "Action-man," although members in this category are not exclusively male. Ian, the Doctor's first male companion, embodies this type. The Doctor was old, and not likely to run around or fight. Ian was able to do this, to perform a combative role. He was envisioned as a hero.[13] Even when the Doctor was played by a younger actor, his character was not aggressively physical, particularly in the original episodes. He was not a man who liked to fight. Companions like Harry Sullivan or the Brigadier could take action when the Doctor couldn't, or wouldn't in some cases, do so. "The 'punching' role of the male companion has only survived at all because the Doctor has been, philosophically, a pacifist."[14]

The male companion, regardless of his other qualities, usually undertakes the job of physically defending the Doctor, but the most action-related companion the Doctor had was Leela, a female warrior. She was not bothered by taking charge in times of danger, and frequently sensed the danger before the Doctor did. She was armed and was often seen defending the Doctor against physical threat. This included using deadly force, which was not appreciated by the Doctor. But he was not above using this martial ability to his advantage. In "The Invisible Enemy" (#93), he deliberately used her innate hunting ability and instincts when cloned and miniaturized to combat the Nucleus of the Swarm, which established itself within the Doctor.

Captain Jack was the most recent companion to embody the action-man. He knew how to handle himself in all sorts of dangerous situations and was able to deal with all sorts of weaponry. He was more apt to action than the Doctor, although in the new series the Doctor is more willing to confront situations head on. This is evident in the episode "Parting of the Ways" (1.13) when the Doctor is trying to set up a technical solution to destroy the Daleks: Jack is sent to physically defend the Game Station from the Daleks. He uses more conventional weapons and is killed for his troubles.

Eye Candy

Casting of companions was influenced by their physical attributes, and from time to time producers believed that these would attract more viewers. Not that any of the companions were ugly, but some were chosen more pointedly for their physical beauty. This was emphasized by the choices made in the costuming. Liz Shaw, while a scientist, was most often seen in short skirts and high-heeled boots, not necessarily practical for the physical requirements of a companion or a scientist. And who can forget the famous image of a naked Katy Manning wrapped around a Dalek (although this photograph was taken after she had left the series). Sex sells.

The character of Leela was perhaps the most overt use of costuming to attract male viewership. All the warriors of the Sevateem shown in the episode "Face of Evil" (#89), which introduced her character, wore animal skins, but while the men in the tribe were dressed in pants and vests, Leela, the only female warrior present, was placed in a tight, short-skirted ensemble. The animal skins could be explained by her primitive upbringing, but the short skirt was a clear attraction for male viewers. All her publicity photos emphasized this view.

Romana was introduced to viewers in "The Ribos Operation" (#98), wearing a long, form-flattering white dress with furs. The first glimpse viewers have of her is a long body shot up to her face. The playing up of the physical appeal of the companion was most evident during the tenure of producer John Nathan-Turner. He was producer for the last season of the fourth Doctor to the end of the original series with the 7th Doctor. Under his direction, companion Tegan Jovanka spent much of the 20th season in a white tank top and shorts. The costume gave the impression that gravity would eventually win out. The audience's first view of Perpugilliam Brown in "Planet of Fire" (#134) was in a wet bikini. Later costume choices were decidedly tight and short. According to Muir, this is a sexist visual distraction called "keeping fathers interested."[15]

In the new series, Captain Jack Harkness stands out as the companion who uses looks the most within the narrative, and his looks were an attraction to viewers as well. The character himself is a flirt and will seek companionship with any and all, regardless of gender or species; he refers to himself as omnisexual. During the episode "Bad Wolf" (1.12), Jack is brought into a *What Not to Wear*-type television show and stripped naked. All of these aspects were played up in the scripts and in the publicity for the series. His popularity led to the creation of a spin-off series, *Torchwood*.

There has been some backlash among fans for the use of sexual stereotypes with the companions. Some of this centered on the costume we first see the adult Amy Pond wearing. In the episode "Eleventh Hour" (5.1) she wears a kiss-o-gram constable's costume, featuring a tight blouse and a very short skirt. One interesting comment made about this costume, its brevity, and the implications of the job it represented came from the blog "Whovian Feminism" which first underscored the lack of discussion concerning Amy's career path after her introduction as an adult in the costume, "As a result, it appears to me that Amy's career as a Kissogram was never intended to be any serious part of her characterization and was only intended to provide the audience with an opportunity to ogle the sexy companion in a sexy outfit."[16] Sexualizing the companions places the character at a disadvantage, lacking more dimension and power in the relationship with the Doctor. In addition is the possibility that the companion is simply there as a lure for viewers—window dressing—and little else.

Romance

If there were a lot of companions whose good looks were highlighted, not all of them were cast as romantic interests for the Doctor. There was a decided hesitance on the part of the series' producers to have the Doctor be romantic, and particularly romantic with his companions. The earliest incarnations of the Doctor tried especially hard to shift romantic focus off the Doctor by having larger groups of companions surrounding him, and having some of the companions pair off. Producer John Nathan-Turner was categorical in his refusal to show such a relationship, arguing that the fans, especially children, would not accept it.[17]

Only Jo Grant, in the old series, had what one would call a romantic relationship with the Doctor, played by Jon Pertwee. The relationship with the Doctor was never portrayed as a romance per se, but it was clear that the Doctor had strong feelings towards her. He even was obstructionist in her dating, luring her away from a date with Capt. Mike Yates of UNIT, to go on an adventure in "The Curse of Peladon" (#61). The romance was never consummated; it was shown more as a crush on the part of the Doctor and not reciprocated by Jo. But her departure from the series, in the episode "Green Death" (#69), gave the audience a glimpse of the Doctor's grief. The last scene in the episode shows a happy Jo telling the assembled that she is marrying Dr. Jones and, while the rest of the group is celebrating the moment, the Doctor walks off looking decidedly unhappy.

It was perhaps a great mistake on the part of producers to leave out the idea of romance between the main characters. According to a study of *Doctor Who* fans by Tulloch and Jenkins, the lack of romantic interest in Doctor Who leaves some female fans cold.[18] Certainly it is unrealistic to assume that amongst all of the companions he had travelled with, the Doctor did not once have or act on feelings of love or lust. By cutting the character of the Doctor off from a romantic or sexual life he is minimized, this when it is clear at one point he had children, as Susan was his granddaughter. It has been said that sex was taboo because of the broadcast time for the series, Saturdays in the afternoon,[19] however that should not have been an impediment for romance.

In the television movie, the Doctor had his first on-screen kiss, with companion Dr. Grace Holloway. A great deal was made of this moment, as it was a distinct departure from the original series' view of Doctor-companion relationships.[20] But, it was only with the new series that the idea of romance is fully explored. Rose and the Doctor were obviously an "item" by the time David Tennant took over the role. For the most part, their relationship was off-screen, with a touch of flirting to liven up the dialogue. The relationship is clearly shown with Rose's departure. Much like Jo Grant's departure in the original series, the Doctor was greatly upset by her leaving. In accepting another person to be his companion, it is clear that the Doctor is still in love with Rose, and he was reluctant to begin another relationship even if it was only friendship.

Martha Jones' unrequited love for the Doctor during her tenure as companion shows the other side of the romantic companion relationship, which was previously unexplored. The lack of reciprocity was a source of tension between the characters. This one-sided relationship, though, has its downside for the character, as Graeme Burk and Robert Smith point out: "Martha is hampered ... by her instant crush on the Doctor. She's established as an extremely likeable, competent career woman, but that's immediately undercut by having her make puppy-dog eyes at the Doctor."[21] Astrid Peth, was also a nice flirtation for the Doctor, who "seems to enjoy the frisson of sexual tension."[22]

The Doctor's relationship with River Song was perhaps the oddest of romances to play out, as it was a romance in reverse. When the character is first introduced in the episode "Silence in the Library" (4.8), River has already met and married the Doctor. For the next few seasons River appears again—for her, the first episode has yet to happen. The Doctor romances her off-screen and at various times, and in the episode "The Wedding of River Song" (6.13) he marries her. While there is romance here, it is not a romance that is easily seen or understood; but, it clearly depicts the Doctor as a sexual being with a companion as an obvious focus of his attention.

Familial Bonds

The Doctor states, during the episode "The Doctor's Daughter" (4.6), that he certainly has been married before and he has children. This is made clear from the first episode of the series with the introduction of Susan Foreman, who was described as the Doctor's granddaughter, and as such was the only member of the Doctor's biological family to travel with him. However the definition of family can be taken here to be much broader, encompassing created familial bonds amongst those who are not related by blood. A number of the Doctor`s companions held familial roles in the TARDIS family. Vicki was a clear replacement for Susan, taking on a pseudo-granddaughter role, which worked well with William Hartnell's Doctor. She was a similar age and disposition, to Susan; her lines clearly indicated that she saw the Doctor as a father-figure and that he saw her as a daughter-granddaughter. Zoe too, with Patrick Troughton's Doctor, related as father-daughter. Adric, in a limited sense, took on the characteristics of a son. Ace, if not playing a child role in the Doctor's life, certainly saw him in a mentoring role. These characters assumed a pseudo-familial role and, to a great extent, this relationship explained why they traveled with the Doctor.

Companions' Successful Characteristics

From the analysis of these characteristics, it is clear that the majority of the Doctor's companions are portrayed in a way so as to emphasize his greater skill, experience and intelligence. Not to say that the Doctor is always shown as an omnipotent being, but that the companions are chosen and used in such a way as to highlight his otherness and his position of authority. These are choices made by producers though; creating and casting characters based on what they believe will serve the narrative, and of course keeping their viewing audience interested. But are these choices the best ones? What kind of companion achieves the success that the producers envision?

Adam Mitchell was created by Russell T. Davies as a "rubbish" companion, showing what didn't work.[23] Self-centered and greedy, he clearly did not fit in with the Doctor. He could now be considered the ultimate in bad companions, but the choice was deliberate. Peter Davison, in his special "the Ultimate Companion," believes that the best companion was: keen on adventure, adaptable, heroic, likeable, and unique but ordinary.[24] Russell T. Davies stated that "a likeable character is shorthand to get you into the story fast. An unlikeable companion, for example, is going to rail against the conventions of the show, so holds you up."[25]

The intent and creativity of the producers and writers aside, the type of companion that works best is the companion that captures the imagination of the viewers. The end product and its reception is the way in which the viewer reacts to the companion and their relative popularity. If the fans are taken into consideration, the average has a place, but it is more complex. One way to determine the success of the companions is to survey the fans about their opinions.

To that end, I created a survey that was published and distributed online through various social media outlets and interest-specific organizations; it asked questions on the series and character preferences. Questions posed allowed space for comments.[26] To supplement the responses I received, I also consulted a number of similar websites to determine which companions were the fan favorites, and likewise those that were the least favorites. This included a number of top 5 lists and the like, as well as a number of articles written about companions, many published around the time of the 50th Anniversary in 2013, when interest was particularly focused on the series.

The results of my survey, which appears at the end of this essay, were influenced by the familiarity of the respondents to the old and new series. This can also be assumed for the results of those online surveys conducted by fan magazines and fan websites, although this is not stated. Because *Doctor Who* has had two lives on television, with a large gap of time in between, there are groups of individuals who are not aware of the original series, or have not as yet watched it in its entirety. The availability of the original series on streaming services and DVD is not complete, so such a breadth of knowledge is not common. Many of those surveyed had not started watching *Doctor Who* until the new series began in 2005, so their responses were more likely to be of companions from the new series than the old series.

When asked who their favorite companion is, Sarah Jane Smith,[27] Donna Noble, Amy Pond and Rose Tyler top most of the lists. As can be seen by the type of characteristics previously mentioned, all these companions are female, human, and from contemporary England. Only one of these women was a romantic interest. If we take into account that this was the most common type of companion over the history of the series, the reason for their predominance is clear: it works.

These companions are popular though for a reason, and if they are considered beyond their initial characteristics, then their success is not only based on gender and relative technical inexperience. Ian Marter proposed that the more intelligent and challenging a companion is, the better they make the Doctor look.[28] And these companions are considered by the fans to be bright and challenging.

When ranking the companions for his article, Dan Martin placed Sarah Jane Smith as number one. He stated: "We may have our own personal favourites, but everyone agrees that nobody was better than Sarah-Jane; smart, brave, but also human and vulnerable."[29] Seb Patrick saw Donna's character and its evolution in the series in a similar light: "the story of how a mouthy, annoying office worker from West London would gradually, through her experiences with the Doctor, reveal the intelligent, sympathetic and warm character underneath."[30] A successful character was one that smartly provoked the Doctor, but maintained his or her humanity and perspective.

The bias of new series companions in these lists can be seen two ways. The first is that as stated previously, a lot of *Doctor Who* viewers have not seen enough of the old series to have formed an opinion. The second is that the new series takes a different ideological view of the companion from the old series. In "The Ultimate Companion," companions from the old series, Janet Fielding and Sarah Sutton, stated that they felt that the companions in the new series were given more opportunities for character development, and that they were more of a focus in the storylines. This is certainly an opinion echoed by Executive Producer Steven Moffat. When asked about his casting for the new companion Clara, Moffat said "Doctor Who is always more the story of the companion. It's her take on the Doctor, her adventure that she goes on with the Doctor that's the story we tell."[31]

This bias is also clear in various surveys which list the worst companions, but in a completely opposite way. The surveys listing the worst companions tend to rank companions from the old series as the worst. Rose Tyler occasionally makes these lists, as does Amy Pond, K-9, and Kamelion, but the most consistently disliked companion is Melanie Bush, who appeared with the 6th and 7th Doctors. "When her memorable traits are 'scream on key' and 'loves carrot juice,' she just never had a chance."[32] Adric is, of course, a name that comes easily to mind as one of the worst companions, and his name appears on all the worst lists found. As a boy genius, he was not well liked, because "No one likes a know-it-all."[33]

Table 1. Companions and Characteristics

Legend: Human+ indicates modified human; X indicates coming from the contemporary broadcast time; and F indicates unspecified future time.

Name	Gender	Species	Nationality	Technical Abilities	Action
Ace—Dorothy Gale McShane	F	Human	English	Y	Y
Adam Mitchell	M	Human	English	N	N
Adric	M	Alzarian	n/a	Y	N
Amy—Amelia Pond	F	Human	Scottish	N	N
Astrid Peth	F	Sto	n/a	N	N
Barbara Wright	F	Human	English	N	N
Ben Jackson	M	Human	English	N	Y
Brigadier Gordon Alistair Lethbridge-Stewart	M	Human	Scottish	N	Y
Capt. Jack Harkness	M	Human +	Boeshane Peninsula	Y	y
Clara Oswin Oswald	F	Human	English	N	N
Dodo—Dorothea Chaplet	F	Human	English	N	N
Donna Noble	F	Human	English	N	N
Grace Holloway	F	Human	American	N	N
Harry Sullivan	M	Human	English	N	Y
Ian Chesterton	M	Human	English	N	N
Jackie Tyler	F	Human	English	N	N
Jackson Lake	M	Human	English	N	Y
Jamie McCrimmon	M	Human	Scottish	N	Y
Jo Grant	F	Human	English	N	N
K-9		Mechanical Dog	n/a	Y	Y
Kamelion	n/a	Android	Zeriphas	Y	y
Katarina	F	Human	Troy	N	N
Leela	F	Human	n/a	N	Y
Liz Shaw	F	Human	English	Y	N
Martha Jones	F	Human	English	N	N
Melanie Bush	F	Human	English	N	N
Mickey Smith	M	Human	English	N	Y
Nyssa of Traken	F	Traaken	n/a	Y	N
Peri—Perpigilliam Brown	F	Human	American	N	N
Polly Wright	F	Human	English	N	N
River Song—Melodie Pond-Williams	F	Human +	n/a	Y	Y
Romana—Romanadvoratrelundar	F	Timelord	n/a	Y	N
Rory Williams	M	Human	English	N	N
Rose Tyler	F	Human	English	N	Y
Rosita Farisi	F	Human	English	N	N
Sara Kingdom	F	Human	Mars	N	N
Sarah Jane Smith	F	Human	English	N	N
Steven Taylor	M	Human	English	N	Y
Susan	F	Timelord	n/a	Y	N
Tegan Jovanka	F	Human	Australian	N	N
Turlogh Vislor	M	Trion	n/a	Y	Y
Vicki	F	Human	English	N	N
Victoria Waterfield	F	Human	English	N	N
Zoe Heriot	F	Human	English	N	N

Intentional Eye Candy	Romance with the Doctor	Familial-Type Relationship	Profession	Time Period	Doctor
N	N	Y	Student	20C–X	7
N	N	N	Catalogued alien technology	21C	9
N	N	Y	Student/mathematician	32C	4,5
Y	Y	Y	Party entertainer	21C–X	11
B	Y	N	Waitress	X	10
N	N	N	History Teacher	20C–X	1
N	N	N	Seaman–Royal Navy	20C–X	1,2
N	N	N	UNIT-Commander	20C–X	2,3,4,7
Y	y	N	Time Agent	51C	9,10
N	Y	N	Au Pair/Teacher	21C–X	11,12
N	N	N	Unknown	20C–X	1
N	Y	N	Temp	21C–X	10
N	Y	N	Doctor	20C	8
N	N	N	Doctor–navy	20C–X	4
N	N	N	Science Teacher	20C–X	1
N	N	N	Unknown	21C–X	9,10
N	N	N	Mathematics teacher	19C	10
N	N	N	Piper	18C	2
Y	Y	N	UNIT-civilian	20C–X	3
N	N	N	n/a	F	4
N	N	N	n/a	F	5
N	N	N	Servant	1200BC	1
Y	N	N	Warrior Sevateem	F	4
N	N	N	Scientist-medicine physics	20C–X	3
N	Y	N	Doctor	21C–X	10
N	N	N	Computer programmer	20C–X	6,7
N	N	N	Auto mechanic	21C–X	9,10
N	N	N	Unknown	F	4,5
Y	N	N	Botany student	20C–X	5,6
N	N	N	Personal Assistant	20C–X	1,2
N	Y	N	Archaeologist	52C	10,11
N	N	N	Bureau of Ancient Records	X	5
N	N	N	Nurse	21C–X	11
Y	Y	N	Sales clerk	21C–X	9,10
N	N	N	Prostitute	19C	10
N	N	N	Space Security Service Agent	40C	1
N	N	N	Journalist	20C–X	3,4 (10)
N	N	N	Starship pilot	23C	1
N	N	Y	Unknown	F	1
Y	N	N	Airline Stewardess	20C–X	4,5
N	N	N	Student	X	5
N	N	Y	Orphan	25C	1
N	N	N	Unknown	19C	2
N	N	N	Astrometicist/astrophysicist	21C	2

If we judge those most often listed as least favorite companion by their chief characteristics then many are outside of the norm. Adric was a male alien. K-9 and Kamelion were mechanical. But these lists also include contemporary British females, particularly Mel. She fit the norm, but her character did not connect with the viewing audience, who felt that she did not work well with the Doctor as he was played by Colin Baker and Sylvester McCoy. Rose, another contemporary British female, was both popular and unpopular. Her character is rather divisive, and it seems to center on the portrayal of her romance with the Doctor. As evidenced by a thread on "Fan Fiction" her character is appreciated for her gumption in the first season of the new series, but as soon as romance properly blooms in the second season, the character loses face with some of the fans. Some do not appreciate any romance; some don't like that Rose becomes jealous of other women who the Doctor encounters.[34] Love changes the female companion in ways not evident in the Doctor.

While some companions may have some technical knowledge, it is not required, and those who are the most popular have none whatsoever. Characters who embrace action are never the most popular of characters, but neither are they the least popular. Male characters have only occurred when paired with other female companions, and they were often left with role of action. Some were more successful than others. Captain Jack is probably the most popular of the male companions, followed by Jamie McCrimmon. Sex may sell, but unless the character has more to it, it does not succeed with audiences. There is no magic formula for what makes the perfect companion, but what seems to work and catch the imagination of the viewers is the contemporary British female companion. It seems that the audiences prefer the unequal relationship of the Doctor as the leader, with a younger female, who for better or worse, relinquishes her control and allows the Doctor to take her away on adventures far away from a norm that the audience could understand.

Notes

1. Latin for "in place of the companion."
2. Cartmel, *Through Time*, 5.
3. Muir, *A Critical History of* Doctor Who *on Television*, 14.
4. Nathan-Turner, *The Companions*, 4.
5. Cartmel, *Through Time*, 96.
6. http://www.bbc.co.uk/doctorwho/classic/episodeguide/companions/ (Accessed May 18, 2015).
7. Tardis Data Core, "Sara Kingdom," http://tardis.wikia.com/wiki/Sara_Kingdom (Accessed May 18, 2015).
8. Matt Smith was born in 1982 and was the youngest actor to be cast as the Doctor, being only 27 years old at the time. Karen Gillan (Amy) was born in 1987; Arthur Darvill (Rory) was born in 1982; and Jenna-Louise Coleman (Clara) was born in 1986. Dating information comes from IMBD.com (Accessed May 18, 2015).

9. Tulloch and Alvarado, *Doctor Who*, 210.
10. http://www.blastr.com/2013-8-5/why-steven-moffat-thought-casting-woman-doctor-who-didnt-feel-right (Accessed May 18, 2015).
11. She stated in "Ribos Operation" that she was 140, but then in "City of Death" that she was 126. http://tardis.wikia.com/wiki/Romana (Accessed May 18, 2015).
12. Nathan-Turner, *The Companions*, 33.
13. Tulloch and Alvarado, *Doctor Who*, 34.
14. *Ibid.*, 229.
15. Muir, *A Critical History of* Doctor Who *on Television*, 63.
16. *Whovian Feminism*, "Amy Pond, AKA 'The Legs.'" http://whovianfeminism.tumblr.com/post/63318845126/amy-pond-aka-the-legs, October 6, 2013 (Accessed July 22, 2015).
17. Road, *Doctor Who*, 9.
18. Tulloch and Jenkins, *Science Fiction Audiences*, 92.
19. Muir, *A Critical History of Doctor Who on Television*, 14.
20. Leach, *Doctor Who*, 87.
21. Burk and Smith? *Who is the Doctor*, 132.
22. *Ibid.*, 191.
23. "Adam Mitchell," http://tardisinfo.weebly.com/adam-mitchell.html (Accessed July 15, 2015).
24. "The Ultimate Companion."
25. Davies and Cook, *A Writer's Tale*, 46.
26. The survey can still be seen here: https://docs.google.com/forms/d/1s4S0zjjFNN4MQL2rmN-TgKn-XxeA7xEhmXdrP7sjAAM/viewform.
27. Noting of course that Sarah Jane was a companion in the original series, but had guest starred in a few episodes of the new series, and had her own spin-off series, *The Sarah Jane Adventures* starting in 2007. See chapters 5 and 6 in this collection for more on Sarah Jane.
28. Muir, 270.
29. Dan Martin, "The Definitive Ranking of 'Doctor Who' Companions," http://www.buzzfeed.com/danmartin/the-definitive-ranking-of-doctor-who-companions#.usMp59oNb (Accessed July 25, 2015).
30. Seb Patrick, "Best of *Doctor Who* 50th Anniversary Poll: 10 Favorite Companions," http://www.bbcamerica.com/anglophenia/2013/11/best-doctor-50th-anniversary-poll-10-favorite-companions/ (Accessed July 25, 2015).
31. As cited in Geoff Berkshire, "'Doctor Who' Returns: Steven Moffat Talks New Companion Clara and Jenna-Louise Coleman." http://blog.zap2it.com/frominsidethebox/2013/03/doctor-who-returns-steven-moffat-talks-new-companion-clara-and-jenna-louise-coleman.html (Accessed May 13, 2013).
32. "List of the Worst *Doctor Who* Companions," http://where-there-had-been-darkness.blogspot.ca/2015/02/list-of-worst-doctor-who-companions.html (Accessed July 25, 2015).
33. "Doctor Who: 5 Best & Worst Companions" http://whatculture.com/tv/doctor-who-5-best-worst-companions.php (Accessed July 25, 2015).
34. "Fan Fiction," https://www.fanfiction.net/topic/36179/3049919/She-s-Not-As-Good-As-Everyone-Thinks (Accessed July 26, 2015).

"It's bigger on the inside"
Verisimilitude and Companion Reactions to the TARDIS

Craig Owen Jones

In common with other makers of television science fiction, writers of *Doctor Who* have had to contend with the problem of introducing mass audiences to concepts and ideas of which they may be unaware, or only imperfectly understand. The TARDIS, with its ability to travel through time and space, and its mind-bending quality of being "bigger on the inside than it is on the outside," is one such element in the series. While the craft is for the Doctor (and indeed some of his alien companions) a mundane mode of transport, for others—especially humans from the viewer's own time—it represents the apotheosis of other-worldly wonder and amazement. As Matt Hills has pointed out, *Doctor Who*'s current executive producer Steven Moffat defines the program in terms of "moments," even going so far as to characterize it primarily in this fashion and offering the archetypal "reveal" of a monster at the end of an episode as an example.[1]

The reactions of companions and visitors to the TARDIS constitute a further example of this. Given the extraordinary variety of responses exhibited by the dozens of principal cast members and guest stars who have gained access to the Doctor's ship over the years, it is surprising that this facet of the characters' narratives—central to so many of *Doctor Who*'s most iconic serials and episodes—has never received the attention it deserves. The Doctor's companions, after all, serve a crucial function in the program, not only asking the questions in the minds of audience members in moments of confusion (or when technologically obscure exposition is required), but also frequently serving as plot complications, by being variously threatened, possessed, imprisoned, or simply creating difficulties for the Doctor to overcome via their ignorance of the realities of the situation at hand, the functioning of the TARDIS, or both. In the post–2005 series, companions have in addition merited their own story arcs, exhibiting more than the token character development so often meted out to companions in the show's past, such as the first Doctor's granddaughter, Susan Foreman, perfunctorily written out of the show at the end of 1964 through what for Philip Sandifer was to all intents and purposes a forced marriage.[2]

The companions' initial reaction to the TARDIS, therefore, orientates the audience, helping to establish a dominant reading of the character at an early point in the story. However, it also fulfills another critical role. The various characteristics of the reactions by these individuals to the Doctor's ship—disbelief, fear, exuberant enthusiasm, or occasionally a mere phlegmatic acceptance—are also indicative of something else: a persistent emphasis on the TARDIS' status as an alien spaceship. This is an important distinction. Other science fiction programs and film franchises set on spaceships—the starship *Enterprise*, *Babylon 5*, and the like—often treat these spaces in a way analogous to a drama set on *terra firma*, to the point where fans apprehend textual and metatextual references to a given locale as "home." In *Doctor Who*, however, companion reactions often militate against this tendency, instead providing constant indirect reinforcement of the Doctor's alien origins. Finally, the emotional tenor of companion reactions can be seen to change over time, reflecting the vicissitudes of popular culture more generally. The following seeks to characterize these tendencies in more detail.

Companion Reaction and the Viewer's Gaze: Conspicuous Neophytism

We may begin with a brief discussion of the role of the TARDIS in storytelling. Like any setting in an episodic series, the audience becomes habituated to its peculiar characteristics over time. It is this process of slow habituation that allows us to reconcile Hills' view of the TARDIS as "provid[ing] unearthly sanctuary for the Doctor and his companions"[3] with Jonathan Bignell's contention that the *mise-en-scène* of the TARDIS' interior comes to connote "homelike safety and familiarity"[4]: clearly, both notions apply, and the compelling factor in this equation is the passage of time. The viewer does indeed become increasingly comfortable with the TARDIS' interior, coming to perceive it as ordinary even as it accomplishes extraordinary things. Yet once this cozy image has been established, every so often it fetches up against reality with a bump. While the viewer becomes accustomed to the conceits implicit in the TARDIS' abilities, neophytes—be they incidental characters or new companions—are required to negotiate the seeming contradictions of its existence directly as they encounter them.

In *Doctor Who*'s case, it is interesting that although we, as viewers, need not necessarily be privy to this process, we usually are. I shall term this tendency *conspicuous neophytism*—the dwelling of the action on the neophyte, for reasons other than characterization. One of the purposes of conspicuous neophytism may be to advance the audience's understanding of the plot and its elements. This occurs in particular in "An Unearthly Child" (#1), where the Doctor's very first companions—schoolteachers Ian Chesterton and Barbara Wright—react with disbelief to the TARDIS' interior, mirroring the audience's disbelief on this initial encounter with the show's central conceit, and thus serving a critical expository role in this opening serial. It is also a central theme of *Doctor Who: The Movie* (1996), in which Chang Lee's confusion over the TARDIS' fantastical properties arguably makes him more susceptible to the Master's manipulations. However, conspicuous neophytism can also function as a source of light relief, and also—crucially—to maintain verisimilitude. It was the BBC's head of drama, Sydney Newman, after all, who averred that the program's "audiences ... always want to believe in the particular life-and-death situation that Dr. Who [*sic*] and his companions find themselves in."[5]

It seems to me to be constructive to connect this notion in the first instance with the idea of the viewer's gaze for two reasons. Firstly, the object of desire here is less any particular character (although, as Chapman, Bignell, and many others have made clear, the Doctor's companions have often been designed to appeal to particular audience elements) than the TARDIS itself. Teresa Forde has drawn attention to the extraordinary success of the Doctor Who Experience, a tourist attraction based near the program's studios in Cardiff, Wales, pointing out that elements of the attraction, such as interactive game-playing within a mock-up of the TARDIS control room and a pseudo-interactive Doctor (played back on a screen), are intended to parallel the experiences of companions—and this is merely one way in which the audience's fascination with the TARDIS manifests itself.[6] Secondly, one of the central conceits of science fiction is the tight focus on what Polish science fiction novelist Stanislav Lem, in a now celebrated 1973 essay, has called "the consequences of fictive hypotheses." Though Doctor Who frequently finds itself on the wrong side of Lem's definition of science fiction—that there is no place in it for "inexplicable marvels," "transcendences," or "devils or demons"—it is nevertheless true of the show that "the pattern of occurrences [in it are] verisimilar,"[7] or at the very least, self-consistent. For a program now entering its second half-century of existence, *Doctor Who* has maintained this self-consistency surprisingly well. Nevertheless, these characteristics of the show must be learned; and for the *Doctor Who* fan, in common with other elements of the science fiction audience, much pleasure is derived from watching others go through the same process of acquisition one has already experienced.

The experience of the neophyte naturally forms the central theme of countless science fiction and fantasy films such as *Back To The Future* (1985), *Flight Of The Navigator* (1986), *Stargate* (1994), *The Matrix* (1999), and many others. The compelling distinction between these examples and those in *Doctor Who* is that of scale. In the above examples, the greenness of the protagonists emotionally underpins the action, and the audience accompanies the neophyte on their journey of discovery. By contrast, once the characteristics of the TARDIS have been established—a process that probably takes a newcomer to the program a handful of episodes or less—this dynamic no longer obtains. Therefore, the introduction of companions to the mysteries of the TARDIS, having been shorn of its didactic qualities, could just as easily be accomplished off-screen. That this seldom occurs[8] is indicative of *Doctor Who*'s polysemic properties—of the engagedness of the text, so to speak, with the role of the neophyte insofar as it constitutes a single but noteworthy element in a complicated patchwork of connotative imagery.

Perhaps the archetypal instance of a companion reaction to the TARDIS in this mode is that provided by Vicki Pallister in the 1965 serial "The Rescue" (#11). The character was introduced to the show to occupy what Chapman refers to as "the role of the teenager"[9] and what Tulloch and Alvarado call the "screamer" role[10] in the light of Susan Foreman's departure in late 1964, a loss precipitated by the conviction of the actor who played her, Carole Ann Ford, that her character was not being developed. Designed to fulfill these functions—to appeal to the youth audience and to provide a character who could serve as a plot generator by getting into perilous situations—Vicki's appearance normalized attitudes towards companions for the foreseeable future. Although several companions in late 1970s and 1980s *Doctor Who* and the post–2005 series of the show in some ways challenged this formula,[11] Susan and Vicki represented the first in a long line of characters that were invariably understood in terms of their youth, callowness, and vulnerability.[12]

"The Rescue" establishes Vicki as an orphan, stranded on the planet Dido with Bennett, an astronaut. At the serial's conclusion, Bennett dies, and as Vicki no longer has either a family or a home, she is invited on board the TARDIS by the Doctor, producing the show's first instance of a new companion's introduction to the ship. The gendered arrangement implicit in the usual juxtaposition of an (authority figure) male Doctor and a (subservient) female companion is here supplemented by the inference that Vicki is joining a family.[13] For Susan—who is not the Doctor's daughter, but his granddaughter—the characters of Ian and Barbara could be seen as functioning as surrogate parents, a role that continued, particularly for Barbara, in relation to the orphaned Vicki. The blocking for the scene reinforces this impression. In the moments immediately prior to Vicki's entry, the Doctor, Barbara, and Ian are formed in a huddle, emphasizing their togetherness, an impression further underscored by the Doctor's declaration that they are all of one mind in inviting Vicki to join them. The focus then switches to Vicki as she walks through the TARDIS' doors; her shapeless dress at once evokes the miniskirt and also hides her figure, reinforcing perceptions of her as a child. The camera angle for this shot is from within the TARDIS, not outside it, making the viewer complicit in welcoming Vicki to her new environment. As she utters her first lines on board, trailing off in wonder—"But it's huge! And … the outside is just…"—she advances towards the camera, and the others make room for her and then close reassuringly around her as the Doctor operates the TARDIS console.

For the first time, then, the viewer's gaze is informed here by the same knowledge possessed by the protagonists, allowing us to apprehend Vicki's astonishment from both the privileged perspectives of "old hands," and as vicarious members of the TARDIS' family. This introduction to the TARDIS also underscores the differences between it and Ian and Barbara's introduction in "An Unearthly Child": where the earlier *mise-en-scène* dwelt on the otherworldly aspects of the TARDIS, including lengthy tracking shots of the interior, Vicki's introduction is shot conventionally, composed of shot/reverse shot photography and a "tight four" shot of the characters at the sequence's conclusion.

The Companion's Gaze: Technological and Cultural Awareness and the Maintaining of Verisimilitude

Yet this was not the only way in which a companion could be introduced to the TARDIS in a believable fashion. Indeed, over the years, countless departures from the narrative model outlined in the above scene have been depicted in *Doctor Who*. It could not have been otherwise. Viewers have memories, and fandom has a collective memory. If verisimilitude is to be maintained, companion reactions must not only reflect the personalities of the characters involved—or else we fall foul of James Blish's "idiot plot," which feels no compunction in moving away from "fictional credibility"[14]—but also a level of technological and cultural awareness on their part that is commensurate with the times. This is especially true today, when the audience, well versed in the tropes of science fiction after the televisual and cinematic "sci-fi explosion" of the 1990s and early 2000s, expects the human characters they see on screen to be similarly aware. Hence Lily's exclamation in *Star Trek: First Contact* when confronted with a phaser: "It's my first ray gun." Hence, indeed, Martha Jones' pragmatic response to the uprooting of her hospital workplace to the Moon in "Smith and Jones" (3.01), in which, far from adopting Ian and Barbara's disbelieving response to the TARDIS in "An Unearthly Child," she not only displays knowledge of the Moon's physical properties, but also correctly deduces that the occurrence is due to alien interference as opposed to an illusion or hallucination (*pace* some of her predecessors).

In fact, this dynamic occurred in a different form from the 1970s onwards, as various characters sought to rationalize the TARDIS' properties by drawing on knowledge and expertise acquired in the course of their profession. The air hostess and long-serving companion Tegan Jovanka's encounter with the TARDIS is of this type. Having chanced upon the ship in "Logopolis" (#115), her exploration of its interior spans the first two episodes of the four-part serial. A full eighteen minutes of transmission time goes by from her entry to her first meeting with the Doctor, during which she attempts to make sense of her ordeal. She—like the Concorde crew of "Time-Flight" (#122)—correctly apprehends the TARDIS as a ship or airplane of some sort from the outset. In the console room, and (we presume) drawing on her training, she manages to locate a communications device on the console, and tries to use it to "speak to the pilot." Searching in vain for "the crew," she shortly gets lost in the TARDIS' corridors.

Despairing of finding her way, she eventually chances upon the cloister room, where she witnesses a TARDIS materializing. The ground shaking beneath her feet, she exclaims: "This is too much! Crazy idiot of a pilot— wait 'til I have a word with him!" She again tries to find a way out of the TARDIS, this time by using deductive reasoning—"I definitely came in this way, so this must be the way out"—before finding herself back in the cloister room, a victim of the TARDIS' skewed spatial environment. Eventually, she runs into the Doctor in the console room.

Tegan occupies what for *Doctor Who* is an intriguing historical moment. There were several precedents for the arrival of a professional woman as companion, most notably in the form of scientist Liz Shaw, who was a companion to the third Doctor in 1970, and Sarah Jane Smith, a newspaper reporter who accompanied the Doctor later in the decade. However, Tegan represented an instantiation of a rather different sort of careerist: unlike Liz Shaw's stand-offish blue-stocking persona, or Sarah Jane Smith's journalist with second-wave "feminist credentials,"[15] Tegan stands as a prototypical 1980s "career woman," "an 'independent' woman from a supersonic age"[16]—even if that career only extended to being a trolley dolly, as the actor who played her, Janet Fielding, once suggested.[17] That Tegan grounds so much of this extraordinary first encounter with the TARDIS in the mundane—conceiving of "pilots" and "crew," and the hierarchical organizational structure this implies— seems to fulfill the requirement for her introduction to be verisimilar. For all of her misconceptions, she leaps to the correct conclusions, perceiving the TARDIS as a ship and the Doctor as the person "in charge." For viewers, the sequence's significance surely lies in the fact that Tegan's deep knowledge of the mores of the 1980s' world she inhabits enables her to impose meaning on a new, fantastical one.

This lengthy excursive sequence is also noteworthy in that it reveals a surprising—indeed, unparalleled—amount of the TARDIS' interior for a dramatic episode of this sort. What we see is both familiar, in that the audience was by 1981 well acquainted with the bright walls and trademark 'roundel' design of the TARDIS' interior, but also strange: witness the maze-like interior corridors and the ancient-looking cloister room, overgrown with weeds and apparently possessing the paradoxical quality of an entrance giving onto a corridor that leads back to the same entrance. As Kevin S. Decker recently opined,

> [T]he TARDIS's status as a mobile headquarters for the wanderings of Time Lord and companions is a further gesture towards the *unheimlich* themes of *Doctor Who*. Efforts at fleshing out the daily life of the TARDIS crew by showing bedrooms, food machines—even a swimming pool—never seem to last for long. Just as the location of the Doctor's vehicle is constantly in flux, so the interior seems to be as well.[18]

This is not "a maximally livable, convenient space," as Hardy and Kukla might have it in their analysis of fan conceptualizations of *Star Trek*'s starship *Enterprise*,[19] and in which terms it might conceivably have been thought of in earlier eras of the show. It is, rather, a recursive space riven with paradoxes, a theme that received more attention in the serial, "Castrovalva" (#117). Thus, it is not Tegan's wonder at the physical impossibilities of the TARDIS, but the physical impossibilities themselves that now come to serve as the device that reminds the viewer of the ship's otherness. This time, our gaze matches Tegan's: we, too, are seeing the TARDIS for the first time.

The Doctor's Gaze: Companion as Initiate and the TARDIS Doorway as Liminal Space

Tegan's reaction on this occasion arguably defines her character in the years to come—sheer incomprehension is shortly replaced by a persistent, if practiced, fortitude. It is as if the character has undergone a rite of passage of the type described by Arnold van Gennep and Victor Turner in their celebrated anthropological studies[20]; and indeed, this would also seem a viable framework in which to view the TARDIS and companion reactions to it if we accept the contention that it is a liminal space. Philip Sandifer among others has written about it in these terms, and we certainly see evidence of this in "Logopolis" in the guise of the ship's position in a recursive loop, nestling in on itself like so many Russian dolls. As Sandifer notes, the TARDIS' "basic concept" has been rooted in liminal experience—for him, it is not merely a time machine, but "a portal that joins two mutually incompatible places together."[21]

My final example is particularly instructive in this connection. In "Rose" (1.01), the episode that marked the return of *Doctor Who* to television screens after a sixteen-year hiatus,[22] the creators introduce a new generation of fan to the TARDIS through the story of Londoner Rose Tyler, shortly to become the ninth Doctor's companion. On the run from an Auton, Rose reaches an apparent dead-end: an alley in which the TARDIS is situated. Initially refusing the Doctor's suggestion to follow him into the ship, on the grounds that they could not hide in what to her still appears to be nothing more than a wooden box, at length she runs inside. As with Barbara in "An Unearthly Child," the camera, positioned inside the TARDIS, allows a close-up of her uncomprehending face as she stands in the doorway, lit in a vivid blue by the TARDIS' interior. Then, like Chang Lee in the 1996 telefilm, she turns on her heel and goes outside, unprepared for the sight of the disparity between the interior and exterior of the TARDIS. She runs round it, surveying its four walls, unable to comprehend its form; she stares at its door again, hesitating for a moment. The Auton, now on the verge of breaking through a door into the alley, forces her hand: she runs into the TARDIS, the camera at her shoulder, until she stops, again in the doorway. The camera now moves past her to catch her expression and begins a lengthy pull out, all the more noticeable for the disjunction with the rapid cutting of the preceding scene, into the roof space of the console room, the whole cued by an ethereal music.

As Chapman suggests, the character of Rose both exemplifies and contradicts any postulated conception of a 'new' type of companion. As a product of the so-called "'Girl Power' generation ... determined, outspoken, opinionated and independent,"[23] her persona is at odds with that of the stereotypical companion of old, bearing obvious resemblances to that of Ace, the Doctor's final companion before the series went on hiatus in 1989, who was explicitly imagined as a companion intended to break the mold by being strong and capable, and have agency independently of the Doctor. However, Rose's characterization has been problematized by Dee Amy-Chinn, who points out that, for all her intelligence, bravery, and fortitude, Rose's role as a giver of care and compassion places her agency in question. Comparing the Doctor's universalized sense of ethics with the person-specific manner in which Rose discharges her moral responsibilities, Amy-Chinn asserts that "she—and other female characters—... remain smaller moral actors than the Doctor."[24]

I would like to modify Sandifer's suggestion somewhat, but in doing so, it is as well to bear Amy-Chinn's analysis in mind. It is difficult not to view Rose's entry into the TARDIS in terms of Turner's *limen*, the threshold whose agency as a site of individuated change carries so much weight in his work. During the history of *Doctor Who*, almost a dozen companions tarry at the door on their initial entry into the ship for a few seconds or longer,[25] and many more incidental characters do the same. Might it be that we can interpret not the TARDIS so much as its doorway as a liminal location, where journeying into another mode of existence can either be embraced or shied away from? This interpretation is of particular moment in connection with the post–2005 series, in which the doorway plays a far more prominent role, and also undergoes a substantial remodeling: where the TARDIS doorway was previously designed to match the rest of the interior, in the post–2005 series it can be seen from inside as it appears from outside, as a police box door, thus emphasizing the juxtaposition of realities that it embodies. One is also reminded of the function of the porch in the medieval church, used from medieval times until well into the early modern era as the setting for the first part of marriage ceremonies; only once the spousal was complete were the couple allowed to move inside the church to the altar in order to take communion.[26]

It is not, however, the idea of a solemn union with the Doctor that I wish to explore here, but rather, a union with the TARDIS, or perhaps even with the institution of time travel. In recent times, several companions have been given their own key to the TARDIS, allowing them to come and go at will, and some, such as Rose and Clara Oswin/Oswald, have even been instructed by the Doctor in use of his sonic screwdriver. The comparison with "the transformation that was understood in the use of ring and hat" by brides-to-be,[27] their adoption of the wedding band and coif used to cover their heads standing as symbols of matrimony, needs no elaboration. Over and above this is the entry into the TARDIS proper: the console, teeming (to the companion's eye) with form and function that remains mysterious, and occupying an obviously integral space within the whole, serves as a focal point for activity much as the altar in the wedding ceremony. This would then allow us to position the companion as initiate in the spatio-temporal ritual of time travel—a notion that perhaps carries more weight in light of Executive Producer Russell T. Davies' pronouncements on religious parallels in the post–2005 series,[28] and would surely benefit from further enquiry.

Perhaps we should not be surprised at this resonance, particularly in the field of televisual science fiction. In his recent study of the burgeoning musical subgenre of psytrance dance music, Graham St John has recently drawn attention to what he refers to as the "liminal ambience of outer space" in popular culture, remarking that this ambience plays a pivotal role in "orchestrat[ing] … self-awakening and empowerment" among the subgenre's adherents.[29] It is in keeping with *Doctor Who*'s preoccupation with its "very moral discourse"[30] in general and these issues in particular that so many of the Doctor's companions leave the TARDIS at the conclusion of their adventures all the more enriched, enabled, and enlightened for having accompanied him on his travels. If the doorway is indeed a liminal space, when a character leaves the TARDIS it can also function as a place to pay one's respects, as a "sacred site"[31] in which one can somberly reflect on all that has transpired.

Conclusion

The foregoing survey is of interest because it is symptomatic of the way in which modes of story-telling in televisual science fiction are changing. Exposition in *Doctor Who* and its small-screen science fiction contemporaries may not be dead, but it is not at all well. The ground that was covered over the space of one or even two episodes in serials of the 1960s and 1970s is now traversed, often at breakneck speed, in the space of a conversation, or even a single, frenetic line. This tendency is in keeping not only with the accelerating pace of contemporary life, but is also of a piece with Hills' "endlessly deferred narrative."[32] The "deferred" suspense over the Doctor and his personal narrative is paralleled in the maintenance of suspense through the very fabric, the *delivery*, of the expository exchanges central to the plot—did the viewer "get" the explanation? Do they "follow" what the new information means?—rather than alleviating pressure through emphasized and unequivocal revelation.

So, too, with companion reactions to the TARDIS. Brian Williams' shock at his sudden arrival in the TARDIS—instantaneously transported from atop a ladder in his suburban home to the ship, new light bulb still in hand—in "Dinosaurs On A Spaceship" (7.02) is conveyed by the simple expedient of a disbelieving stare and a locked-down camera shot of his dropped bulb shattering on the TARDIS' floor: another of Moffat's "moments," perhaps, that is meant to cater to an audience long familiar with this trope. The fans of *Doctor Who*, as with an increasing number of contemporary drama shows, identify to a substantial degree with such moments. It shall be interesting to see to what extent the tail is allowed to wag the dog in future iterations of the companion introduction.

Notes

1. Hills, "The Dispersible Television Text," 26.
2. Sandifer, *Tardis Eruditorum*, 131–32.
3. Hills, "The Dispersible Television Text," 33.
4. Bignell, "The Child as Addressee," 48.
5. Quoted in James Chapman, *Inside the TARDIS*, 38.
6. Forde, "'You Anorak.'"
7. Lem, "On the Structural Analysis of Science Fiction," 28.
8. A notable exception is Mel, who on her first appearance in the 1986 serial "Terror of the Vervoids" (#143) is depicted as already being acquainted with the TARDIS.
9. Chapman, *Inside the TARDIS*, 55.

10. Tulloch and Alvarado, *Doctor Who: The Unfolding Text*, 210.

11. Notably Tegan Jovanka (1981–84), whose (infrequent) "screamer" moments were counterbalanced by her feistiness and pluck, and Ace (1987–89), whose destruction of a Dalek with a baseball bat has become part of the program's mythology. Moreover, Brigid Cherry has written persuasively of Martha Jones, companion to the tenth Doctor (2007, 2008), in terms of her "apostolic" relationship with the Doctor, "bear[ing] witness and preserv[ing] memory" in the two-part episode "Human Nature/The Family of Blood" (3.08, 3.09), and ultimately walking the Earth—literally—to spread his message of hope in third series finale "Last of the Time Lords" (3.13); see "You're this Doctor's companion," 87.

12. Ross P. Garner's recent reappraisal of the late 1960s companion Zoe has offered a corrective, observing that this "future-coded" character, though often required to be a "screamer," also commits frequent acts of bravery, and fulfills an important ancillary role for the Doctor due to her technological knowledge and eidetic memory.

13. For example, see John Tulloch and Henry Jenkins, *Science Fiction Audiences: Watching Doctor Who and Star Trek*, pages 110–112 on attempts by audiences to gloss the Doctor in terms of a parent. Bignell, "The child as addressee," page 48 makes reference to the Doctor's "pseudo-parental relationship" with his companions in the context of the show's 1960s serials.

14. Wolfe, "Coming to Terms," 18–19.

15. Chapman, *Inside the TARDIS*, 80.

16. Tulloch and Alvarado, *Doctor Who: The Unfolding Text*, 101.

17. As discussed in "Girls Girls Girls!: The 80s," an extra feature on the *Doctor Who* DVD "Paradise Towers."

18. Kevin S. Decker, *Who is Who?*, 39.

19. Hardy and Kukla, "A Paramount Narrative," 181.

20. van Gennep, *Rites of Passage*; Turner, "The Center out There: Pilgrim's Goal."

21. "Civilizations of Pure Thought (Planet of Evil)." October 17 2011. http://www.philipsandifer.com/2011/10/civilizations-of-pure-thought-planet-of.html. Last accessed November 5 2014.

22. The appearance of a telefilm starring Paul McGann in 1996 notwithstanding; see Chapman, *Inside the TARDIS*, 173–83 for a comprehensive survey.

23. Chapman, *Inside the TARDIS*, 192.

24. Amy-Chinn, "Rose Tyler," 232.

25. Including Ian, Barbara, seemingly Polly and Ben Jackson (though the episode containing their entry into the TARDIS does not survive), Sergeant Benton, Ace, Rose, and Donna Noble.

26. For example, see Christine Peters, "Gender, Sacrament and Ritual."

27. *Ibid.*, 65.

28. See Chapman, *Inside the TARDIS*, 207; Miller, "The Monstrous and the Divine in *Doctor Who*;" Balstrup, "*Doctor Who*."

29. St John, "Aliens Are Us," 186.

30. Amy-Chinn, "Rose Tyler," 232.

31. Turner, "The Center out There," 195.

32. Matt Hills, *Fan Cultures*, 157.

"The battle-scarred, the insane, the ones even you can't control"
Disability and the Female Bodies of the Doctor's Companions

Kimberley McMahon-Coleman

The British television series *Doctor Who* remains one of the most well-loved science fiction television programs around the world. It features the Doctor, an alien Time Lord—a two-hearted, self-proclaimed "madman in a box"—who travels through time and space and, at the point of death, is able to regenerate into a different body, conveniently allowing the show to continue when the lead actor opts to pursue other projects. Running from 1963 until a long hiatus beginning in 1989, *Doctor Who* was then itself regenerated by Russell T. Davies in 2005. The new version, complete with new iterations of the Doctor, companions, monsters and adventures, has brought the series to another generation of fans. In 2010, Davies left the series to pursue his work on spinoff series *Torchwood* and *The Sarah Jane Adventures*, and former writer Steven Moffat took over as head writer and Executive Producer. Moffat has proven to be something of a controversial figure among Whovians, who appear to either love him or loathe him, with very little middle ground in between. One of the recurring accusations leveled at Moffat is that of misogyny, with a secondary and related issue being flawed characterization and what appears to be one of the cardinal sins of Science Fiction: occasionally ignoring facts which have become part of the series' canon.

The latter charge is an interesting one, in that it describes a phenomenon that has existed for almost the entirety of *Doctor Who*'s 50 years, yet seems to be leveled at the latest Executive Producer, in particular. As Paul Booth and Jef Burnham argue, the Doctor's character has always been "free-flowing and enigmatic,"[1] noting that the Doctor's second heart was not mentioned until the third Doctor's tenure, and that the lore about Time Lords only being able to regenerate twelve times was established with the Fourth. They argue that this kind of discontinuity is inevitable with different writing and production staff over a long period of time, and that all Davies and Moffat have done, in effect, is to compress some of these character developments into a shorter time span.[2]

The first charge, of sexism and/or misogyny, is one of the key focuses of this essay. Despite the Doctor's characterization being largely established by the divergent series of actors who have played him, he has always "conform[ed] to standard patriarchal, racial and heteronormative representational modes."[3] Through thirteen[4] male incarnations the Doctor, he has been accompanied on his adventures by a variety of mostly female, mostly human companions. As Alyssa Franke argues, the Doctor/Companion relationship is one predicated on power imbalance because the Doctor is "practically immortal," and has an "encyclopedic knowledge of the universe, and the ability to travel through time and space."[5] His companions, on the other hand, cannot travel through time and space without his intervention, and are more vulnerable to attack.[6] In the Steven Moffat era, it has become increasingly clear that female companions are also vulnerable to acquiring illness and debilitating conditions. Companions Idris (Suranne Jones), Amy Pond (Karen Gillan) and Oswin/Clara Oswald (Jenna-Louise Coleman) have all developed varying degrees of physical and mental disability, largely attributable to the impact of continued travel through time and space on fragile human bodies.

Idris and Oswin, two of the more recent characters in the BBC television series, have shared some of the iconic Doctor's idiosyncratic character traits: manic speech, social awkwardness, and occasional truculence. Elsewhere, these might be read as symptomatic of mental health disorders or differences. Rapid speech peppered with alliterative word associations, for example, is symptomatic of a manic episode; being oblivious to social niceties and conventions, as Idris is, is often read by audiences as autism spectrum disorder. In the Whovian universe, however, these traits are used to align the characters with the non-human Time Lord. Further, these differences have been overshadowed by their physical differences: their mechanized hybridity. Idris in "The Doctor's Wife" is revealed to be a humanoid manifestation of the TARDIS, ultimately unable to survive in that form. More recently, Jenna-Louise Coleman's Oswin (also known as soufflé girl, the Impossible Girl and later, Clara Oswald) is revealed to have been unwittingly converted into a very powerful Dalek, a race of enemies of the Doctor. Long-term companion Amy Pond also finds that her travel with the Doctor physically impacts on her body. In a prolonged story arc, she is held hostage for the duration of her pregnancy with daughter Melody, and develops secondary infertility as a result of her experience. In a rare moment of vulnerability, she reveals the extent of her resultant mental anguish around this. This paper questions, therefore, whether gender is the most useful lens through which to view recent companions Idris, Oswin and Amy, and posits that using a twin focus of disability and gender is ultimately more productive.

Gender and the Doctor

Debates around gender cannot be dismissed where the Doctor and his long list of (largely female) companions is concerned. Certainly it is raised regularly by Moffat himself in interviews, buying into debate about whether it is time for a female Doctor: "It is part of Time Lord lore; it can happen. Who knows? The more often it's talked about, the more likely it is"[7] and through onscreen allusions to the possibility of a future female Doctor, which establishes said lore. I would suggest, however, that the lens of disability is perhaps less examined, and is valid given the storylines assigned to these characters. The intersection of gender and disability studies, then, allows for a more nuanced reading of rather complex characters.

As with many other television series in recent years, fans of *Doctor Who* have had unprecedented access to the Executive Producers and series writers via social media sites such as Twitter. In September 2012, debate about the characterization of women in the work of Steven Moffat suddenly (re)appeared on the internet. The quotation that was circulated read, in part:

> There's this issue that you're not allowed to discuss: that women are needy. Men can go for longer, more happily, without women. That's the truth. We don't, as little boys, play at being married—we avoid it for as long as possible. Meanwhile, women are out there hunting for husbands.[8]

This contentious quote, predictably, caused quite an uproar and has since been cited in many online arguments as to whether or not Moffat is a misogynist, particularly given that the storyline of companion Amy seemed to largely center on courtship, pregnancy and marriage.[9] Moffat defended himself via Twitter, explaining: [I was] "quoted out of context in the original. I was talking about [character] Patrick in *Coupling*, not ME!"[10] In September of 2012 another bout of hate messages in the Twittersphere prompted Moffat to ask how you could block or limit incoming tweets,[11] and his Twitter account was deleted not long afterwards. In his absence, fans debated whether Moffat was a misogynist destroying the classic telefantasy franchise, or a writer of singular vision and talent. A few voices did point out that Moffat does not write every single episode, nor create every female character (as is the case with Idris, who appeared in a Season 6 episode written by Neil Gaiman), but this was largely overlooked.

Both lines of argument—that Moffat is a misogynist destroying the Doctor's legacy; and that he is not, because he has some strong female characters—seem rather simplistic in light of the complexities of the show and its storylines. Indeed, such a demarcation does little to examine the ways in which a "strong" woman might be constructed or represented. In her analysis of the furore, journalist Jill Pantozzi suggests that a reasonable next step would be to examine the body of work to see if the allegations of misogyny hold up, and further argues that there are a number of strong females in the new *Doctor Who* franchise.[12]

Clearly, *Doctor Who* has always included a consistent female presence; indeed, some of the female companions have been intelligent, well-educated career women (Barbara Wright, Sarah Jane Smith, Martha Jones); others are feisty (Rose Tyler, Donna Noble) or rule-breakers (River Song). A number of scholars are beginning to look at the tenor of the relationships and conversations between the female characters, often using the Bechdel test. The concept was originally created in a 1985 Alison Bechdel comic strip wherein one female character told another that she would only watch a movie if it had at least two women in it, those women spoke to each other, and their conversation was about something other than a man.[13] Some variations on the test include whether or not the characters are named. It has since become a common benchmark for trends about female representation in popular media.[14]

The application of the Bechdel test to new *Who* produces some unpredictable and even counterintuitive results. For example, episodes featuring River Song—a strong female presence who often knows more about the Doctor than he does himself—typically fail the test as her conversations are largely with or about the Doctor. As Alyssa Franke notes, more than 70 percent of the episodes that aired between 2005 and 2009 did pass the test outright, and every one had at least two named female characters.[15] Franke found, however, that once Moffat took over from Davies, the majority of episodes began to fail the test.[16] Rebecca Moore and others found much the same thing: the Bechdel test pass rate during the Rose era was 74 percent and during Martha's time on the TARDIS was 78 percent; every single Donna Noble episode passed (possibly because Donna was the first companion in the new era to be categorically not interested in a romantic relationship with the Doctor, creating a different dynamic and allowing for the Doctor-Donna storyline where she and the Doctor were equals). Yet Amy's time as the main companion, which began in Season 5 when Moffat took over, shows that only half the episodes passed the test, and that the average speaking time of the female companion per episode (which peaked with Donna) also dropped by the more than a minute per episode, to its lowest level ever.[17]

Of course, the Bechdel test is a rather crude measure, as both Franke and Moore acknowledge. It requires some editorializing on the part of the person applying the test (for example, what constitutes a conversation "about" a man? If the man is only mentioned in passing and is not crucial to the purpose of the conversation, how does that sit with the criteria?). Perhaps its biggest limitation is that it is merely quantifying conversation. Measuring the quality of those conversations is, of course, quite a different matter and is by its very nature, a subjective task.

In this essay I want to focus on three female characters from the Moffat era: Idris, Oswin/Clara, and Amy Pond. Amy, then known as Amelia, had first met the Doctor as a young girl, and had patiently waited for his return, even as her family and friends tried to convince her that he was no more than an imaginary friend on whom she had built a mentally unhealthy reliance. Appearing alongside the eleventh Doctor (Matt Smith), Idris and Oswin have rather fluid identities that are not at first fully understood by the Doctor, Amy or her husband Rory Williams (Arthur Darville). Both Idris and Oswin are mechanized hybrid figures, for Idris is revealed to be a temporary humanoid manifestation of the Doctor's spaceship, the TARDIS, and Oswin is revealed to be a human who has unwittingly been converted into one of the Doctor's sworn enemies: she is a very powerful Dalek. Oswin later reappears in the Christmas 2012 special "The Snowmen" as Clara Oswin Oswald, where she is again physically disabled, and ultimately succumbs to her injuries, only to reappear a third time as the ongoing companion and find that in her debut episode in that guise, her mind is once again altered without her knowledge or permission by sinister alien others. Idris and Oswin are figures whose mental health is questioned, either directly and repeatedly, in the case of Idris, or rather more implicitly, as with Oswin's location in the Intensive Care unit of an asylum for war-damaged Daleks. In addition to their mechanized hybridity and physical differences, Idris and Oswin share some of the iconic Doctor's more idiosyncratic character traits: manic speech, high intellect, social awkwardness, and stubbornness.

Disability and the Doctor

Disability is defined as "a state of decreased functioning associated with disease, disorder, injury, or other health conditions, which in the context of one's environment is experienced as an impairment, activity limitation, or participation restriction."[18] Each of the characters examined here experiences some form of disorder or injury. But as Rosemarie Garland-Thomson argues, Western thought since Aristotle has "conflated femaleness and disability, understanding both as defective departures from a valued [male] standard."[19] Garland-Thomson thus posits that "[d]isability studies can benefit from feminist theory and feminist theory can benefit from disability studies. Both feminism and disability studies are comparative and concurrent academic enterprises."[20] As I have argued elsewhere, non-physical impairments are viewed with even greater suspicion, for Victorian society, in particular, problematized mental illness as "madness" and grounds for institutionalization, effectively removing the individual from society.[21]

Certainly in the episodes on which I wish to focus here—primarily "The Doctor's Wife" and "The Asylum of the Daleks"—we see Idris, Amy and Oswin as having weak or deficient bodies. Idris, the physical manifestation of the TARDIS matrix, warns that her human casing "may blow" at any time. She is referred to as the "mad, bitey lady" who is "doolalley." Oswin, much like her malformed soufflés, is ultimately "too beautiful too live," her genius IQ and quirky personality constrained by her conversion into a Dalek, albeit one who continues to protest its humanity. The Dalek is, of course, an image which has long been associated with disability in *Doctor Who* lore, since their creator, Davros, fashioned the Daleks after his own mobile life support system. It is worth noting, in this context, that the Daleks and the Cybermen, the Doctor's nemeses in both the original and the rebooted series, have their roots in the technology of body replacement. Similarly, an ailing John Lumic is prompted by genuine medical need to create a race of "upgraded" cybernetically-enhanced humans. Lumic is a wheelchair user in danger of imminent death, who anticipates that the cyber-conversion technology will allow him to overcome human frailty and mortality. Both Davros and Lumic, of course, are still presented as evil—as "powerful, immoral characters who harness technology for apparently immoral purposes" and demonstrate a "perverse will."[22] Idris, Amy and Oswin are also each held in some kind of restorative stasis. The difference for the viewer is that these characters are configured as victims without agency in the process; they have the medical procedures done to them, whereas Davros and Lumic are active participants and willing to allow others to determine the safety of the process before taking that risk themselves. The gender divide here with regard to agency cannot be ignored: Idris, Amy, and Oswin are depicted as damsels in distress who require the protection and salvation of the Doctor.

Idris

In episode 4 of Season 6, "The Doctor's Wife," viewers are introduced to the character of Idris. Despite only appearing on screen in this form in a single episode, Idris is arguably the Doctor's longest and truest companion, since she embodies the matrix of the TARDIS, with whom he has travelled for seven centuries. His constant companion for over 700 years, the TARDIS is, therefore, the "Wife" of the episode title, presumably only able to be parted from him by death. The show plays on this motif, using stereotypes as shorthand for characterization; the TARDIS is the one who tidies up—she has archived consoles the Doctor has not even made yet—and argues with him about the need to read instructions.

The episode, scripted by Neil Gaiman, has been described as a "love letter" to *Doctor Who*.[23] Certainly, the episode's junkyard location (which recalls the discovery of the TARDIS and Doctor in Totters' Lane in the first ever episode, "An Unearthly Child," in 1963) and the use of Jon Pertwee's line "old girl" when speaking to the TARDIS, among other details, do seem to be an homage to the show's long history.[24]

The eleventh Doctor follows a distress call sent by another Time Lord, the Corsair, to an asteroid that is actually a parasitic, sentient being named House. Living on House is a family: Auntie (Elizabeth Berrington) and Uncle (Adrian Schiller), who are Frankensteinian creatures patched together from other travelers lured to the asteroid; Nephew (Paul Kasey), an Ood; and Idris, a young woman dressed in Victorian/steampunk style. The episode opens with the young woman having her soul drained and declaring that she is scared, but she is told by Auntie not to worry because both a new soul and a Time Lord are coming.

When regenerating from Ten (David Tennant) to Eleven, the Doctor articulated every thought that came into his head: from riffing about his new appearance to his experiment with a meal of fish fingers and custard as he attempted to process his new likes and dislikes. In a moment which has become central to the female regeneration debate, Smith's Doctor, upon discovering his longer hair, squeals, "I'm a girl!" before touching his Adam's apple and sighing (with apparent relief): "Not a girl." Similarly, Idris, now containing the TARDIS' stolen matrix (or soul, as the Doctor explains) recognizes the Doctor immediately, and voices her ideas as they come to her. She greets him with an accusation of being a thief, and "Goodbye!" Throughout the episode Idris continues to call the Doctor "Thief," much to his confusion as he does not believe that they have ever met before. The rest of Idris' opening monologue is equally confusing: "You are stealing me. Oh, tenses are difficult, aren't they? … Biting's excellent! It's like kissing, only there's a winner!" Both Aunt and Uncle immediately apologize on Idris' behalf, referring to her as "off her head" and "doolalley." Idris thus loses agency through the infantilizing act of having "relatives" apologize for her behavior as though she is a child, and she is then further marginalized by the suggestion of mental incompetence. The language of madness is repeatedly and explicitly used throughout the episode. This purposeful Othering of the individual also clearly aligns her with the alien Other, the Doctor himself.

Certainly, the Doctor sees Idris as unreliable, dismissing her claim that she is (at least partially) the TARDIS, correcting her: "No, you're the mad bitey lady. The TARDIS is up-and-downy stuff in a big blue box." In this one example, he uses both gendered language and an unreconstructed term for mental illness as reasons to ignore her assertions. It is only when she demonstrates that she has information about the model of "his" TARDIS and the circumstances of its theft that he begins to believe her. Even then, his relationship with her is, rather bizarrely, reduced to one of carnality, as intimated in Amy's arch response to his explanation that his TARDIS is now a woman: "Did you wish really hard?" Further, when he and Idris work together to build a new TARDIS console and escape House, it becomes apparent that Idris is racing against time: "I don't belong in a flesh body. I could blow the casing in no time." Only then—after 700 years, as Idris archly points out—does the Doctor think to ask if she has a name. She tells him that he calls her "Sexy." The objectification of the TARDIS when it is still the TARDIS, that is, an actual object, is perfectly understandable; that the Doctor's suddenly human "wife" is reduced to being "Sexy" and having a limited lifespan, less so.

The model of marriage depicted in Moffat-era *Doctor Who*—primarily through married companions Amy and Rory, but also secondarily through the Doctor and Idris, in this episode, and later, the Doctor and River Song, is one of the areas where gendered power differentials are explored and often critiqued. The marriage and "pregnancy" of Amy and Rory will be considered in more detail later. The idea that the feisty, independent, resourceful archaeologist River Song is progressively reduced to a caricature of a femme fatale whose very *raison d'etre* is to seduce and kill the Doctor is one that is disappointing to many viewers of the show. In "Let's Kill Hitler" (6.8), she is even aligned with the dangerous seductress Mrs. Robinson from *The Graduate*, a role that she embraces, calling the Doctor "Benjamin" and celebrating her newly curvaceous body as "all kinds of mature."

In this instance, the chaste marriage of the Doctor and his TARDIS is depicted as one based on frustrated bickering. When building a TARDIS console out of the available remains in the junkyard, Idris offers advice, which only serves to make the Doctor irritable. She argues that he "never reads the instructions," noting that for 700 years he has been ignoring the "Pull to Open" sign on the front door of the TARDIS. This quickly devolves into an argument about his childishness and then he accuses her of unreliability, of not always taking him where he wanted to go. Idris replies that she always took him where he *needed* to go. This domestic power struggle is cut short, however, as Idris stumbles and reports that "one of the kidneys has already failed ... this body has about 18 minutes left to live." Unfailingly, every time Idris says something that draws the Doctor's attention to her new, female form, that human body demonstrates its frailty.

Despite its focus on continuity and the show's long history, the episode does alter some canon: introducing the notion of the gender fluidity of Time Lords with a reference to the Corsair's different regenerations, and having the TARDIS declare that it was she who stole a Time Lord, rather than the other way around. Here, Idris, "the mad, bitey lady" is aligned explicitly with "the mad man in the box." Her agency—in choosing to steal a likely Time Lord and in deciding where he should go—has hitherto always been limited by her inability to speak, and is now limited by her ailing body.

Yet there is still much debate as to whether these stereotypes are misogynistic or even glorifying particular gender roles, when they appear to be being played for humor and are contrasted with the marriage of Amy and Rory, which is, at least in some ways, less traditional. Rory is depicted as the carer and the follower, and the Doctor insists on calling him Mr. Rory Pond, rather than calling her Mrs. Williams. Arguably, however, this relationship is also not unproblematic, since, as we shall see, Amy's storylines center around her relationship with and marriage to Rory, her pregnancy and her (admittedly highly unusual) relationship as a mother to River Song (Alex Kingston).

Amy

As a child, Amelia Pond (Caitlin Blackwood) prayed to Santa for a policeman to come and fix a crack in the universe that had appeared in her bedroom wall. When the Doctor arrived in his police box to rescue her, she believed her prayers had been answered. He promised to return in five minutes, and young Amelia packed a bag and waited. Owing to the vagaries of time travel, however, the Doctor overshot the mark by some twelve years. Aged 19 and now known as Amy, "the Girl Who Waited" has been subjected by her family to psychiatric treatment because of her belief that the "Raggedy Man"—her childhood description of the Doctor—was not, as they thought, an imaginary friend. Amy is thus framed within the discourse of mental illness from the outset. In terms of gender politics, the beginning of her time as the companion is also somewhat less than auspicious. Dressed as a police officer, it seems, at first, as though she has a challenging career (and indeed, one that aligns her with the Doctor in his police box). This is undermined for humor, however, when it is revealed that she works as a kissogram messenger, rather than an actual police officer.

Amy does choose to join the Doctor on an adventure, and two years later agrees to ongoing travel as his companion. She opts to leave for space and time travel on the eve of her wedding to Rory Williams, and after helping the Doctor save the universe, attempts to seduce him. This sets up a complex dynamic as there is some confusion over whether Amy loves the Doctor or Rory more, eventually resolved through a number of complex storylines that involve sacrifice, waiting (in Rory's case, for some two thousand years), and alternate timelines. Indeed, Amy forgets the Doctor himself until her wedding day, when the rhyme about "something old, something new, something borrowed and something blue" reminds her of the existence of the TARDIS—one of the few things in the universe that fits all four criteria simultaneously.

Amy's story arc seems to be inexorably grounded in her relationship and marriage—from the pan back to see her wedding dress hanging in her room after the Doctor returns her, to her delighted shout of "I remember you, my Raggedy Man!" at her wedding, to the alternate timeline wherein she and a be-mulleted Rory are expectant parents. Further, the plotline where Amy is revealed to be the birth mother of River Song is one which seems to be predicated on the assumption that if Rory and Amy are newlyweds, "the narrative has to jump straight to domesticity and babies."[25] For most of Season 6, Amy's pregnant or not-pregnant state is unclear, and even the Doctor's sonic screwdriver cannot explain this anomaly. It transpires that a *doppelgänger* is on board the TARDIS and the real Amy is being held hostage on Demons' Run; sedated and heavily pregnant, she awakes in labor and is instructed to "push." The lack of bodily autonomy and agency here is palpable—she is held captive, unaware of her pregnancy, and wakes in pain with no time to adjust to the idea of being a mother. Her child is then taken from her, and it will be some time before she learns what happened to baby Melody Pond.

The fallout from this drama is seen in "Asylum of the Daleks" (7.1), when Amy, now a model, is interrupted at work by the arrival of Rory, bearing divorce papers. The papers are never filed, however, as they are kidnapped by a pair of Dalek puppets and transported to the parliament of the Daleks because, as they are told by the Dalek Prime Minister, "It is known that the Doctor requires companions."

The asylum, it is revealed, is a fully automated planet that has become legendary in that it is where the damaged Daleks—"the battle-scarred, the insane," the uncontrollable ones—are housed. Believed to be impenetrable, it seems that there has been a breach since someone is now broadcasting Bizet's *Carmen* from its very core. The Daleks, who believe it would be offensive to "extinguish such divine hatred" as that shown by the battle-hardened and traumatized Daleks in the asylum, propose to teleport the Doctor and his companions to the planet so that they might lower the force field, allowing any intruders—including, of course, the Doctor and his companions as well as the person behind the transmission, Oswin—to be eradicated. When pressed on his counter-plan, the Doctor lists the saving of the marriage of Amy and Rory among his goals, alongside neutralizing the Daleks, rescuing Oswin, and escaping the planet.

The three time travelers are all issued with a bracelet that neutralizes the nanocloud that converts all organic matter, living or dead, to Dalek puppets. The conversion process, it is explained, is about subtracting love and replacing it with anger. This allows further exploration of the state of Amy and Rory's union when she loses her bracelet, prompting Rory to offer his, reasoning that "I love you more than you love me, which today is good news because it might just save both of our lives." This awkward attempt to quantify love goes some way to explaining why the Amy-episodes score so poorly on the Bechdel test—many of her conversations are with Rory and/or the Doctor, and many are also about her relationships with Rory and the Doctor. Yet Amy reveals here that the reason why she ended their marriage was not because of Rory, his behavior or even that she was no longer in love with him; rather, it is because of her acquired impairment, telling him: "You want kids.... And I can't have them.... Whatever they did to me at Demon's Run— I can't ever give you children." Arguably even more disappointing, then, than Amy's characterization being based largely on her role as a wife, is her apparent belief that her worth is tied to her reproductive capacities.

In the same episode Amy, hitherto a strong and feisty character who is wont to take the lead and direct both the Doctor and her husband Rory in the majority of their interactions, is carried, unconscious, in the arms of the heroic Doctor. For fans of Moffat, these moments of vulnerability were read as being particularly poignant, since viewers knew that the departure of Amy and Rory was imminent, and that Jenna-Louise Coleman (who plays Oswin in this episode) was to become the new companion. For others, this was seen as a calculating attempt to trade on that dynamic which ultimately did not work as it seemed quite out of character for Amy. Indeed, elsewhere in this episode Amy's hardheadedness is such that Oswin worries that Amy may be being converted into a Dalek, asking "doesn't she seem angry to you?" to which Amy replies: "Well, *somebody's* never been to Scotland!"

The Bechdel test scores get progressively worse over Amy's tenure as the companion, and this episode—towards the end of her time in the TARDIS— exemplifies why. Despite moments when she appears more switched on than the Doctor—realizing, for example, that they are in imminent danger from the deceased Dalek-puppets in the escape pod—much of the dialogue in this episode is given over to examining the entrails of her marriage. Further, Amy seems to lose agency and gain uncharacteristic vulnerability in this episode— she becomes not the partner in adventures, but the damsel-in-distress, requiring both physical and emotional rescue. For this reader, at least, the image chosen to promote this episode—of the heroic Doctor striding through broken and burning Daleks and carrying a prone Amy—encapsulates the elements that have led to the accusations of sexism and misogyny leveled at Moffat.

Oswin

"Asylum of the Daleks" marked the first on-screen appearance of Jenna-Louise Coleman, who had been announced as the actress to play the new companion, replacing the departing Karen Gillan; the "Impossible Girl" stepping in to replace the "Girl Who Waited" (one wonders if there are any circumstances in which these "girls" might be viewed as adult women). She is introduced in a chatty, cheerful voiceover, declaring that it is "Day 363" and that "the terror continues," even as she is seen watching a music box ballerina and attempting to bake a soufflé. In her voice diary, she notes that it is her mother's birthday and remarks, "I did make you a soufflé, but it was too beautiful to live." This comment proves prescient for Oswin, whom the Doctor dubs "soufflé girl." From the outset, Oswin Oswald seems improbable to the Doctor; a junior Entertainment Manager on her first voyage, holding off the Daleks for almost a year after being shipwrecked, hacking into Dalek technology, and persisting in her quest to make a perfect soufflé despite the lack of fresh ingredients. The Doctor and Oswin are deliberately aligned when she explains away her talent for hacking, asking, "is there a term for total screaming genius that sounds modest and a tiny bit sexy?" to which he replies: "Doctor." She was also deliberately aligned with the Doctor in press promoting the show, as Moffat noted in an interview that, "It's not often the Doctor meets someone who can talk even faster than he does, but it's about to happen."[26]

In a reversal of the usual gender stereotype, Oswin uses her genius intelligence to save a screaming Doctor as the Daleks set in on him, hacking into the pathweb to erase the memory of him from the mind of every single Dalek. He enters her cell, at the very center of the intensive care unit, to be faced with the truth: that Oswin's genius was so useful to the Daleks that they did a full conversion. The scenes where Oswin's lines as she hears them, safe in her enclave, are intercut with the chained Dalek completing her sentences are poignant. In an effort to maintain a last shred of her humanity, Oswin gives the Doctor a final instruction: "I am Oswin Oswald. I fought the Daleks and I am human. Remember me."

Oswin's frailties, both mental and physical, are less clearly delineated than those of Idris. Nevertheless, they are evident. Oswin is found in a Dalek asylum, a place for the "battle-scarred, the insane." Further, she is at the very heart of the Intensive Care Unit, reserved only for those who have survived catastrophic wars with the Doctor. Her entire existence within that space is delusional; as the Doctor gently explains, "You dreamed it for yourself because the truth was too terrible." Her final insistence that she is human, is her attempt to still be the Oswin Oswald she was before her profound physical change; to not let her acquired dis/ability alter others' perceptions of her.

Oswin is a proactive character who is capable of opening locked doors, hacking into the Dalek pathwebs and advising the Doctor, Rory and Amy how best to survive. Despite all this, she does take on the damsel in distress role to some degree, requesting: "Rescue me, Chin Boy, and show me the stars," which appears to be a traditional and gendered stereotype.

Further, all that Oswin can do, she does from behind a control panel, constrained by what appears to be a very small apartment but which is, in reality, a Dalek unit. Thus the Dalek unit, with its historical allusions to wheelchairs established in the 1960s era stories about Davros, seems to be implying that wheelchairs, rather than promoting mobility, are actually reminders about impairment and immobility.

Oswin is also able to move through time and space, and it is implied at this point that she may be able to regenerate or reincarnate in some way. As previously noted, Jenna-Louise Coleman plays both the one-off character of the soufflé-girl, Oswin Oswald, and the ongoing companion, Clara Oswald. Clara later appeared as a Victorian governess in the 2012 Christmas special, *The Snowmen*. Even within this one-off episode, her identity remained fluid, for she was a governess moonlighting as a barmaid. She also shows a certain amount of ingenuity when she follows the Doctor and discovers his TARDIS on a cloud high above London. The Doctor—who never saw Oswin, and thus does not recognize Clara as being another incarnation or regeneration of her—is intrigued by her and offers her the key to his TARDIS, a tacit invitation to become his regular companion, explaining "I never know why, I only know who." Clara, however, is dragged from the cloud by a sinister ice manifestation of the episode's enemy, the Great Intelligence, and plummets to the ground, sustaining paralyzing and life-threatening injuries.

The Doctor, for his part, seems to be in denial about the seriousness of her condition. When the evil mystical snow generated by the Great Intelligence suddenly turns to salty rain, he intuits that Clara's death is imminent, as only the sadness of an entire family crying on Christmas Eve could have such an effect. He returns in time for Clara to utter her final words—"Run, you clever boy, and remember"—which were also the final words of Oswin. Here, the language used actually demeans the male Doctor, rather than the female companion, by infantilizing him and using a patronizing tone. At Clara's grave, the Doctor learns that her full name was Clara Oswin Oswald, and so he sets off to explain the impossibility of "the Girl Who Died Twice," once as Clara in the Victorian era, and again as Oswin in the futuristic asylum. It is made very clear to the viewer that this new companion shares not only the Doctor's propensity for rapid-fire speech, but also his superior intellect and problem-solving capabilities and the capacity for time-travel, independently of the Doctor and his TARDIS.

When next we see Clara, it is in "The Bells of St John" (7.7) as a contemporary young woman in London, assisting a recently widowed friend to raise his children. Clara is at first shown to be IT-challenged, despite her genius IQ. The Great Intelligence, however, is uploading certain people to the Internet, a process which the Doctor manages to interrupt, meaning that Clara is returned with increased computer awareness and skills (which, presumably, are what help her hack into the Dalek pathweb as Oswin in the distant future). At the time of writing, Clara is still the ongoing companion, now adjusting to life with the twelfth Doctor (Peter Capaldi). He had entered the Doctor's timeline on Trenzalore, thus dispersing her identity through time and space, assisting the Doctor in all of his incarnations and explaining why Eleven had seen three different versions of her during their adventures together. Thus Clara's very purpose in life, like River's, seems to be inextricably linked to her function within the Doctor's life.

Conclusion

Although implicit, it has become lore that travels through time and space will eventually cause decreased functionality in the Doctor's human companions. In the case of his female companions in the Moffat era, these consequences seem to be particularly prevalent; in the instances canvassed here, mental illness, kidney failure, paralysis, and infertility have all been written as the price to pay for the privilege of travelling with the Doctor. Whether this is adequate evidence to support the charges of misogyny leveled at Moffat, it does seem clear that issues of dis/ability and gender are working in tandem, and that they are, at times, problematic. In what are necessarily complex storylines, it seems Garland-Thomson's exhortation to integrate disability analysis and feminist analysis, both areas of study which allow us to compare the human, female companions' frail bodies against the benchmark of the Doctor's (thus far) male bodies, does indeed lead to enriched understanding.

NOTES

1. Booth and Burnham, "*Who* are we? Re-envisioning the Doctor in the 21st Century," 203.
2. *Ibid.*, 214.
3. *Ibid.*, 209.
4. The current doctor played by Peter Capaldi is known as the Twelfth, but during the fiftieth anniversary episode "The Day of the Doctor" it was revealed that there was a previously unacknowledged version of the Doctor, the War Doctor (John Hurt) between Doctors Eight (Paul McGann) and Nine (Christopher Eccleston).
5. Franke, "Clara in Control."
6. *Ibid.*
7. Utichi, "BBC's Doctor Who."
8. Pantozzi, "Steven Moffat."; The Scotsman, "Time Lad."
9. *Ibid.*

10. Moffat via Twitter. This source has since been deleted.
11. *Ibid.*
12. Pantozzi, "Steven Moffat."
13. Ulaby, "Bechdel."
14. Steiger, "No Clean Slate," 104.
15. Franke, "The Bechdel Test."
16. *Ibid.*
17. Moore, "University Study."
18. Leonardi, Bickenbach and Ustun, "The Definition," 1219.
19. Garland-Thomson, "Integrating Disability," 6.
20. *Ibid.*, 2.
21. McMahon-Coleman, "I was hoping," 149.
22. Decker, *Who is Who?*, 51.
23. Anders, "Doctor Who."
24. Hills, *New Dimensions*, 83.
25. Franke, "Their Stories."
26. Itzkoff, "Doctor Who's Companions."

"There's nothing *only* about being a girl"
Learning to "Play" the Doctor's Companion

DAVID BOARDER GILES and AMY PELOFF

> *The Doctor: Liz was a highly qualified scientist. I want someone with the same qualifications.*
> *Brigadier Lethbridge Stewart: Nonsense. What you need, Doctor, as Miss Shaw herself so often remarked, is someone to pass you your test tubes and to tell you how brilliant you are.*
> —"The Terror of the Autons" (#55)

Liz Shaw, the third Doctor's first full-time accomplice, was hardly the first strong woman in the Doctor's life. Ever since Barbara Wright boldly pushed her way into the TARDIS 50 years ago in search of her missing student, the Doctor's travels have been filled, on screen and off, with confident, clever, and trailblazing women—from Verity Lambert, the show's first producer, to Ace, his proto-riot grrl[1] travelling companion (and demolitions expert). And yet these role models have just as often been reduced to a (usually screaming) plot device by the writers and sidelined by the Doctor's own paternalism, eccentricity, and ego. The writers admit as much in the scene above, ironically putting in Miss Shaw's mouth their own reasons (as we'll see below) for writing her out of the show.

For all this chauvinism, his companions have always found redemptive moments to assert themselves, to step in and save the universe, and even rescue the Doctor on occasion. Nonetheless, this essay suggests that some companions' importance lies not only in their classical heroism, but in their everyday performances of gender, onscreen and off—particularly in response to the characters' and production teams' everyday sexism. Like Liz Shaw's absentee critique, such moments speak in several voices at once: from the writer's pen, they smack of casual sexism; from the characters' (and actresses') mouths they read as feminist jabs at that very sexism. (It is all the more ironic, then, that Shaw's retort is delivered by proxy, by the affably paternalistic Brigadier.)

This essay explores some of these poly-vocal moments and characterizations, through which the overt paternalism of the program was undermined, contested, or superimposed against more liberatory (or, at least, less two-dimensional) interpretations and embodiments of gender—not only in spite of the sexism of some of its writers or producers, but within the very gendered roles carved out for the Doctor's companions. Here, we pay particular attention to the possibilities exploited by the actresses to read between their lines and complicate the show's often patriarchal savior narrative. Indeed, fan favorites like Elisabeth Sladen and Janet Fielding—who played Sarah Jane Smith and Tegan Jovanka, respectively—made lasting impressions precisely because they transcended the roles of damsel-in-distress or vacant audience proxy ("What on earth is *that*, Doctor?") so often written for them.

In a way, of course, every performance is a cacophony of voices. A constellation of participants leave traces on the story told. But on *Doctor Who* perhaps more than most the show has been defined by change, by the comings and goings of players, production teams, and entire historical eras. Like the Doctor himself, the show's strength has been that it can transform—not only from Doctor to Doctor, or companion to companion, or even from writer to writer, but in genre and format, both within seasons and across the show's history. Built into this Rube Goldberg machine of evolving components, then, are interstices and slippages that both record and reinvent the historical contexts in which it is embedded. And in these slippages and interstices, the vortices of genre, narrative, and identity are reified, distorted, multiplied, queered, and reinscribed. In other words, *Doctor Who* is both a cipher for the historical moments it inhabits and a mechanism for change. (Change being, after all, the only certainty in the universe.) Below, then, we have taken an approach that is quasi-ethnographic and quasi-historical, assembling from a broad, popular archive of interviews, biographies, documentaries, and audio-commentary something of a "thick description" of the gendered meanings and diverse social relationships that made *Doctor Who*.[2]

Is It Still the Same Broom? Doctor Who, Disjuncture and the Patriarchal Continuum

At the risk of sounding trite, we start from the assumption that the world has changed, and *Doctor Who* with it. The continuities in narrative and audience over that time are, of course, what allow it to continue *qua Doctor Who* (certain cranky purists notwithstanding). The story of a heroic alien vagrant with a magic travelling box has been broad in its appeal to audiences' imaginations (with the implicit critique of the here and now). Within such consistency, however, the differences, too, are significant. Indeed, perhaps more than any other contemporary narrative-media phenomenon, *Doctor Who* is built on difference. In one particularly meta-textual moment, the Doctor himself asks the question hiding in plain sight: "If you take a broom and replace the handle, and then later replace the brush, and you do it over and over again, is it still the same broom?" ("Deep Breath" 8.1). Having travelled across half a century in real time, is *Doctor Who* the same program? The Doctor's answer: "Of course it isn't, but you can still sweep the floor."

The format of the show, therefore, has evolved—both onscreen and behind the scenes. And in the process, each new actor, writer, director, producer, and so on, have in various constellations made their mark on the singular genre that has become *Doctor Who*. Indeed, virtually before the ink was wet on the BBC's initial premise—which emphasized the show's historical content and absence of "Bug-Eyed Monsters"—producer Verity Lambert had reimagined it and (over creator Sydney Newman's objections) introduced *Doctor Who*'s first and most popular bug-eyed monsters, the Daleks.[3] Fifty years later, the proverbial broom now represents the interplay of innumerable gravitational forces.

This multiplicity might amount to what anthropologist Sherry Ortner calls a "serious game"—a metaphor she uses to describe the shared social codes and protocols which scale up to reproduce existing social structures like gender and sexism, or perhaps, on a more modest scale, like *Doctor Who*.[4] The strength of the metaphor is that it allows us to imagine the agency of individual players to strategize and occasionally to renegotiate the rules of the game. Ortner imagines the serious game as an alternative to two schools of thought—one commonly identified with poststructuralist theory, and another which she calls "practice theory."[5] Practice theory accounts for social structures based almost entirely on the scale of the rational individual agent, in contrast to poststructuralism, which focuses on larger social and linguistic systems. Where poststructuralist theory often obscures personal agency, she says, practice theory fails to account for structures of power and oppression that are systematic and not reducible to individual practices or decisions. She suggests, for this reason, practice theory often suffers from the same static vision as poststructuralism. "One can do practice analysis as a loop," Ortner writes, "in which 'structures' construct subjects and practices, but subjects and practices reconstruct 'structures.'"[6] In contrast, she suggests what she calls "subaltern practice theory," which opts "to avoid the loop, to look for the slippages in reproduction, the erosions in long-standing patterns, the moments of disorder and outright 'resistance.'"[7] Thus, for Ortner, "subaltern practice theory" and its "serious games" emphasize "the disjunctions in, rather than the coherence of the structure, [and] the creativity of women within the limits of their traditional politics...."[8]

Indeed, the slippages, interstices, disruptions of continuities, and the shifting of players may often add up to a multiplicity of games according to whose rules different agents might play at any given moment. Above all, as Ortner points out, these layered games do not necessarily amount to wholesale challenges to the predominant social structures. Rather, she says, the multiplicity of games affords players a sense of alternatives. Consider the example of Caroline John, who played Liz Shaw. While in the role, she took efforts to argue for scripts and direction befitting Liz's highly skilled character—including a minimum of screaming and a more practical costume than the short skirts and tall boots in which she was often outfitted. At the same time, her approach for landing the part in the first place represented a different stratagem for the same playing field: she found the BBC finally responded to her letters of application once she began including a photograph of herself in a bikini.[9] What is important for Ortner is not whether any strategy or game prevails over the others, but, rather "that they exist and thus prevent closure."[10] Ortner is imagining these games writ large. Patriarchy itself, for example, is one of the macro-social systems she ascribes to these playing fields. But in microcosm, as we will see, such lack of closure in the format and production process became openings for performers like Elisabeth Sladen and Janet Fielding, as well as for their respective production teams, to embody and extrapolate the contradictory experience of gender in the historical moments of which they and their characters were a part.

Of course, in macrocosm, those historical moments were no less full of slippages and disjunctures than *Doctor Who*. Fifty years on, "patriarchy" itself is not the same proverbial broom. In 1963, as *Doctor Who* premiered, the "long" fifties[11] were coming to a shockingly violent end, with John F. Kennedy's assassination the previous day portending a very different decade to come.[12] Agitation for social change was growing, as the complacency of the post-war recovery period gave way to simmering discontents. By the end of the decade, social movements had emerged around a broad range of social justice issues. While in the U.S., the civil rights, student, and anti-war movements predominated, in Britain the activism focused less on racial equity than on issues of class. In both regions, sexism within these social movements alienated female participants, spawning a reenergized feminist movement.[13] British feminism experienced significant legislative successes with the Equal Pay Act of 1970 and the Sex Discrimination Act of 1975, which ironically led to strong popular resistance to ongoing critiques of gender roles. The sense that formal equality had already been achieved, thus rendering feminist activism and the Women's Liberation Movement unnecessary, was frequently communicated via popular media. As one letter to the *Daily Mirror's* editor argued, "[F]rom a financial viewpoint, women have never been so well off, nor had such equality of opportunity. Are these liberationists merely frustrated females?"[14] This sense that social inequity had been sufficiently resolved proved to be a difficult one to challenge, and as the Seventies wore on, the Backlash against feminism and its proponents became the dominant frame through which gender roles were viewed.[15]

We can find traces in *Doctor Who*, then, of the feminism of the early Seventies and the backlash of the late Seventies and Eighties. As the Doctor explains in "Blink" (03.10), linear progress is a myth. History is complicated, and largely obscured by attempts to reduce it to a neat narrative. To wit, the shifts that occurred during this period in British society's understandings of gender roles are enmeshed in "a big ball of wibbly wobbly ... time-y wimey ... stuff." We look to the experiences of Sarah Jane Smith and Tegan Jovanka, as well as the actors who played then, to explore this "stuff"—to illustrate how women navigated these changes and used the lives they portrayed on screen to interrupt, reinterpret, and contest characterizations of gender.

Production Teams and Evolving Playing Fields

The classic pre–1996 era of the show has sometimes been derided by critics and fair-weather fans alike as backwards in comparison to recent seasons—in terms of writing, acting, effects, and particularly in terms of gender. But in spite of its moments of casual sexism and two-dimensional, screaming plot-devices in miniskirts, the show nonetheless also allowed for a variety of spaces and voices to express and contest a continuum of gendered perspectives, and perhaps even to speak back to and shape the ground rules in subtle ways. This has made *Doctor Who* itself not so much a vehicle for explicit feminist critique (although it did occasionally achieve this) as for a plurality of subjectivities that did not always take the male gaze of the producers, writers, or audience for granted. Indeed, some of these casual sexisms were the occasion for the actresses' more strategic and subtle critiques of paternalism and inequality (in fleeting moments, perhaps, or behind-the-scenes jockeying).

The playing field of the classic era offers sharp contrast with that of contemporary television, of course. Since the rise of Joss Whedon's groundbreaking series *Buffy, the Vampire Slayer* in the late-nineties (1997–2003), the idea of an auteur-helmed television show has become the norm in network-produced science fiction and fantasy.[16] The rebooted *Doctor Who* has adapted this structure, so that recent seasons are strongly identified as a product of visionary Executive Producer Russell T. Davies, and later Steven Moffat.

Whereas neither can lay claim to the same creative control that marks the bulk of Whedon's work, there has been an identifiable shift from the earlier period, whose staffing was often at the whim of the BBC. The growing agency of these 'show-runners' might be indexed by the charismatic monikers and online chatter afforded to "R.T.D." or "the Moff" by contemporary fans and bloggers, many of whom have been quick to observe the ways in which the tenure of these auteurs has coincided with different styles of characterization and embodiment for gender and sexuality. Indeed, a spate of fan conversations have been critical of the ways in which female characters have been written in Moffat's episodes—only 57 percent of which stand up to the benchmark "Bechdel Test" for three dimensional female characters (which asks simply: [a] whether more than one female character is given a name; [b] whether they speak to each other; and [c] whether they talk about something other than a man).[17] While Russell T. Davies' episodes fared far better by this test (eighty-nine percent pass), it is perhaps just as telling that the very first seasons of *Doctor Who* far surpassed even Davies' work, with practically every episode passing.[18] This was not necessarily due to explicitly feminist intent (although Verity Lambert, as the BBC's first female producer, was hardly unmindful of sexism). Rather, as the BBC's original briefs demonstrate, the introduction of recurring female characters was an early guideline intended to appeal to the middle-aged female demographic—indexing the composite nature of the show's authorship.[19] This does not, therefore, mean that in 1963 *Doctor Who* was simply less sexist (nor does it mean that Steven Moffat is a raging misogynist—many of his episodes, after all, focus on the companion's outgrowing her dependence on the Doctor, in contrast to the devotion of Davies' companions to a vaguely messianic Doctor). However, it does highlight some of the potential slippages and interstices afforded by the decentralized shape of the classic era's production teams.

In a way, then, *Doctor Who* until the 1980s suffered at times from an oddly salutary case of "too many cooks in the kitchen." The relationship, for example, between the producer and the script editor—who reviewed scripts for tone and consistency, often rewriting them in part or wholly—was collaborative, fluid, and central to the creative process in a way that is distinct from the present relationship between the head writer and the producer. Discussions between these two players were vital to the development of the series' tone and characterizations and to the sorts of scripts that were commissioned. With this in mind, some of the ambiguity, slippage, and leeway in the gendered inflections of various characters emerged out of the dialogue between these two key players. Certainly, as we will see further below, some of the ambiguities of Sarah Jane Smith's character emerged from mild creative differences between Barry Letts, who was amenable to the influence of Women's Liberation, and Terrance Dicks, who was unabashed about the companions' passive damsel-in-distress role. As we will suggest, these ambiguities were also openings for actors like Elisabeth Sladen to invest companions like Sarah Jane with nuance and gendered complexities. Sladen herself described the creative authority she felt within this constellation of different perspectives. "You just have that moment of clarity," she wrote, "where you realise, *I know this character better than this week's rent-a-writer or director-for-hire. I'm the one who plays him or her all the time.*"[20]

In a similar manner, the rotating ensemble nature of the production team allowed for fluidity and disjuncture in the relationship between the companion and the Doctor, corresponding to the relationships developed between the actors who played them. For Elisabeth Sladen, "the arrival of a new Doctor actually gave me the freedom to regenerate Sarah Jane as well."[21] While Jon Pertwee's fatherly (or less generously, paternalistic) attitudes towards her manifested in their on-screen relationship as clear, hierarchical Doctor-Assistant roles, for example, Tom Baker brought much more camaraderie to the position. According to Sladen, the relationship between her and Tom allowed their characters to develop a true partnership, with "[her] Sarah and Tom's Doctor [fitting] together so naturally, hand in glove."[22] She points to "The Sontaran Experiment" (#77) as the serial in which their on- and off-screen rapport fully gelled into something "so much more than master and pupil. Tom's Doctor allowed me to have fun but there were plausible parameters, just as there would be in real life between two companions."[23] Baker's Doctor even came to refer to Sarah Jane as his "best friend," a new emotional depth in the role of the companion that would be influential on every other companion that came afterwards, and can be arguably traced to the actors' distinctive partnership.

While even in recent seasons, the opportunity remains for actors to develop new relationships in the wake of the Doctor's recasting, the less centralized production team of the classic era perhaps allowed for more of that leeway to bleed through into the finished product. Consider, for example, Sarah Jane's farewell scene, which Philip Hinchcliffe and Robert Holmes left unwritten, as they considered Elisabeth Sladen and Tom Baker the only two people who knew the characters' relationship well enough to decide how to end it. The resulting scene is both touching, and yet prefaced by a domestic quarrel with the Doctor after one-too-many casual demands to hand him the sonic screwdriver. (Many an underappreciated housewife may have sympathized.) One wonders if the same degree of agency would ever be allowed to, say, Jenna Coleman or Peter Capaldi under the current auteur-driven model of production.

Along with the recent centralization of creative decision-making has also come a parallel shift to a "single-camera" format, which affords a great deal more agency to the editorial process, in which separate takes of different performers and perspectives are seamlessly integrated into a single scene. The casual viewer will notice the greater frequency with which new shots are introduced and cut together compared to the older three-camera format (now largely reserved for soap operas and sitcoms). Indeed, in the earliest days of BBC drama, television functioned much more like live theater in front of a camera, with cuts and retakes discouraged or disallowed. While this relaxed a little over the show's first decade, with episodes and scenes beginning to be filmed out of sequence with the introduction of color and a new Doctor in 1970, the inflexibility of the multi-camera format still meant limited takes and limited opportunities to revise what made it into any given shot. Yet this playing field also allowed actors distinctive strategies for taking control of their own performances: each of the women, for example, who played opposite Jon Pertwee's third Doctor, recalled being taught by him to deliver a four-letter word if they felt they needed to stop to retake a scene. "I said 'Jon, I daren't,'" recalled Caroline John, "and he said 'Well, it's the only way they'll stop.' And he was right."[24]

Similarly, the infrequency of cuts and the correspondingly inexorable shooting schedule was sometimes matched by the director's inattention. Sophie Aldred, who played Ace from 1987 to 1989, recalled *Doctor Who* attenuated direction: "People tend to assume that the directors tell you what to do, but they don't. They're looking at their shots."[25] And, indeed, in some scenes, companions were left entirely to their own whims as to what to do in between lines—as Elisabeth Sladen recalled, of shooting 1983's "The Five Doctors" (#129), the episode's ultimate climax involved several Doctors' efforts to save the day while several Doctors' companions hung in the background with nothing to do. Indeed both Sladen and Janet Fielding (about whose Tegan we will hear more shortly) meet on the set in this scene, and mime a brief conversation about the situation which, if the audience had heard it, might have made the difference between this episode's passing the Bechdel test or not! While these moments were often frustrating to the actors, they also allowed actors a certain autonomy in their self-presentation—one curtailed in contemporary scenes, whose impact is largely the result of careful selection and editing from among numerous takes, all framed by a single camera.

The three-camera format and inflexible shooting regime, the evolving relationship between actors in an ensemble, and the pluralism built into the role of producer and script editor, are of course only a few examples of the ways in which a distinct production regime may also confer distinct possibilities for agency. And, of course, it would be too simplistic to suggest that one production regime is simply more liberatory, or confers more agency to women, than another. Undoubtedly there are new and different ways in which contemporary women on *Doctor Who*, and in television more generally, find the agency to express and reimagine their femininity. However, as the examples above suggest, the classic period of the show was a rich period and a complex playing field within which to perform and to read gender.

Sarah Jane Smith, Women's Liberation and the Changing Role of the Companion

The people involved in the production of *Doctor Who*—producers, script editors, writers, directors, and actors—were immersed in the larger social debate over gender roles, whether they wanted to be or not. As our opening epigraph illustrates, the writers were very conscious of how the relationship between the Doctor and his companions was being read through the lens of the feminist movement. The waffling between strong and weak women in the representations of the Doctor's various companions mirrors that ambivalence towards changing gender roles that the larger British society held. In 1970 Liz Shaw's role as an intellectual (almost) peer to the Doctor was unappealing to producer Barry Letts, even when she was clad in surprisingly short skirts. As actor Caroline John explained,

> Jon came, and this was a new Doctor, so they wanted to upgrade the show so dads would watch. So they started saying, we're not going to have a boy companion [as had previously been the norm], we're going to have a woman, like *The Avengers*.... They wanted to make it more adult. And to make her a scientist. She was intelligent. And then when Barry [Letts] came on the scene, he thought, she's too intelligent, really, so they got rid of me.[26]

Her replacement's subordinate status was established in her very first scene by the Doctor, who calls Jo Grant a "ham-fisted bungler" when she puts out a fire that he has created ("The Terror of the Autons" #55). Any suggestion of her potential competence is immediately squashed as her effort to take initiative by responding to a small explosion (which she assumed was out of control since the Doctor cried "Oh, no!" and began choking on the smoke) is ridiculed by his arrogant assertion of her idiocy, which he proceeds to emphasize by explaining how she had destroyed his experiment in jargon-laden techno-babble. From this inauspicious start, Jo Grant's character (who appeared on the show from 1971–1973) is relegated to the role of flighty blond who requires frequent rescuing, despite her credentials as "a fully qualified agent" with expertise in "[c]ryptology, safe breaking, [and] explosives."

Eventually the producers felt that they needed to try once again to address the social changes wrought by feminism in Britain, replacing the pre-women's liberation Jo Grant, who happily abandoned her career as a UNIT agent to support the work of her new husband ("The Green Death" #69), with the single, independently-minded journalist Sarah Jane Smith.[27] Then-producer and director Barry Letts explained, "We want Sarah to be very much her own person, someone of today, with her own job, and always questioning everything."[28] Sarah Jane was initially imagined to be, if not the Doctor's scientific peer (like Liz Shaw), then at least his social peer. According to Letts, "It was somebody who almost by accident—and indeed, in the first story, by accident—got involved with him, and got involved with the story. And so they became friends."[29]

However, this was not a universal attitude held by the entire production team. Writer and script editor Terrance Dicks, for example, opined, "Somewhat to my disgust, there was the onset of feminism, you see. Now Barry was okay with this. *I* feel the right place for the heroine is strapped to the circular saw, screaming her head off til the Doctor comes to rescue her. Or the railroad tracks, as the case may be. But it was becoming obvious we couldn't get away with that anymore."[30] Sladen herself was ambivalent about her role as the voice of feminism on the show: "What that [being a journalist] meant was that she could stand up for herself. And I hate the word 'women's lib,' but sometimes I did have to stand up for myself. Sometimes I was the only girl there. And you learn how to *play* that."[31] Sladen's particular brand of feminism (despite her resistance to that label) was emblematic of the national attitude towards gender roles. Unequal pay and sex discrimination were accepted as wrong, but the day-to-day expressions of sexism often defied that kind of clarity. Jon Pertwee's paternalistic behavior towards her, as well as the indignity of having her professional credentials challenged regularly on set, drove her mad. As she wrote in her memoir,

> Patronising isn't really the word. (Actually, yes it is—it's the perfect word.) Unfortunately, this wasn't something that disappeared with the first episode. A constant turnover of directors, crew and production personnel meant I repeatedly encountered new people who assumed I'd been hired from a modelling agency and not from a background of twenty-odd years, girl and woman, on the stage.[32]

Throughout her tenure on the show—which ran from 1973–1976, encompassing the heyday of British second wave feminism—Sladen recognized that she would need to stand up to what she referred to as the "casual sexism on the show" both for herself as an actor, and for Sarah Jane as a character.[33] In her first on-screen conversation with the Doctor, she sets very clear boundaries, both for the Doctor and for the audience, with her strong negative response to the Doctor's suggestion that she could make herself useful by making some coffee ("The Time Warrior" #70). Even with the show's clear mandate to change the role of the companion, Sladen faced an entrenched sexism on the set. As she soon discovered, "Doctor Who in those days could be a bit of a boy's club, I think it's fair to say. A lot of my predecessors were written to be supplementary to the action. I needed to shoehorn Sarah Jane into the action as quickly and firmly as possible—and that had to start with the boys of UNIT...."[34] The physical demands of the role gave her the opportunity to physically express Sarah Jane's spunk, attacking "each hurdle with gusto" and "showing she was as much of a swashbuckler as any man—or Time Lord."[35]

Sladen worked hard to make her character believable, showing vulnerability when appropriate, but never allowing that to prevent her from taking action. When, in "The Ark in Space" (#76), she gets stuck in a ventilation shaft, Sarah Jane starts to panic and cries out of fear and frustration. Yet the Doctor understands that the best way to motivate her is by taunting her with the possibility of failure: "That's the trouble with girls like you. You think you're tough, but when you're really up against it, you've no guts at all."[36] Enraged by his insults, Sarah Jane saves herself. Having "guts," being a strong woman who cannot just keep up, but can hold her own with the Doctor, was fundamental to how Sladen enacted Sarah Jane Smith.

While Sarah Jane occasionally vocalized an explicit feminist position—as in "The Time Warrior" when she tries to foment revolution among the women working in the kitchen, exhorting them to "set yourselves free," or when she lectures the Queen in "The Monster of Peladon" (#73) that "There's nothing *only* about being a girl"—Sladen primarily worked to embody a strong female character in a male-dominated universe through her delivery of lines and physical movements. (Of course, as Sherry Ginn points out, despite the explicit feminism of Sarah Jane's statement, there is a sort of paternalism in both the ethnocentrism of a white Briton decreeing what women's liberation ought to look like in an alien culture, and—as Elisabeth Sladen herself acknowledges—in the fact that these words were scripted for her by men.[37])

Arguably, it was Sladen's subtle expressions of agency (often snatched from within the long takes and wide shots of the three-camera format) rather than her scripted feminism, which waxed and waned according to the whims of male screenwriters, that gave her character such depth and such longevity in the fans' memories. Her snarky "Ooooh, I know you're a 'Time Lord'" comment in response to the fourth Doctor's self-important "I walk in eternity speech" from "The Pyramids of Mars" (#82)—accompanied by face-making, eye-rolling, and laughing—took some of the wind out of his portentousness. Similarly, Sladen drives home the Doctor's intractable childishness in "The Brain of Morbius" (#84), punctuating the line "Stop being so childish" by blowing a raspberry at him and mocking him with a flippant kick of her leg. Her exit stayed true to this principle, for both Sladen and for Sarah Jane. Rather than kill her or marry her off to write her out of the show—options that Sladen believed "would have undone all the 'strong woman' messages we'd delivered over the years"—Sarah Jane says an emotional but stoic goodbye and walks out of the TARDIS calmly, under her own steam.[38]

Brave Heart, Tegan: The Backlash

One the few companions to rival Sarah Jane Smith for fans' enduring love and nostalgia was the brash Australian air stewardess Tegan Jovanka—but against all the odds. A mere four years after Sarah Jane's departure, the game had changed: 1980 introduced new companions, a new Doctor, and a new producer, John Nathan Turner, with whom some of the women co-starring on the show would find it difficult to work. Meanwhile, where the explicit influence of feminism on the show had waxed with Sarah, it had decidedly waned with Tegan—who describes herself as a "mouth on legs" ("Earthshock" #121). Where Barry Letts' openness to Women's Liberation and Elisabeth Sladen's subtle and strong embodiment of the character had been subsequently answered by several strong, capable companions, Tegan inaugurated seven years' bad writing for the Doctor's female companions: until Ace broke the spell with her boom box and penchant for explosives in 1987, the Doctor's female companions weren't vested with much agency. In other words, Tegan's tenure ushered in the Backlash. The attenuated agency represented onscreen ran parallel to both a growing cultural cold shoulder in Britain turned to feminist critiques of gender roles, and to a casual behind-the-scenes disregard for the gains of the show's previous era on the same fronts.

It is all the more remarkable then, that thirty years after her departure from the show, Tegan took first place in a 2014 poll for favorite companion.[39] Even Fielding herself was surprised.[40] Sarah Jane came in second. Given the relatively limited palette of motivations written for her, Tegan's popularity has to be ascribed to the spunk and wit invested in her by Fielding. "I'd always wanted to play Lucy in Charlie Brown," Fielding explained, so she decided that Tegan would be "an Australian Lucy."[41] It is a testament to Fielding's intuitive, sympathetic, and confident portrayal of Tegan that what might have, on paper, read as a fairly constant stream of complaining and nay-saying instead reverses the polarity, sounding a note of much needed challenge to the Doctor's aloof intransigence—and probably a testament as well to Peter Davison's "feckless charm," as the sixth Doctor would later describe it ("The Twin Dilemma" #136), that more viewers weren't turned off by the chauvinism scripted for him, particularly at Tegan's expense.

Whereas both Sarah Jane and Tegan were career women, Tegan's authors forewent the veneer of professionalism so natural to Sarah Jane and the fourth Doctor's subsequent companions. Her first appearance on the show is a madcap effort to even make it to her very first day of work ("Logopolis" #115). Tegan and her aunt are written as 1980s Lucys and Ethels who struggle to drive cars, close doors, and change tires. Tegan's frustrated efforts to take care of things on her own comes across as Fielding's own irritation at being written into a role from which common sense and basic competence are being withheld.

You can arguably sense the actress struggling to temper her irritation at the diminutive role by which she is constrained. Her portrayal, therefore, invested these scripts with a more profound voice. Her farewell scene—when Tegan has finally had enough death and mayhem—reads on the page as a reflection of Tegan's own growing traumatization by the dangers of space/time travel. But in action, the scene indicts not Tegan's squeamishness, but the Doctor's desensitization to it all ("Resurrection of the Daleks" #133). Similarly, when Adric dies, it is Tegan who indicts the Doctor's aloofness, refusing to let him sail away from the loss without comment, like he has from so many other deaths along his travels ("Time-Flight" #122).

Fielding's portrayal, however, was not simply a case of strong characterizations onscreen. Rather, like Sladen before her, she had to "play," strategically, albeit upon a much different playing field. Where many of the moments of leeway for expression and character development described above were characteristic of *Doctor Who* during the 1970s, Fielding's were wrested from a noticeably harsher climate on- and offscreen for women's agency. That Fielding was still able to do so in the climate of the 1980s backlash against feminism is indicative of some of the same slippages and playing fields we have already described.

One of the key determinants of those playing fields was producer John Nathan Turner himself—by some accounts as intransigent as the Doctor. "At first, it was awful," commented Sophie Aldred, on their working relationship, "He didn't really understand me, because he came from the world of Joan Collins–ish type glam, the Kate O'Maras of this world, and Bonnie Langford. And he didn't really understand at all why I didn't want to shave my armpits, y'know."[42] Anticipating the show's later, centralized production model, Turner developed a reputation for making creative decisions somewhat autocratically, without consulting the performers (the seventh Doctor's rainbow-colored costume being the most infamous example). Fielding, for one, was highly critical of the costumes chosen for her by Turner. Of the beige "boob-tube" ensemble from season twenty, she commented: "I had that unspeakable costume that John designed. It was neither warm nor sexy nor interesting nor flattering. I cannot find a good word to say about this costume."[43] The costumes, indeed, are a useful index of the show's historical context and its reflection in the casual sexism in the production team, as Fielding and her costar Sarah Sutton—who played Nyssa—both recalled Turner altering their costumes over time in response to viewers' letters asking to see more of them, literally. Sutton commented that Turner replaced her more comfortable, practical pants during her first season with a skirt in response to letters asking "where have Sarah's legs gone?"[44] (Compare this to Sladen's experience, in which she was given the leeway to work with the costume designer and choose Sarah Jane's outfits—gradually evolving from her initially conservative pantsuits to more outlandish ensembles, to reflect the Doctor's bohemian influence.[45])

The creative control extended beyond costumes, of course. Fielding noted that, unlike during other eras of the show, Turner wouldn't let performers watch themselves on the studio monitors. Indeed, as she said bluntly, "nobody helped you," explaining that while on other programs the directors and producers would give guidance to the performers on everything from characterization to blocking, on *Doctor Who*, there was little creative dialogue between producers and performers.[46] In this context, Fielding distinguished herself, by initiating some of that dialogue herself, particularly in an effort to afford Tegan more onscreen agency. "I can remember having fights with John about the way the girls were treated," she recalls, describing for example a scene in *The Five Doctors*: "As originally written, the girls went off to make the tea.... I got it changed so that Mark [Strickson] also went off to make tea with the girls."[47] Indeed, Fielding's savvy behind the scenes continued on afterwards as she eventually gave up acting to work as an agent. In that role, and as recurring commentator at *Doctor Who* conventions and productions, her vocal critique of gender roles on *Doctor Who* and in the industry has continued. "When I was an agent," she commented, "there weren't that many roles for women, and they dried up when you got beyond the ingénue stage. And it hasn't changed *that* much."[48]

Fielding's approach to Tegan, then, reflects a valuable critique of gender explicitly played against that of the writers and producers, a strategy better suited to the playing field of 1980s Backlash Britain than to the 1970s under the influence of the Women's Liberation Movement. Her exit, too, is a testament to the on-going need for women's voices as a corrective, not just to the Doctor's behavior, but also to the production of the show and the larger British backlash-enmeshed society. Tegan's final line on the show, an echo of the Doctor's common rejoinder to her, was written as a nostalgic epitaph for her tenure: "Brave heart Tegan," she says as the TARDIS vanishes ("Resurrection of the Daleks"). Fielding's own response to the line is just as much an epitaph of her vocal critiques of gender and paternalism on the show. While commenting on this episode, Peter Davison and Peter Grimwade, the director, both rate this scene as touching, and the line as iconic. Fielding's rejoinder is simply, bluntly, "What an awful line."[49]

Conclusion

As we have argued throughout, such spaces and slippages emerged from the structure of *Doctor Who's* production team and format during the classic era. They enabled the actors to play out their own resistances to frustrations experienced within the show, and in the process to inflect their characters with additional gendered dimensions that embodied neither unequivocal empowerment nor two-dimensional sexism, but rather the contested, polyvocal politics of their day. The cacophony of voices and interpretations made possible by the show's production created opportunities for ambivalence about, confusion around, resistance to, and embrace of feminist notions that were percolating in each era to shine through. Elisabeth Sladen's vacillation, for example, between discomfort at being cast as the voice of women's liberation on *Doctor Who* and chafing at the on-going humiliation of the day-to-day sexism she encountered on set was presumably matched by much of the audience, which was also struggling to make sense of rapidly changing gender roles in Britain during that period. Her ambivalence reflected the on-going debates over women's roles in a country which had comparatively quickly embraced legal correctives to sex discrimination, while simultaneously resisting calls for more sweeping changes to existing social roles. In turn, the fight to be treated equitably and professionally that so marked Elisabeth Sladen's (and Sarah Jane Smith's) tenure on *Doctor Who* was echoed in Janet Fielding's (and Tegan Jovanka's) uphill struggle against diminutive characterizations and a societal backlash while reasserting her right to those gains won by an earlier generation of companions and actresses.

The influence of their labors lives on not only in the fans' memories, but in the precedents set for future narratives. The affection and collaboration between Rose Tyler and the Doctor was arguably only thinkable in the wake of the camaraderie between the fourth Doctor and his "best friend." Similarly, Clara Oswald's recent reinvention as the Doctor's moral compass (quoth the Doctor: "She cares so that I don't have to" ["Into the Dalek" 8.02]) is hard to imagine without recalling Tegan's open skepticism and critique. The behind-the-scenes work of these actors, and their respective production teams, therefore, succeeded in reshaping the playing field for future generations of actors, writers, and audiences. And, of course, the place of the heroine continues to change. Whereas auteurs and editors now exercise much more agency upon the show, slippages and disjunctures are nonetheless inevitable within any ongoing cultural production, and therein will be time and space for agency. Who knows what continuums of gender will emerge from such vortices? *Who*, knows?

Notes

1. "Riot grrl" is deliberately misspelled by self-identified participants in the subcultural movement of the same name.
2. Geertz, *The Interpretation of Cultures*, 3–30.
3. Braybon and Frick, "Report" to Donald Wilson.
4. Ortner, *Making Gender*, 12.
5. *Ibid.*, 11–12.

6. *Ibid.*, 17.
7. *Ibid.*, 17.
8. *Ibid.*, 18.
9. "Girls! Girls! Girls!: The 1970s."
10. Ortner, *Making Gender*, 19.
11. Wini Breines posits several potential markers of the end of the 1950s, including Kennedy's assassination, the Beatles' arrival in the US, or the publication of Betty Friedan's *The Feminine Mystique* in her book *Young, White, and Miserable*, xii.
12. Leach, *Doctor Who*, 1.
13. For more about this see: Bouchier; Meehan; Mendes.
14. Quoted in Mendes, "'The Lady Is a Closet Feminist!,'" 556.
15. Susan Faludi's seminal book *Backlash* (which popularized the term) explores this phenomenon in detail in the US context, and constitutes an important point of reference for Mendes' analysis of British feminism and the British backlash against it.
16. Hammond and Mazdon, *The Contemporary Television Series*.
17. Moore, "University Study on Sexism in Doctor Who." Note that while we have cited the reports of fan-bloggers whose research methodologies are not wholly transparent, the Bechdel test is itself only an approximate guide, and a straightforward one at that, designed for home use. (See also Bechdel.)
18. "How Sexist is *Doctor Who*?: Part One."
19. Webber, "Science Fiction."
20. Sladen, *Elisabeth Sladen: The Autobiography*, 209. (Author's emphasis.)
21. *Ibid.*, 155.
22. *Ibid.*, 189.
23. *Ibid.*, 162.
24. "Girls! Girls! Girls!: The 1970s."
25. "Girls! Girls! Girls!: The 1980s."
26. "Girls! Girls! Girls!: The 1970s."
27. Sladen, *Autobiography*, 83.
28. *Ibid.*, 83
29. "Beginning the End."
30. *Ibid.*
31. "Doctor Who Stories: Elisabeth Sladen Part 1." Interviewee's emphasis in original.
32. Sladen, *Autobiography*, 100.
33. *Ibid.*
34. *Ibid.*, 100
35. *Ibid.*, 94.
36. In her autobiography, Sladen seems to explain that this iconic moment was unscripted and that she had actually become stuck in the shaft, and that her escape was managed with both of them remaining in character: *Ibid.*, 165–66.
37. Ginn, "Spoiled for Another Life: Sarah Jane Smith's Adventures With and Without Doctor Who."
38. Sladen, *Autobiography* 215. (It is worth noting that Sarah Jane's composure and agency in her farewell episode is somewhat undermined by the retconning (i.e. retroactive reimagination in a show's continuity) of Sarah Jane's implicit heartbreak and romantic intentions towards the Doctor when she encounters him in 2006's "School Reunion" (2.3).
39. Candy Jar Books, Online Poll Results, "Vote for Your Favourite Companion."
40. Martin, "Tegan Voted Best 'Doctor Who' Companion Ever," *Cultbox*.

41. "Girls! Girls! Girls!: The 1980s."
42. "The Den of Geek Interview: Sophie Aldred."
43. "Girls! Girls! Girls!: the 1980s."
44. *Ibid.*
45. Sladen, *Autobiography*, 196.
46. "Girls! Girls! Girls!: the 1980s."
47. *Ibid.*
48. *Ibid.*
49. Peter Davison and Janet Fielding, audio commentary, *Doctor Who: Resurrection of the Daleks.*

Life Post–TARDIS?
The Case for Jo Grant and Sarah Jane Smith

Sherry Ginn

Doctor Who, according to Steven Moffat (qtd. in Lacob), has always been about the companion. The companions who travel with any given Doctor serve as a substitute for the viewer and a person with whom the viewer can identify, the person who will be transported into the past or into the future to share the Doctor's adventures. These companions may be male or female, human or alien, young or old, but they must always be ready and willing for the adventure of a life-time. During that adventure the companions will face danger and terror and learn about their strengths and weaknesses. Each will grow as a person and the assumption is that each will leave the Doctor's company better for having made the journey. However, Lynnette Porter notes that each companion pays a price for travel with the Doctor. "They lose their innocence, and quite often they become physically or emotionally injured as a result of their travels.... The Doctor, however, seldom follows up to 'heal' the wounds his companions suffer."[1] But is that necessarily true? Certainly we have watched numerous companions over the five decades of *Doctor Who*: some choose to leave him on their own terms as Jo Grant did. Some sacrifice themselves to save the Doctor, their planets, their friends or families, such as River Song. Some are forced to leave him, like Donna Noble. And, he has even, on occasion, been forced to leave them.

Such is the case with one of the most popular of the Doctor's companions, Sarah Jane Smith, who traveled with both the Third and Fourth incarnations of the Doctor (1973–1976).[2] Portrayed by Elisabeth Sladen, Sarah Jane figured in 18 adventures before 'retiring' from further travel. Attempts were made briefly to revive Sarah Jane, but those efforts were unsuccessful. Sarah Jane was reunited with the tenth Doctor in three episodes: "School Reunion" (from which the CBBC launched *The Sarah Jane Adventures* in 2007), "The Stolen Earth," and "Journey's End"; and the eleventh Doctor when invited to his funeral.

Sarah Jane provides a glimpse into the aftereffects of travel with the Doctor, as we are able to examine the life of this woman during those travels as well as afterwards. Despite the laments of various companions, notably Rose Tyler, as to how they could ever live without the Doctor, Sarah Jane did have a life after she left the Doctor, as we learned during her reunion with the tenth Doctor and her subsequent adventures on Bannerman Road.

In addition, we learn about her life after her adventures with the Doctor when we encounter Jo Grant (Jones) when she comes to the Doctor's funeral in the *Sarah Jane Adventures* two-part episode "The Death of the Doctor" (4.3). Jo Grant traveled with the third incarnation of the Doctor (1971–1973). Portrayed by Katy Manning, Jo Grant figured in 15 adventures before leaving the Doctor to marry scientist Clifford Jones. Not only do Sarah Jane and Jo bond over their status as companions, we learn that Sarah Jane has attempted to find other companions from Earth, telling Jo what she discovered. Information about Jo's life is not as well-delineated as is Sarah Jane's, but we can examine the information available to give us a glimpse into what happened to her following her departure from the Doctor's travels. The purpose of this paper is to examine briefly Sarah Jane's and Jo's lives, to see how each changed from our first meeting with them, their first meeting with the Doctor. To do this I will examine their lives through the lens of Psychosocial Developmental Theory, as proposed by Erik Erikson, and Life-Course Developmental Theory, as proposed by Daniel Levinson.

"Whether it's a world, or a relationship.... Everything has its time. And everything ends."[3]

Two theories that dominated psychology during the twentieth century were Sigmund Freud's Theory of Psychosexual Development and Jean Piaget's Cognitive-Developmental Theory. Freud was particularly interested in elucidating the stages through which the individual's personality developed from birth into adolescence. Piaget, on the other hand, was concerned with the changes that occurred in the way children and adolescents think. Each theory was important for shaping the field of developmental psychology; however, neither postulated development past adolescence, proposing instead that human beings' personality and cognitive structures were molded by childhood experiences. Neither proposed that significant changes occurred beyond adolescence and into adulthood.

One theorist who did propose that human development continued throughout the lifespan was Erik Erikson. In the tradition of Freud and Piaget, Erikson postulated that psychological development occurs in a series of stages that are heavily influenced by biological and cultural constraints. Erikson believed that development proceeds in eight stages from birth until death, with each stage characterized by a crisis that the individual must overcome in order for development to proceed in a healthy manner. For the purposes of this essay on the lives of Jo Grant and Sarah Jane Smith, three of the adult stages are important.

During adolescence one confronts the questions "Who am I and why am I here?" The heart of the fifth stage of development, Identity vs. Role-confusion, is the identity crisis. The adolescent must confront the roles that he or she has played in his or her life thus far and incorporate them into a cohesive identity. To this end the adolescent must be allowed to explore new and different roles or different paths in previous roles. Failure to synthesize an identity leads to the inability to find direction in life and pursue a meaningful future. Following identity development the adolescent enters young adulthood, in which the overwhelming social pressure is to find a mate. Increasingly intimate relationships with friends and the drive toward marriage and procreation characterize this stage. Thus, young adulthood is the period of childbearing and childrearing. Generativity vs. Stagnation, the stage encompassing middle adulthood, is characterized by launching one's children into the world. Some middle-aged individuals may now feel a need to "give-back" to the world, and these people become concerned with future generations, a concern that may manifest as charitable work. However, the primary task of this stage is helping younger generations of people develop useful and productive lives.

When we meet Sarah Jane Smith in "The Time Warrior," she is 23 years old and working as a journalist.[4] For some time after that, representing three years in our world, she travels with the Doctor until she is forced to return home. Sarah Jane has apparently resolved her identity crisis and is comfortable with her career choice, which has led to her experiences with the Doctor. As we meet up with her over the next ten years or so, we find that she has continued her work as a journalist and she is apparently quite good at it. She drops names of very respected journals and magazines, letting us know that her career has proceeded very well. However, the two times we encounter Sarah Jane between her adventures with the Doctor and those on Bannerman Road ("K-9 and Company," "The Five Doctors") we do not learn very much about her private life. Nor will we learn anything about her private life until she meets the Doctor again in "School Reunion." Unlike Rose Tyler or Martha Jones, Sarah Jane never indicated that she harbored romantic feelings for the Doctor. Nevertheless, she expresses the depth of her feelings toward him in "School Reunion," telling the tenth Doctor how devastated she was when he never returned for her.[5] She tells him that he was her life, and his cryptic response is that he could not come back for her because everyone died. Before leaving again the Doctor invites Sarah Jane to come along with Rose and him, but she says no, it is time that she stopped waiting for him and found a life of her own. Little does she realize that the new life she finds will include a teen-age son.

When the Doctor asked her about her life and she replied that no, she had no children, she never had time (although why the Doctor would have to ask such questions is a mystery, as shouldn't he already know?), Sarah Jane was not contemplating changing her life in such dramatic fashion. Apparently Sarah Jane has not resolved the crisis of Erikson's Stage Six of development, as she does not seem to have developed a close relationship with a person of either the opposite or same sex. She appears to have completely skipped Stage Six. Several theorists, including Erikson, have proposed that women sometimes flip Stages Five and Six. That is, women will sometimes enter into an intimate relationship with another person prior to establishing a clear sense of identity. However, it does not appear that such is the case with Sarah Jane, much as "School Reunion" makes it appear that she would have liked a relationship with the Doctor. Indeed, Nina Allan complains that the "script [of this episode] still manages to convey the sense of a life wasted, of a woman who has spent much of the last 20 years awaiting the Doctor's return."[6]

Examining Sarah Jane's life in the present, she appears to be in Stage Seven, Generativity vs. Stagnation. Although Sarah Jane does not have biological children, she adopts a son who was created by aliens using human DNA, and a daughter who is not human; each was left with no one to take care of them. Sarah Jane is clearly mentoring a group of young people, teaching them to question things that are not quite right, how to investigate, and to be brave and resourceful. Much as she was the Doctor's companion for a number of years, she has four teens, five if we count Maria, acting as hers. It is during the time of her adventures on Bannerman Road that we begin to see Sarah Jane re-assessing her life and questioning some of the decisions that she made when younger. This time of reflection, a crisis we could say, is not unique to Sarah Jane. According to Daniel Levinson both men and women have several times in their adult lives when they experience transition points, or shifts, in their developmental trajectories.

Jo Grant Jones also appears to be Stage Seven of Erikson's theory, although by her own account, her life is anything but typical. Like Sarah Jane, when we first encounter Jo she has apparently resolved her "identity crisis" and is ready to begin her adult life. Jo was about 18 or 19 years old when her uncle—apparently a well-placed uncle—pulled some strings and got her a job with UNIT ("Terror of the Autons" #55). Joking, or perhaps not, the Brigadier assigns her to be the Doctor's assistant, knowing that what the Doctor needs is someone to fetch his tea and tell him how brilliant he is. Liz Shaw, the third Doctor's first companion, was a scientist, rather too brilliant for the Doctor, hence the Brigadier's search for a new assistant. Jo promptly destroys an experiment conducted by the Doctor, setting the stage for much of their future together. She is "scatty," notes Katy Manning, who played the part of Jo, adding "I'm supposed to crack safes and pick locks, *Avengers*-style … but really I need looking after."[7] Katy Manning is extremely near-sighted, refusing to wear her glasses on camera. This fact led to Jo's apparent clumsiness and frequent tumbles on screen; Mike Yates refers to her as "Jemima Bond: License to Spill" in the audio adventure "The Doll of Death." These characteristics would eventually endear her to the Doctor and contribute to his paternal (and paternalistic) feelings toward her. As a matter of fact, Barry Letts and Terrance Dicks note that UNIT provided the third Doctor with a family.[8]

Jo's mission—to serve as the Doctor's assistant—is one she fulfills brilliantly throughout her tenure with the third Doctor. Jo becomes very attached to the Doctor, often risking her life to save him from danger, and even offering to sacrifice herself to save his life on more than one occasion (such as in "The Dæmons" #59). Unfortunately in a series with multiple writers and no writers' Bible, á la *Star Trek*, her character changes from story to story. Sometimes she is confident and not at all ditzy, sometimes even resilient, self-sufficient, and almost bright. For example, in the episode "The Mind of Evil" (#56) she actually fights physically when threatened. However, in the very next story "The Claws of Axos" all she does is scream, wear an extremely short skirt, and reveal the color of her knickers—a lot! It is also amusing to read early interviews with Katy Manning, in which she states that "I really need looking after.…"[9] Commentaries on "her" episodes of the series inevitably have her recalling Jo as much more accomplished and less scatter-brained than we remember. For example, in the commentary for "The Mind of Evil," Manning states that Jo exhibited "spot-on caring," that she was really solid and very capable, often taking the side of the under-dog (and exactly where did the idea of her being dizzy come from?, she asks). Plus, she states that Jo was much smarter than anyone gave her credit for in the commentary to "Colony in Space" (#58). In a recent tweet, Katy Manning posted "I liked Jo! so oft misunderstood! Thought she was funny feisty brave clumsy & always ready to lay down her life for the doctor."[10]

As befitting a young woman in the 1970s, Jo is quite open-minded. She can suspend belief, as when meeting an alien "monster," and is willing to believe in the supernatural, although the Doctor chides her on being so superstitious (as in "The Dæmons").[11] However, she is still a young woman and can be quite naïve as well as too trusting. In her earlier adventures with the Doctor she has a tendency to see things in black and white, with no shades of gray, but becomes less rigid in her thought-patterns as she becomes more mature and has more adventures with the Doctor. Nevertheless she is frightened when first entering the TARDIS, pleading with the Doctor to return them to Earth ("Colony in Space"). Her trust in the Doctor—that he will protect her and that everything will work out properly—deepens his feelings toward her. As Steve Tribe notes, the Doctor warmed up to Jo over time because he quickly recognized "that every setback made her more determined to succeed next time."[12] Although Katy Manning thinks that there was "something" between the Doctor and Jo, Jon Pertwee insisted that it was more a fatherly/familial thing, even when she left him to marry Clifford Jones at the end of "The Green Death."

Jo is a healthy young woman and she has a number of flirtations with various men encountered in her adventures with the Doctor. Captain Yates was originally meant to be a love interest for her, but their relationship remained platonic.[13] Her various flirtations and her eventual decision to marry Clifford Jones—perhaps he seemed to be a younger version of the Doctor—situate her squarely within Erikson's stage of Intimacy vs. Isolation during her tenure with the Doctor.

Irrespective of her faults, she exhibits two character traits that will follow her throughout her time with the Doctor and her life with her family afterwards. These are compassion and loyalty. Although the Doctor sometimes tells Jo to look after someone in a story, he does not always have to tell her to do so. She is good when taking this maternal role—even though she is such a young woman—and is visibly upset when those placed in her care die, such as in "The Mind of Evil" when she bonds with Barnham, who later sacrifices himself for everyone. In addition, her loyalty to the Doctor means that she will place his agenda above all others. However, that does not mean that she follows him blindly nor does it mean that she does not question his motives or his actions. The Doctor is proud that she becomes more independent with time, but is not happy that she becomes independent of him.

"Last time I saw you, Jo Grant, you were what— 21, 22? It's like someone baked you!"[14]

Although Erik Erikson's Psychosocial Theory provides a framework for examining the lives of both Jo Grant and Sarah Jane Smith, each character's life can also be analyzed using a different theory, called Life-Course Developmental Theory. Daniel Levinson and his colleagues developed this theory following the completion of extensive and in-depth interviews with men and women at various times in their adulthood, beginning in late adolescence and continuing until late middle adulthood. Based upon the interviews with his sample of women, Levinson separated women into two categories: a homemaker sample, or those with a Traditional Marriage Enterprise, and a career woman sample, or those with an Anti-Traditional Marriage Enterprise. Those women who espouse the Traditional Marriage Enterprise marry at an early age either directly after high school, in college, or shortly after college and begin having children shortly after marriage. They generally do not work outside of the home once their children are born; however, they may seek a job after their children reach school-age. Like their husbands these women believe that a woman's primary responsibility is to her children and therefore she should not work outside of the home. Those that must work outside the home due to financial constraints are generally unhappy. Nevertheless some of the women found that they enjoyed this outside work and transitioned from part-time employment to full-time as their children aged.

The women who espoused the 'Anti-Traditional Marriage Enterprise' in Levinson's sample were career women who worked in corporate America or academia. The women in this category were quite diverse as far as their lives were concerned; they were less likely to be married, have children, and be involved in a traditional marriage. They believed in what Levinson called the Successful Career Woman myth, which stated that women could have it all: career, marriage, family, and leisure, everything if they just worked hard enough. However, by middle age, during a period referred to as the Mid-Life Transition (approximately 40–46), these women were questioning this myth, realizing that instead of being a Successful Career Woman, they were actually Jugglers, "who managed to keep several spheres moving at the same time, but who had a very restricted life and little connection to her self and her inner spheres."[15] This is a period of time when career women begin to question and reconsider what it means to have a career or a marriage or a family, perhaps asking the question "Is this all there is?"

Unfortunately Levinson's sample did not study women much older than 50; however, it is my belief that both Jo and Sarah Jane, even though they are older than Levinson's sample, fit nicely into the mid-life transition described above. Sarah Jane has had a satisfying career as a journalist; she is apparently well-respected and well-connected. She is good enough at her job that she has been able to continue it for almost forty years. Yet, she also realizes, once she meets Luke, that the decisions she made earlier in life—to have a career and not a family—might not have been the best decision. Hence, her decision to 'adopt' Luke and later Sky, her obvious love for Luke, and her continued mentorship of the teenagers Maria, Clyde, and Rani, indicate that Sarah Jane has reached a transition point in her life, where she reassesses her life and decides to follow a different path. As mentioned earlier, Sarah Jane's life would also reflect Erikson's Stage 7 of Generativity, where she begins to "give back" to the next generation: her knowledge of what is "out there," her curiosity, her refusal to take no for an answer coupled with her refusal to accept anything at "face-value." Her life also reflects Levinson's Life Course Theory which proposes that developmental transition points occur periodically throughout one's life, when one examines the decisions made and determines if a new trajectory is called for.

Despite her work with UNIT and her travels with the Doctor as well as living during a time when opportunities for women were exploding, Jo leaves the Doctor, choosing to marry a man who would show her adventures on her favorite Planet ("The Green Death" #69). Jo and Clifford apparently have a successful marriage; they are still married when Jo meets Sarah Jane.[16] They raise 7 children and now have 12 grandchildren, with a 13th on the way. She brings one of the grandsons, Santiago, to the Doctor's funeral. He has fond words for his grandmother, although is quite aware of how ditzy she can be, an adjective used to describe Jo during her early-twenties as well. Jo certainly appears to have followed Erikson's trajectory of adult development, learning about herself and growing into a more competent woman during her time with the Doctor, then developing an intimate relationship with a spouse, rearing and caring for children, while also giving back to the world through her activism, instilling in her children and her grandchildren the importance of caring for Planet Earth and all of the creatures inhabiting it.[17]

Levinson would place Jo squarely in the Traditional Marriage Enterprise camp—marrying soon after school by choice and then choosing to raise children. Indeed Jo apparently never questioned the decision to marry and have a family. Her primary regret with respect to the Doctor was that he never contacted her again following her departure. Kate Flynn notes that Jo's remarks to the Doctor are that he promised he would keep in touch with her and he broke his promise, a childish lament that indicates her relationship with the Doctor was parental. I have suggested the same with respect to Sarah Jane and the Doctor. One could say in the language of pop psychology that Jo and Sarah Jane's meeting with the Doctor at his "funeral" allowed them closure, indeed giving each woman a renewed sense of purpose and a sense that each had finally achieved independent adulthood.

Sarah Jane Smith, although only a fictional character, provides the viewer with many positive exemplars of a woman living life on her own terms. However, those terms include having a large amount of money and teenage children, the first to allow her the luxury of not having to worry about how to pay the bills and the second of not having to worry about diapers and childcare. Obviously intending to appeal to children and adolescents, *The Sarah Jane Adventures* does provide this audience with several positive role models of women: Sarah Jane is an investigative journalist, with a secret life; Rani Chandra is a teenage girl who plans to have a career and is not constantly obsessing about boys; and, Rani's mother, Gita Chandra, owns her own flower shop. Given that over 60 percent of the female population in the U.S., Canada, and Britain work outside the home, even those with young children, a television series that portrays women in the work force does reflect the reality of contemporary life.

Jo, unlike Sarah Jane, fell in love with a man who clearly loved her and with whom she shared a common vision of service to Planet Earth. She shared in his adventures, which included living among the natives in Brazil and traveling to such places as China and Africa. They raised children together, something that is increasingly less likely to happen in the 21st century, when fewer people are marrying, choosing to have children, or having children while married. It would seem that Jo continued to be "traditional" in the sense that she was a mother who supported her husband in his endeavors and was apparently happy to do so.

Nevertheless, these women were privileged, beyond their tenure in the TARDIS. Both were obviously educated, even if Sarah Jane appears to have been the better student. Each also appears to have advantages that the average Briton did not have during the 1960s, a time when the country was still suffering the financial ill-effects of the Second World War. Middle-class in the traditional sense of the world, Sarah Jane and Jo both had connections that helped them establish themselves in life. For Sarah Jane it was relatives with money and for Jo it was relatives with connections. As mentioned earlier, money helped Sarah Jane pursue her search for aliens' presence on Earth. Having press credentials allowed her access for exploration, but being able to work free-lance allowed her the independence to pursue stories of her own choosing. For Jo it was an uncle who got her the job with UNIT that allowed her to have adventures—if she were male we would say she was "sowing wild oats"—before settling down to married life, although we could hardly say that she "settled down" following her marriage to Clifford Jones.

What Jo Grant Jones and Sarah Jane Smith also provide us with are examples of women who made choices that shaped their futures. We met each character during a time of great political turmoil with respect to women's lives. Based upon both her beliefs and her actions, Sarah Jane would be labeled a feminist. The timing of her tenure aboard the TARDIS would coincide with the rise of Women's Liberation and what is now referred to as second-wave feminism.[18] Jo Grant is not quite a feminist, but I do not think she thought of herself as a doormat. She certainly believed in fighting for what she thought important. As a matter of fact, one could almost label Jo a third-wave feminist, one who will insist upon having it all (before it becomes clear that such a plan is not possible).[19] Each woman took a different trajectory with respect to her life, thus each embodied a core tenet with respect to feminism—women have choices and those choices should be respected. What we have here are two of the Doctor's companions who did not suffer following their departure from the Tardis, who lived full lives, apparently on their own terms. At least with respect to Jo Grant and Sarah Jane Smith we have examples, not of life imitating art, but rather art imitating life.[20]

NOTES

1. Porter, *Tarnished Heroes*, 228.
2. *The Telegraph*'s poll places Sarah Jane Smith as the number one Doctor's assistant and Jo Grant as number eight.
3. "School Reunion."
4. The portions of this essay about Sarah Jane were originally published in *Doctor Who in Time and Space: Essays on Themes, Characters, History and Fandom, 1963–2012*, 242–252, edited by Gillian I. Leitch. Used with permission. A much shorter version of this essay was presented at the "Walking in Eternity" Conference held at the University of Hertfordshire, September 2014.
5. Some fans, including this one, were decidedly upset at the way Sarah Jane's relationship with the Doctor was "rewritten." See also Giles and Peloff, this collection.
6. Allan, "Forever Playing Second Fiddle," 145.
7. *Radio Times*, 1972, 8; *Radio Times People*, reprinted from "The Dæmons" Special Feature, Disc 2.
8. *Life on Earth* Special Feature, "Terror of the Autons."
9. *Radio Times People*, reprinted from "The Dæmons" Special Feature, Disc 2.
10. @ManningOfficial, May 5, 2014.
11. I agree with Sleight about this episode: The Doctor is even more condescending than usual, not only to Jo but to others, such as Miss Hawthorne, as well.
12. Tribe, *Doctor Who: Companions and Allies*, 28.
13. See for example the commentary from "The Mind of Evil."
14. "The Death of the Doctor."
15. Levinson, *Seasons of a Woman's Life*, 372.
16. Katy Manning has stated that Jo would never have actually married him; she would leave him in the middle of the Amazon and go off on her own adventures (*PanoptiCon '93* interview, "The Three Doctors," DVD special feature).
17. Joan Frances Turner discusses what Jo learned from the Doctor, and what the Doctor learned from her, in her essay "Where in Eternity … is Josephine Grant Jones." Turner notes that one thing Jo learned from the Doctor is that all of our choices have consequences; her choice to make a difference on Planet Earth is an example of the positive effect the Doctor has on his companions.
18. See Tong, *Feminist Thought*, for a thorough review of feminist theory.
19. See Dicker and Piepmeier as well as Baumgardner and Richards for information on third-wave feminism.
20. I was invited to attend a "Celebration of Doctor Who," hosted by Paul Booth, at DePaul University in 2013. I talked about Sarah Jane at one of my panels and I remember someone in the audience making the comment that I talked about her as if she were a real person. I was taken aback and didn't really know how to reply at first. Of course, we treat our favorite characters (and our not-so-favorite characters) as if they are real. What would be the point of watching a television program if the viewers were not engaged with the characters? For me, I want to see women who are similar to me or who are similar to how I would like to be. And, if the companion is supposed to be a person with whom the audience can identify, then audience members must be able to relate to the companion as if she or he were real.

Rose *Is* England
Nationhood, British Invasion Anxiety and Why the Doctor Will (Almost) Always Rescue His Companions

Tanja Nathanael

With the reboot of the popular British television series *Doctor Who* in 2005, it is perhaps no accident that the first companion to join the Doctor on his new adventures is named Rose. The name Rose is iconic, evoking the English Rose—a suitable symbol for the garden that is England, a place to be cherished and kept safe. The name is also evocative of the Tudor Rose, the symbol of Tudor England, an era when England was becoming aware of itself as a nation and as an empirical force, the new heart of Western civilization. During the reign of Queen Elizabeth I, England as a nation became conflated with the female body, specifically the queen's body. Maps of the British Isles from that period display images of Elizabeth with her foot upon the map of England or with symbols of England on her coronation regalia,[1] or of Britannia, Elizabeth's alter ego, wrapped up in a cloak-like map of England[2]—all suggesting that England is female, not only in the symbolic idea of a political entity, but embedded in the physical geography of the land itself.[3] Anxiety about invasion, although historically always a factor, achieves a new significance: If the land itself is female, then protecting that land from a defiling, foreign invasion is imperative.

The perils of Rose Tyler, then, may be read to signify the perils of England, requiring the Doctor's diligent protection. And yet Rose resists being stereotyped as a damsel-in-distress through empowered action and by interrogating the Doctor's authority. Just as the body of Queen Elizabeth is conflated with England, I argue, the body of Rose is conflated with England. I argue that the Doctor's drive to save Rose is a response to British invasion anxiety and the convention of invasion narratives. I argue that Rose, although empowered, reveals a postmodern discomfort with interrogating the patriarchy, suggesting that England's idea of herself as a nation and as a symbol of Western civilization is undergoing a transformation, one which calls into question the rightful uses of power in a rapidly changing world.

As the focal point of peril, Rose embodies and establishes a new kind of companion—one that exists in a state of tension that results from her need to be protected and her desire to be empowered. In her first act of heroism, she swings down from a high scaffold on a chain, knocking aside the Autons holding the Doctor prisoner and propelling an anti-plastic solution into the heart of the Nestene consciousness ("Rose" 1.01). In her very first episode, Rose saves the world. However, in the following episode, Rose is trapped in a room on the rim of a space station as the sun shields are closing ("End of the World" 1.02). For a good portion of the episode, Rose is menaced with being burned alive and must wait for the Doctor's rescue.

These dramatic moments demonstrate Rose's power and vulnerability and present an uneasiness that resonates with the tension found in George Gascoigne's *The Princely Pleasures* (1576), otherwise known as the Kenilworth plays, light entertainments performed before Elizabeth I in her holiday court. These extravagant court entertainments were based on the chivalrous exploits of King Arthur's Knights of the Round Table; however, they were also meant to be allegorical in nature, illuminating Elizabeth's character and reflecting England's political policies. Further, they revealed the current political tensions in Elizabeth's court.[4] Two of the most intense and politically charged masques were cancelled before their performance and were replaced by ones more suitable, both favoring and favored by the Queen. Later, Gascoigne published his "true copie" of the censored masques, in an attempt to assuage his patron, Robert Dudley, Earl of Leicester.[5]

Susan Frye reports that in Gascoigne's unperformed first version of one of the cancelled masques, the Queen (played by an actor) sends her Captain (played by Dudley) and her knights to rescue the Lady of the Lake from the rapacious Sir Bruse. Gascoigne believed that Elizabeth would appreciate the dynamism of his "military skirmish," even though she was not featured in an active role. However, as Frye notes, "It presents the necessity of a male response to threat by featuring Leicester vanquishing a rapist who threatens the Lady of the Lake and also, by implication, Elizabeth herself."[6] By comparison, in the censored version performed before Elizabeth and the other guests at Kenilworth, the Queen's actions alone disperse the forces of Sir Bruse and free the Lady.[7] By replacing the action of the masque with a non-military device, Frye argues that the masque not only glorifies the Queen's power to overcome threat, but also demonstrates Elizabeth's (mostly) successful move to counteract Dudley's political maneuverings.[8]

Both versions of the "Sir Bruse" masque raise concerns that are problematic. If the Queen is threatened with rape, so too is England, which is a deeply discomforting thought for the audience; however, when the Queen does the rescuing, she is clearly taking the role of a man, an equally uncomfortable reminder of the Queen's (historically male) role as sovereign of England. That England continues to identify itself as female after Elizabeth's time and during the reign of male monarchs is demonstrated in James Gillray's political cartoons (c. 1782–1805).[9] Gillray depicts Britannia sometimes as a child, sometimes as a young woman, sometimes as an old woman, and in varying states of dominance or distress in relation to the predominantly male figures representing other nations. As can be seen, the representation of England as a powerful/vulnerable female body continues to resonate.

I would like to clarify here that I am not conflating Rose with the Queen but drawing a similarity between the way they function as symbols for England.[10] Rose's parallel role of power/weakness demonstrates a kind of postmodern uneasiness with the idea of a companion who can usurp so much of the Doctor's power, and yet anything less would disrupt modern sensibilities regarding empowered female roles. Like Rose, England today struggles with identifications of power and weakness. No longer the global empire it once was, it still remains a potent representation of Western civilization. From its seemingly secondary position as a world power—compared to the former glory of its imperialist state—it is situated to critique the uses of power, both by itself and by other nations.

Britain's dynamic swing between power and weakness has historical precedent. As a cluster of small islands located off of larger mainland Europe, it has always been vulnerable to invasion, as its history plainly shows. Therefore, it should not be surprising to see that when aliens decide to invade Earth in *Doctor Who*, they start by invading England. This invasion is more than just a geographical convenience for the BBC; it is based on a much older historical tradition and one holding deep psychological resonance for the British. The genre of "invasion narratives," as explained by Martin A. Danahay, or what Charles E. Gannon refers to as "future-war" narratives, would appear in the 1870s and continue well into the twentieth century and to the present day. Gannon argues that as "the first true superpower state,"[11] Victorian England "not only 'invented' technologically speculative future-war fiction, but they pursued it."[12] Fueled by reports of the Franco-Prussian War of 1870 and other conflicts in the nineteenth century, the genre of the invasion narrative was born out of the anxieties England experienced about the possibility of invasion.[13]

Invasion narratives were often written by persons with military or naval background and ranged in focus from the horrors of invasion to the advanced technical equipment or strategies used to combat the invaders.[14] In turns, these narratives served as cautionary tales, warnings of the consequences if Britain grew lax in her defenses, or as a celebration of British ingenuity, resourcefulness, and courage. Widely recognized as the first popular invasion narrative, George Chesney's "The Battle of Dorking" (1871) dramatizes the invasion and defeat of England by German invaders and culminates in the destruction of London. Publication of the story touched off a heated debate and sales skyrocketed upwards of 20,000 pamphlets a week.[15] Even after the furor died down, the story was republished and even satirized for years afterward.[16] Nevertheless, Chesney's text set the pattern for the stories to follow and, regardless of whether England won or lost, London met its demise at the hands of the foreign invaders. Danahay observes, "Other invasion narratives such as *The Great War of 189-* (1893) and *How John Bull Lost London* (1882) invariably have as their climax the destruction of London. Since London was the capital city of Britain and the Empire, as well as the center of trade, government and culture, its destruction was seen as the ultimate calamity."[17] Not only a calamity for England, then, but for the whole world.

Additionally, these invasion narratives reveal the feminizing of London in the throes of such calamity and her subsequent sexual vulnerability. In one such invasion narrative, William Le Queux describes the fall of London in *The Great War in England in 1897* (1894): "As the night wore on London trembled and fell. Once Mistress of the World, she was now, alas, sinking under the iron hand of the invader."[18] Gannon contends that the threat of sexual violation of the nation by a male predator "invites readers to perceive their homeland as too innocent and naive to suspect evil motives."[19] The invasion narrative serves once again as a warning of England's "tragic unpreparedness" and yet conversely acts as a strong political proponent for military change and technological development.[20]

By the time H. G. Wells wrote his novel *War of the Worlds* in 1895, he was writing in the convention of invasion narratives already established. Wells was simply the first to make his invaders extraterrestrial. As a result, his text did something that the others did not. Although responding to the same anxieties of invasion as the other narratives, by making the Martians attack England, "Wells is implying that all of humanity is under threat."[21] Thus the peril of London becomes the peril of the whole world. Further, Wells held scant regard of both Church and State; in his novel, England is saved neither by prayer nor military might, but by a lowly virus. Unlike other invasion narratives, Wells' novel challenges assumptions regarding imperialism, technology, and violence.[22]

Consequently, for Wells' Martian invaders to aim for England is perfectly natural, because England is both the heart of the British Empire—a position of power—and the Garden—the female body that must be protected. In "The Garden and Wells's Early Science Fiction," David Y. Hughes argues that "the fundamental use of landscape in *The War of the Worlds* is in terms of an allegory of the world's body."[23] He observes that Wells' language "groups works of man and nature as a single organism."[24] Wells writes of "the skin of our old planet Earth" and how human organizations like the railway and the police dissolve—"guttering, softening, running at last in that swift liquefaction"—in the face of the invading threat.[25] The words "guttering," "softening," and "running ... swift liquefaction" create a visceral connection to the world's body. Wells' London, too, is a feminized body that can be both robed and naked: "All about the pit, and saved as by a miracle from everlasting destruction, stretched the great Mother of Cities. Those who have only seen London veiled in her somber robes of smoke can scarcely imagine the naked clearness and beauty of the silent wilderness of houses."[26] London as Garden, and as the "great Mother of Cities," serves to exemplify all the vulnerability and power of the world.

Emerging as it does from the assortment of invasion narratives, and yet retaining Wells' distinctive perspective, *The War of the Worlds* shaped the science fiction tradition early, and its influence can still be seen today in *Doctor Who*. When the Doctor says, in defiance of her Dalek captors, "Rose, I'm coming to get you" ("Bad Wolf" 1.12), he is reaffirming what all good British believe in their heart of hearts: Rose must be saved, because England must be saved. The Doctor's promise to save Rose is a promise to save England.

Except that he doesn't always make good on that promise. Not always. In the classic series, Sara Kingdom, Katarina, and Adric sacrifice their lives during their adventures with the Doctor and he is unable to save them.[27] But after a moment of grief (which may arguably linger, but the classic series does not comment much upon it), the Doctor and his remaining companions go on to the next adventure. Something the new series does exceptionally well is to set up emotional consequences for the Doctor when he loses a companion or fails to keep him or her from harm. In turn, the companions themselves have been given more autonomy, have more freedom to act and to choose; they are enabled to rescue themselves as sometimes they must. In "The Satan Pit" (2.09), Rose disposes of a menacing enemy by shooting out the front window of a rocket and jettisoning him into space. As we are repeatedly reminded, the universe is a dangerous place, and the companions, and sometimes even the Doctor, are in way over their heads.[28]

Critics and scholars alike have noted Rose's humanizing influence on the Doctor, as well as the universal nature of her working-class social status, making her representative of the average British citizen. However, I would argue that she is more than that. The fact that she is a common woman and not a queen validates the argument that there is a shift in how England sees itself as a nation and provides an illustration for the tension that exists when one starts interrogating the uses of power. At once powerful and vulnerable, the savior and the saved, Rose is the hinge upon which the series swings and reflects back upon itself. In Series 1, she absorbs the power of the Time Vortex and destroys the Daleks, saving Earth, but risks the destruction of her vulnerable human body ("The Parting of the Ways" 1.13). In Series 2, she pulls the switch that opens the void, destroying the Daleks and saving Earth again, but she is lost to an alternate universe ("Doomsday" 2.13). In Series 4, she breaks through the barriers of time and space to save the Doctor, but risks destroying reality itself ("Journey's End" 4.13). By infusing Rose with creative/destructive power nearly equal to that of the Doctor, she is elevated to a position from where she can critique the uses and abuses of power.

Rose's position as the Doctor's judge is most evident in *The Day of the Doctor*, *Doctor Who's* 50th anniversary special released in 2013. In it, the audience finally gets to witness the most pivotal day of the Doctor's many lives, the day in which he used, or is presumed to have used, a weapon of mass destruction to destroy both the Daleks and his own people in order to save the universe. The weapon, called "The Moment," is sentient, possesses a conscience, and has the power to stand in judgment of the person who uses it. The Moment appropriates Rose's image as an interface to speak with the War Doctor and calls itself "Bad Wolf," Rose's powerful alter ego from earlier episodes in the series. She tells him, "I chose this face and form especially for you. It's from your past. Possibly your future. I always get those two mixed up." With this statement she clarifies her identity: she is not the human Rose transported out of space and time; she is the manifestation of the consciousness of a living machine. Additionally, we find that the destruct button on The Moment is shaped like a rose—the design of which closely resembles a Tudor Rose—making the association between The Moment and Rose unequivocal.[29] Bad Wolf warns the War Doctor (so-called because this regeneration is his "forgotten" identity from the Time War) that if he uses the weapon, there will be consequences: His punishment will be to survive the destruction, and that "one terrible night" he will count all the children of Gallifrey who die as a result.

To help him with his decision, which for him has not happened yet and therefore is not ordained, The War Doctor is brought into contact with his future selves, Doctors ten and eleven. In the year 1562, Queen Elizabeth I is prominently featured in the narrative and is duplicated by a Zygon, a member of a shape-shifting alien race. In present day London, Kate Stewart, leader of UNIT, is also duplicated by a Zygon, and her confrontation with her Zygon double results in a standoff of similar catastrophic proportions as the War Doctor's.[30] Kate threatens to detonate a nuclear bomb, choosing to destroy England in order to save the world from the alien threat.[31] Doctors ten and eleven force a peaceful resolution, telling Kate, "This is not a decision you will ever be able to live with." The War Doctor witnesses this event and discovers that Bad Wolf has shown him exactly the future he needed to see. He seeks an alternative solution and does not set off The Moment.

Once again we find Rose/Bad Wolf illustrating England under threat. The choice to not set off the nuclear bomb and destroy England persuades The War Doctor to not set off The Moment, an act that would destroy the Rose/Bad Wolf "body" that has been appropriated for the event. Clearly, Rose/Bad Wolf is conflated with England and it is her interrogation of the right use of power which results in influencing the Doctor's actions. England is saved, but England's image of itself is complicated by the questions raised here. Do the needs of the many outweigh the needs of the few? Does anyone have the right to kill in the name of the greater good? At what point is the cost of power too great? Can nations, and the individuals in them, choose creative alternatives to destructive action? That *Doctor Who* continues to explore these themes suggests that Britain's image of itself as a nation is undergoing a transition as it takes a closer look at its role in a rapidly changing world.

Perhaps the most significant indicator of Rose's role as a symbol for England is bound up in her relationship with the Doctor himself. However, this relationship cannot be seen as a 1:1 relationship between nations. Taking into consideration how the Doctor is presented throughout the series, it would not do to frame him as a mere nation. The Doctor is positioned outside of Earth, a powerful extraterrestrial in charge of space and time. His role is deeply gendered as male.[32] His authority has traditionally been presented as unquestioned and absolute. However, a closer look at how presentation of his authority changes visually and verbally between the classic series and the reboot reveals not only what kind of authority the Doctor signifies, but also signals a shift in prevailing Western attitudes towards that authority.

For example, in a scene from the classic series with the fourth Doctor and his companion, Leela says, "I suppose you're always right, about everything." The Doctor replies, "Invariably" ("The Face of Evil" #89). This quiet exchange—and others like it—assures the viewer that the Doctor always knows best, positioning him in a fatherly role (even "grandfatherly," as the first Doctor begins his adventures in the role of Susan's grandfather) to the human race. Taking into account, also, that the Doctor is often paired with a young female companion, it is no small stretch to understand his role as signifying patriarchal power—a power for good, certainly, and one with knowledge far beyond the humans and other species he encounters—but power that is often taken for granted and only occasionally questioned nonetheless. The companions in the classic series may argue with the Doctor, but more often than not they do what he tells them and look to him for answers.

We are presented with an alternative view of the Doctor in the series reboot. First, visually, his heroic image has expanded considerably from the "cosmic hobo" of the classic series, who may be heard to admit "I save planets mostly" with off-handed humility ("The Pirate Planet" #99). In the series reboot, we are presented time and again with scenes of the Doctor strutting confidently amidst chaos and explosions, as the tenth Doctor does on the space-going cruise ship Titanic in the 2007 Christmas special ("Voyage of the Damned"). When verbally challenged by passenger Rickston Slade, he responds with aggression and self-aggrandizement:

> The Doctor: I'm the Doctor. I'm a Time Lord. I'm from the planet Gallifrey in the constellation of Kasterborous. I'm nine hundred and three years old, and I'm the man who's gonna save your lives and all six billion people on the planet below. You got a problem with that?

Both visually and verbally, the Doctor's status as a messianic god-hero is reinforced repeatedly in the series reboot. He is placed high upon a pedestal, even if that pedestal should be seen to wobble a bit.[33]

And yet the narrative positioning of the Doctor in this seemingly unassailable light invites critique. If the Doctor is at times presented with an over-inflated sense of importance, he is situated then to feel keenly the prick of the pin, which Rose provides. Rose is the first companion to protest the TARDIS' automatic translation circuit, insisting to the Doctor that he must ask permission before invading and altering another person's mind ("The End of the World" 1.02). She also stops him cold when he is hell-bent on destroying what he believes to be the last remaining Dalek from the Time War:

> The Doctor: *[aiming a hand-held cannon at the Dalek.]* Rose, get out of the way now!
> Rose: No. I won't let you do this.
> The Doctor: That thing killed hundreds of people!
> Rose: It's not the one pointing the gun at me ["Dalek" 1.06].

Rose's critique of the Doctor's power ranges from issues of personal agency to that of questioning the use of violence in the face of alternative methods of negotiation. By questioning the Doctor's uses of power, she teaches him to stop taking his own power for granted, even if it is used with the best of intentions.[34]

However, as Deborah Pless is quick to point out, "the Doctor was conceived from the start as an unconventional, non-patriarchal figure, a plan marred only slightly by time."[35] By briefly sketching historical events in the years immediately following World War II, Pless demonstrates that the loss of Britain's colonies and its decline in the international sphere ushered in a new political era, one in which Britain would rely more heavily on diplomacy than military might.[36] Pless argues that the Doctor "represents what Britain hopes it can be: proudly British, while rejecting Britain's exploitative past."[37] Relying heavily on examples of the fourth Doctor, Pless claims that "the Doctor was a character created consciously to bring up the nation."[38] Although Pless claims that the Doctor represents Britain, I do not disagree with her argument overall; rather, I see my argument aligning with hers. We both see the Doctor as a patriarchal figure. In addition, if the Doctor of the classic series was "created consciously to bring up" the Britain of that time, then the reboot series of the twenty-first century may be doing the same thing with Rose. The relationship of Rose and the Doctor complicates the power dynamics initiated between Doctor and companion in the classic series and demonstrates a shift in perception of Britain's self-image.

Arguably, the most significant moment that demonstrates the importance of Rose's role as someone who teaches the Doctor is their fateful leave-taking at Bad Wolf Bay ("Journey's End" 4.13). The Doctor is leaving Rose in an alternate universe with his duplicate, a human-Time Lord hybrid that has been inadvertently created in the course of events. The Doctor tells Rose that this new Doctor needs her—that she needs to teach him the way she taught the tenth Doctor when they first met. The new human-hybrid Doctor desires to be good, behaves heroically and with the best of intentions, but is nevertheless seduced by the siren-call of his own power, making himself judge, jury, and executioner of the Daleks and destroying them all in a flash. The tenth Doctor says that the new Doctor was "born in battle." He tells Rose, "That's me when we first met. And you made me better. Now you can do the same for him" (4.13). The tenth Doctor believes he has learned from Rose to question his own motives, to interrogate his use of power. The tenth Doctor recognizes Rose's contribution to his willingness to wrestle with his own assumptions and believes that she can do the same again. In this moment, reading Rose as England, the narrative suggests that England has a role in the world: to show the world a better way to be.

In the universe of *Doctor Who*, "the world is always ending."[39] Visions of apocalyptic peril threatening England and the world reflect past anxieties of invasion heightened by England's perception of itself as a gendered nation. Whereas the concept of the Doctor as an all-knowing savior is a comforting one, the new series complicates his patriarchal role by not always letting him win or by putting him in situations where he wins only by degrees. Some days he rescues his companions; other days his companions rescue him. On darker days, he may be unable to save his companion at all. Rose, with her human compassion, her empowerment, and her vulnerability, is a companion for the twenty-first century. Other companions may follow, but she sets her stamp on those who come later. She teaches the Doctor how to be, to question his assumptions, to examine alternative solutions. And when the time comes, Rose, like England, is quite capable of saving herself.

Notes

1. See Marcus Gheeraerts the Younger's *Queen Elizabeth I* ("The Ditchley portrait") c. 1592 in the National Portrait Gallery.
2. See Michael Drayton's *Poly-Olbion* (1612, 1622), a topographical poem describing England and Wales. The title page depicts Great Britain as a woman wrapped in a cloak-like map.
3. In Gildas' *De Exidio Britonum* (c. 540 C.E.), Gildas refers to Britain as both an "island garden" and a "bride," setting the precedent for envisioning Britain as both garden and female even before there was a political entity known as England (Staley 1). Writing on Gildas and other texts, Lynn Staley observes that while the metaphor of England as the island garden has been "neither simple nor stable," it was used throughout history to express concerns regarding national identity and anxieties about invasion and isolation (2–3).
4. In fact, many of the court entertainments created by George Gascoigne prominently feature his sponsor, Robert Dudley, Earl of Leicester, and reveal much of Dudley's personal agendas—his criticism of Elizabeth's unwed state, his ambition to be accepted as a suitor, and his criticism of her foreign policy—an attitude both Gascoigne and Dudley may have felt was shared by many in England. Susan Frye notes, "Gascoigne imagines an audience that shares Leicester's impatience with Elizabeth's unwillingness to commit either her physical body to marriage or her political body of England to an interventionist policy that would more closely involve the island kingdom in events on the Continent" (70).
5. Frye, *Elizabeth I*, 62.
6. Ibid., 79.
7. Ibid., 88.
8. Ibid., 79.
9. See the James Gillray collection in the National Portrait Gallery.
10. A correspondence between Rose and Britannia can also be argued. In the two-part adventure "The Empty Child" (1.09) and "The Doctor Dances" (1.10), Rose wears the Union Jack on her t-shirt; the Union Jack figures prominently on the shield of Britannia. For another example of Britannia, see Lady Edith Amelia Wolverton (née Ward) as Britannia (photograph, 1897) in the National Portrait Gallery.
11. Gannon, *Rumors of War*, 5.
12. Ibid., 16.
13. Ibid., 8.
14. Both Danahay and Gannon provide a historical overview of the development of invasion narratives: Danahay more briefly as context to his edition of H. G. Wells' *War of the Worlds* and Gannon in much greater detail in the opening chapters of his book.
15. Gannon, *Rumors of War*, 9.
16. Gannon notes that "The Battle of Dorking" became "fodder for a brief fad in national humor: any small injury was likely to attract the mock-serious inquiry, 'Weren't you wounded at the Battle of Dorking?'" (10). Gannon observes that if the joke is to work, the text must "enjoy immediate nation-wide recognition," a sign that the story has entered the public consciousness (10).
17. Danahay, "Introduction," 22–23.
18. Ibid., 237–241.
19. Gannon, *Rumors of War*, 61.
20. Ibid., 61. Gannon also observes that extreme xenophobia, racism, "othering,"

and "convoluted ethical rationalizing" characterizes many of these narratives (57–60).

21. Danahay, "Introduction," 23.
22. *Ibid.*
23. Hughes, "The Garden," 61. As noted earlier, Hughes is not the first to use "England as garden" metaphor (see Note 3), but is among the first to examine Wells' use of the language of landscape and how it works to connect England allegorically with the whole world.
24. Hughes, "The Garden," 62.
25. *Ibid.*, 62–63.
26. H. G. Wells, *The War of the Worlds*, 182–83 (Danahay edition).
27. In the classic series, Sara Kingdom loses her life while aiding the Doctor in his struggle against the Daleks in "The Daleks' Master Plan" (#21); Katarina sacrifices herself to save the Doctor earlier in that same story, becoming the first companion to die on the show ("The Daleks' Master Plan"); years later, Adric dies while attempting to stop a Cyberman spaceship from crashing into ancient Earth ("Earthshock" #121).
28. There are few moments when the Doctor is rendered genuinely helpless, but on occasion he meets a foe beyond which even his own formidable powers can cope. In addition to the Beast of "The Satan Pit," he is also confronted by an unknown life form in "Midnight" (4.10) and faces real peril.
29. Although it might be said that the Tudor Rose button on The Moment suggests Elizabeth I, the last reigning Tudor monarch who also appears in the episode, I would argue that the image points more directly to Rose: the physical casing of the bomb with its big, red, Tudor Rose-shaped button is the "body" of The Moment and Rose's image is its consciousness or "mind." They are both The Moment. The mind/body connection would more strongly suggest that the Tudor rose is Rose's symbol in this case.
30. There is a lot of duplicating of bodies in *The Day of the Doctor*, which is suggestive of the Jungian shadow. Jung hypothesized that we all have a shadow self—containing our darkest impulses—which must be confronted and embraced in order to be overcome. In the course of the narrative, the Doctor must face, quite literally, himself—and his worst self, as he recalls it—and embrace the past he has been suppressing in order for victory to be achieved. For more on the Jungian shadow, see Jung, *Collected Works*, Vol. 9, 275–289.
31. There is an interesting parallel with the invasion narratives here: Gannon notes a pattern in which the British, in spite of claiming the ethical high ground, ultimately end up fighting as ruthlessly as their foes. He observes, "No matter that the British are fighting to oust a rapacious foe; they ultimately match their foe in the ruthlessness with which they fight, and show at least as great a talent for obtaining objectives through terrorism" (58). In *The Day of the Doctor*, Elizabeth I demonstrates that she can be as equally formidable as her foes by killing her Zygon duplicate and impersonating him, ultimately protecting her England and ridding it of the Zygon threat at her end of the timeline. Kate Stewart, equally as ruthless as the Zygons, threatens to sacrifice London in order to save the world. However, in the midst of the chaotic peace negotiations, Stewart's assistant Osgood and her Zygon duplicate demonstrate that unity can be achieved as they quietly share Osgood's inhaler. Osgood, wrapped in the fourth Doctor's long scarf, can be seen as a stand-in companion, one who shows that alternative solutions are worth seeking.
32. Although many fans have clamored for a woman or a person of color to be cast in the role of the Doctor, with each regeneration he continues to be played by

white male actors. Certainly, if ever the producers of *Doctor Who* experiment with alternative casting, that moment would be a notable indicator of a shift in Western attitudes about power and who is perceived as being capable of wielding it. A recent big development in the *Doctor Who* universe is Missy, the female regeneration of the Master, the Doctor's longtime archenemy ("Dark Water" 8.11). Although this is certainly thrilling progress and may be a strong indicator of the possible selection of a future female Doctor, the power dynamic has not changed. Missy challenges and subverts the Doctor's power, but ultimately the Doctor—along with the white male authority he represents—remains in charge.

33. The Doctor continues to struggle with his desire to exercise ultimate power, as "The Waters of Mars" (15 November 2009), "The Runaway Bride" (25 December 2006), and "Turn Left" (4.11) indicate. The viewer is repeatedly shown instances where the Doctor can be a danger to himself as well as entire worlds when there is "no one to stop him" ("Turn Left").

34. This is not to say that the Doctor of the reboot series is unethical or lacks a sense of diplomacy or empathy. He still possesses the qualities that make the Doctor who he is, but he is perhaps more grim and quick to judge. The Doctor is at his best and is the most right when he is the most selfless, such as when the eleventh Doctor discovers that human refugees from Earth have harnessed the energies of an alien creature to fuel their spaceship. His fury over the abuse of an innocent creature is demonstrated by his simple statement: "No one human talks to me today" ("The Beast Below" 5.02). In cases like this, he is justified in his judgment of the human race.

35. Pless, "The Decline and Fall," 352.
36. *Ibid.*, 353.
37. *Ibid.*, 354.
38. *Ibid.*, 357.
39. This is a complaint that Ianto Jones voices to Captain Jack Harkness in *Torchwood's* "Children of Earth." Since *Torchwood* is a spin-off of the *Doctor Who* universe, the quote serves as an apt description here as well.

Rory Williams
The Boy Who Waited

Teresa Forde

Rory Williams is an established companion within the New Whoniverse: he was initially introduced as Amy Pond's boy/friend and developed into a significant companion, both for Amy and the eleventh Doctor. The boy who waited refers to the extent to which Rory waits for Amy's attention and affection within the series, both as a child and an adult. It also implies that Rory has to wait until his character develops to the point where he becomes a companion as well as Amy's husband. Rory's wait for Amy's affections echoes the way in which other female companions, such as Sarah Jane Smith or Clara Oswald, waited for the Doctor to return to visit them or take them travelling in his TARDIS. It also acts as a counterpoint to the description of Amy Pond as the girl who waited for the Doctor to come back to visit her after their first meeting when she was a child.

When Rory first appears in the series, in "The Eleventh Hour" (5.01), Amy initially introduces Rory to the Doctor as her friend, whereas he refers to himself as her boyfriend, because Amy is still attracted to the world of the Doctor and sees a dichotomy between life with Rory and life in the TARDIS. On board the TARDIS Rory develops his relationship with Amy and becomes intertwined with the Doctor's own personal history as well. Rory and the Doctor share a similarity in their relationship with Amy as they each try to protect her in their own way. This caring attitude may stem from both of them knowing her as a child. Rory has loved Amy since they were childhood friends. The Doctor feels protective towards Amy due to first meeting her as the young Amelia. The issue of Amy's safety also leads to Rory's more angry moments, particularly if he thinks the Doctor is putting her in danger through their adventures. The term Doctor's "companion" is often associated with a female character, whether human or alien. Although this assumption is understandable, as the Doctor has travelled with more women than men, there have been a fair number of male companions, numbering fourteen out of forty-three. Rory has become one of the most popular male companions due to the affection that both the eleventh Doctor and, especially, Amy hold for him. Rory's popularity is also cemented by his love for Amy and by his character as it develops throughout the series.

The Doctor has had a number of male companions who assist him in his adventures. He is often antagonistic towards them, at least initially, and increasingly in new *Who* seems to test them to see if they are worthy suitors for female companions. The second Doctor's relationship with Jamie McCrimmon involved fond and playful banter, often at Jamie's expense. As Jamie was a Jacobite soldier he could provide the muscle to complement the Doctor's brain. Jamie's kilt-wearing provided cause for comment but the Doctor and Jamie became close and Jamie established himself as an important companion. Even in the case of the third Doctor, the figure of the Brigadier Alastair Gordon Lethbridge-Stewart provided the military force to attack the enemy. Although disapproving of military warfare, his relationship with the Brigadier nevertheless became one of mutual friendship and respect. Others, such as Ancient Alzarian mathematician Adric, often challenged the fourth Doctor's authority, as when Adric said to the Doctor "a lot of the time you don't really make sense" in "The Keeper of Traken" (#114).

The sense of antagonism felt by the Doctor is clearly depicted in new *Who* as Mickey Smith, initially Rose Tyler's boyfriend, is ridiculed by both the ninth and tenth Doctors, partly because of his desire to stop Rose travelling in the TARDIS and partly due to his initial fear of the Doctor's world. The tenth Doctor often refers to him as "Mickey the idiot" and calls him "Ricky" to tease him. Mickey is also a boy who waited, as he waited for Rose to come back to him after her travels with the Doctor. However, Mickey's story arc finally establishes him as a significant character and hero. Elements of some of these male companions can be found within Rory's relationship with the Doctor and Amy throughout his story arc.

Cometh the Hour, Cometh the Man

"The Eleventh Hour" introduces Rory to the Whoniverse. His introduction reveals the extent to which Rory is in love with Amy and the way in which Rory might view the world differently from other people. In this episode, the multiform Prisoner Zero has escaped and is hiding within coma patients in order to evade capture. As a nurse from the local hospital, Rory recognizes one of the coma patients who should be in bed but is instead standing in the village green with his dog. Whilst everyone else is looking at the sky and filming the Atraxi, the self-appointed galactic police force hovering in the sky, Rory is instead recording the image of the patient, who has been "possessed" by Prisoner Zero. The fact that Rory is looking in a different direction than everyone else is noted by the Doctor, who then focuses his attention directly onto Rory. It is Rory's role as a nurse that has alerted him to the fact that a coma patient is standing out on the village green as he recognizes the patient from the local hospital. Rory's behavior implies that he will not necessarily follow the crowd and might always view the world in a different way. The Doctor explains that a coma patient is an ideal vehicle for Prisoner Zero to inhabit, due to an apparently dormant brain. As he says this, the Doctor taps Rory's forehead, implying that his brain might also be dormant and clearly echoing that long tradition of Doctors who may be threatened by, and certainly tease, other male characters in the series. The Doctor's approach to Rory detracts from the latter's specialist knowledge about the situation and suggests that the Doctor's might see him as a potential rival.

"The Eleventh Hour" takes place in Leadworth village which is home to Rory and Amy. Prisoner Zero's presence on Earth prompts an international crisis and the eleventh Doctor asks Jeff Angelo, also a resident of the village, to make contact with world leaders and experts whilst on his laptop in his bedroom. The Doctor refers to Jeff as his "best man" as he needs to rely on him to maintain this link to world leaders. When Jeff asks him why, the Doctor replies, "it's your bedroom." This response implies that anyone can fulfill the role of the Doctor's best man if they are in the right place at the right time; but also Jeff knows how to establish communication links so he does have specialist knowledge. The Doctor says that Jeff is likely to get a lot of job offers after this crisis; Jeff undergoes an adrenalin-fuelled job interview set on the world stage as he links world leaders together online in the middle of a global crisis. At the end of "Eleventh Hour" the Doctor presents his own mental resume to the Atraxi, depicting himself as the ultimate defender of Earth and portraying a vision of all the alien foes he has defeated. At the start of the episode it initially appears as if Jeff might become the new companion until we meet Rory. Later, in "Flesh and Stone" (5.05) when Amy reveals her wedding plans, the Doctor asks her if she is going to marry "the good looking one" in the village, presumably referring to Jeff as opposed to Rory, and Amy has to quickly correct him. These responses position Rory as an atypical heroic figure but one who has still already nearly "gotten" his girl.

When he first appears, Rory's dress and demeanor do not initially translate into a traditional action hero. When not dressed in his nursing uniform, or in later costume as a Roman centurion, or as a soldier, Rory dresses casually, appearing in his familiar wardrobe of jeans, shirt, and hooded jacket or body warmer. The generic wardrobe has also been often compared to Marty McFly from *Back to the Future* (1985), due to the blue denim and jacket combination, Marty being another time traveler whose story arc is also nearly erased from history. However, Rory's look is more "geeky" or "nerdy" in the British context than Marty's middle of the road American attire. Rory also dresses differently than the tenth Doctor's more stylish geek chic and the eleventh Doctor's suit and bow tie look. At times Rory also wears glasses and the whole effect gives him the Geek chic look. As indicated in the instructions on a cosplay site entitled "How To Dress Like Rory Williams," apart from the more specialist outfits, Rory's wardrobe should be relatively easy to replicate with everyday clothing. In a review of the Rory action figure, McAlpine observes that, in order to encapsulate Rory's personality, you need to "practise looking a little hangdog, a little unsure of yourself, with flashes of pure steely venom from time to time. Be a good guy, a beautiful guy, who thinks he's a loser, but not a hopeless loser."[1] This description encapsulates the sense that Rory is not the stereotypical action hero but does have flashes of courage, resolve, and humanity. Although Rory does dress up in various other outfits, this more casual look is his default and most comfortable looking style.

The notion of the "beautiful loser" bears close resemblance to the contemporary and popular image of the geek as an alternative to the aggressive action hero or, in music terms, "Rock God." As Rebecca Williams argues in relation to geek and nerd representations: "in the rock or indie music scene there has been a reappropriation of 'geek cool' which displays and valorizes being 'introspective, insecure and self-deprecating.'"[2] In fact, Arthur Darvill, who plays Rory, is a musician and composer whose indie band, *Edmund*, has produced the kind of gentle-voiced, emotional and intelligent music that ensures his indie credentials and "geek-cool" persona are further established.

Science fiction offers the opportunity to see aliens from different worlds and alternative societies so it is possible that traditional gender stereotypes might be challenged or modified. In her consideration of masculinity within popular television, Rebecca Feasey suggests that a male character in science fiction may be "able to present a new image of contemporary masculinity by combining such supposedly feminine traits as emotionality, sensitivity and openness with those supposedly masculine qualities of power, strength and bravery."[3] For Feasey, it is clearly possible to have a heroic figure who also behaves emotionally as a sensitive character. In *Doctor Who*, Rory's story arc also develops to exhibit a balance of qualities in nurturing, romance, bravery, and logic to construct a more "rounded" and contemporary male character. As a somewhat reluctant hero, Rory's actions seem to be founded upon his "emotionality" more than the desire for combat.

The ability to see things differently, particularly from a humane perspective, is a mark of Rory's character and can set him apart from the Doctor. Prior to entering the TARDIS for the first time Rory is not fazed by its dimensions; he has read about scientific theories regarding relativity so he understands why the TARDIS looks bigger on the inside. Rory is also not as fascinated by the Doctor, unlike many other companions, because he sees the Doctor as a potential threat to both his and Amy's future together. As childhood friends, Amy used to dress Rory up as the "Raggedy Doctor" so he has already been in competition with the Doctor in terms of Amy's affections, even though everyone believed that the Doctor was only a figment of young Amelia's imagination. Also, the Doctor's tendency to eschew compassion when necessary is counterbalanced by Rory's conscience and empathy, a trait usually seen in female companions, such as Rose Tyler, Martha Jones or Donna Noble. However, by the episode "The Hungry Earth" (5.08), during the discovery of the Silurian race hibernating beneath the Earth's surface, Rory is more supportive of the Doctor's plans. He is particularly keen that the Silurian and human race do not go to war and so he supports the Doctor, although he is unhappy that Amy is still endangered when she is captured by the Silurians. Rory's protective instinct towards Amy is strong, and he feels that she is going to be in endangered and wishes to protect her. However, it is not really her inability to cope with dangerous situations that Rory fears, as much as her desire to get involved in adventures and risk her life in the first place.

Rory does become a resourceful and effective adventurer, but he does not begin his adventures as a typical action hero. In his first fight with the vampiric Saturnyne Francesco Calvierri in "The Vampires of Venice" (5.06), in an attempt to draw the vampire away from Amy, Rory taunts his foe with playground insults, including one about his mother, and then swordfights him with a broom until Amy comes to the rescue and blows up the vampire. Before firing at Francesco, Amy calls out "mummy's boy" to get his attention, although perhaps there is a playful ambiguity in the object of her call, as Rory lies helpless on the ground almost defeated. Whereas there is a certain gender-swapping in Rory's rescue, it is actually unlikely that Rory will suddenly become a supreme fighter in this adventure with the Doctor and Amy, and more probable that he will be rescued by Amy as she has been having these kinds of adventures longer and actively enjoys facing danger. Even though they had left in the TARDIS on Rory's stag night, the trip to Venice was Amy and Rory's "honeymoon" gift from the Doctor and Rory is still quite new to being a somewhat reluctant companion and potential husband.

At the end of "The Vampires of Venice" Amy refers to her relationship with both Rory and the Doctor as "me and my boys" to which they playfully acquiesce. So there is a sense of camaraderie established between Rory and the Doctor who are deemed to be acting at Amy's behest and in her interest. As they walk into the TARDIS the Doctor asks Rory what he can hear. Rory replies "nothing" and the Doctor knows that the silence is coming, prefiguring Rory's later encounter with the rift in time. It is at this point that Rory and the Doctor seem to fully accept one another as companions and no longer see each other as a threat. In terms of their impending nuptials, Rory's relationship with Amy also playfully inverts the tradition of a woman taking her husband's name when they marry. Rory and Amy are often referred to by the Doctor as the "Ponds" as opposed to using Rory's surname of Williams; Amy is seen as the dominant character, and Rory is sometimes described as Mr. Pond. This is partly because the Doctor often refers to Amy as "Pond," albeit in an endearing manner, and possibly to distance himself from her in a romantic way, since he first met her as a young girl and because, eventually, he is married to her daughter. But, it also emphasizes Rory's initial role as a companion's companion, as Mr. Pond, whose character evolves to become part of a significant story arc. Rory's ties to the Doctor become further cemented as he technically becomes the Doctor's father-in-law when the Doctor finally marries River Song.

The nature of humanity in relation to alien life forms is an ongoing trope within the Whoniverse and many other science fiction films and series. In "Rebel Flesh" (6.05) and "The Almost People" (6.06) Rory is sympathetic to the 'gangers, who are cloned humans, as he is concerned for their welfare. This may be due to his nurse's training but also because he recognizes the validity of their existence as people, accepting their value even though they are not "original" humans. His heroism appears to be automatic; he sacrifices himself at the end of "Cold Blood" (5.09) and saves the Doctor by running in front of him to take a bullet. Rory falls through a crack in time and is erased from history. After he falls into the rift, Amy forgets that he ever existed, although the Doctor still remembers. After Rory is erased from time, Amy is taken to her favorite places by the Doctor as compensation for losing her memory and forgetting about Rory. This erasure from time constitutes a form of death for Rory's character. In "Vincent and the Doctor" (5.10) the Doctor and Amy continue their travels without Rory. They visit Vincent Van Gogh, one of Amy's favorite artists, and Vincent senses Amy's sadness and feelings of loss as she begins to cry for apparently no reason, not realizing that she is actually mourning the loss of Rory. Amy is attracted to Vincent and he provides a surrogate Rory-figure in this episode as he cares for Amy and is emotionally responsive to her.

Mr. Pond: The Man Who Waited

Rory eventually returns to Amy in the guise of an Auton duplicate dressed as a Roman Centurion. Amy lived with a crack in time on her bedroom wall as a child from which the Nestene Consciousness was able to extract knowledge about her interest in the Roman Empire, including an image of a centurion. To a large degree she shapes Rory's behavior, character, and appearance. The Nestene Consciousness drew on psychic residue from Amy as a child in order to construct the Roman Centurion from a picture in one of her school books on the Romans. They used this image to produce a Roman Army in which Auton Rory is dressed as a Centurion. The effect of Amy's memories is encapsulated in the image of Rory as the initially deadly but finally heroic Auton Centurion, reflecting her interest in history. However, she is also attracted to the Roman Centurion uniform for aesthetic reasons and her interest in the Roman Invasion of Britain resulted in a poor grade on a school essay as she had entitled it "The Invasion of the Hot Italians" ("The Pandorica Opens" 5.12). Rory the centurion is a fantasy figure desired by Amy and is effectively dressed up by her through her liking the uniform. The fascination with an almost-fabled hero, and its manifestation, can also be seen in Clara Oswald's desire to travel to Medieval England to see Robin Hood, despite the twelfth Doctor's incredulity that he actually existed. "Robot of Sherwood" (8.03) depicts Robin as the Earl of Loxley and is full of playful banter and bickering competitiveness between Robin Hood and the Doctor. Just as Clara fantasizes about meeting Robin Hood, so the Last or Lone Centurion in the guise of Rory fulfills one of Amy's fantasies.

It is the information from Amy's past that was used to create the Roman Legion and Rory's Auton. Amy eventually remembers Rory when she sees him reappear as the centurion ("The Pandorica Opens"), only for him to turn into a weapon that tries to kill her. Auton Rory still harbors Rory's memories sufficiently to resist the urge to kill Amy. After shooting her, Rory, as the Lone Centurion, preserves Amy in the Pandorica for nearly two thousand years until she is released by young Amelia. She has been healed whilst entombed within the vault. Rory ensures that Amy is safe by guarding the Pandorica through the decades. This protection of the Pandorica leads to the mythologizing of the Lone Centurion throughout history and implies that Rory's centurion Auton is full of loyalty and devotion. Although Rory is a logical and rational individual, his caring side is often depicted, most clearly in his devotion to Amy: when the Doctor says to Rory, "Your girlfriend isn't more important than the whole universe," Rory retorts, "She is to me!" ("The Big Bang" 5.13). Finally the cracks in time are mended and the universe is rebooted and restored. As the Auton held Rory's memories, so the restored Rory remembers his time as the Auton, devoting all those years in the Pandorica to protecting Amy.

By the time Rory faces Adolf Hitler in "Let's Kill Hitler" (6.08), he has undergone so many adventures that he instinctively punches the German Fürher in the face and takes his gun before telling him to "sit down" and "shut up." Still rather dazed by his actions, Rory ends the scene by stating in a slightly bewildered manner that he is "putting Hitler in a cupboard" at the

Doctor's behest. When Amy asks if Rory can ride a motorbike so they can chase River Song through 1930's Berlin, he says that he probably can as "it's that kind of day," before speeding off on the bike with Amy holding on behind. It seems as though Rory can undertake all of these actions because he has to in order to look for his daughter, River Song, and to try to save the Doctor with her help. It also illustrates that Rory still finds his adventures bemusing and bewildering at times.

It becomes clear that Rory has always been waiting for Amy and has always loved her. He has also waited for her in other ways that highlight his somewhat passive character as he "holds a torch for her" without expressing his feelings. This approach to Amy is also revealed to us in "Let's Kill Hitler" when Mels reveals that she has actually been Rory and Amy's daughter all along. There is a flashback to when Rory, Amelia and Mels were young, where Amy and Mels were playing hide and seek with him, and just left him hiding. When Rory confronts Amy about what they did, she says that they were going to find him but "we are just not ready for you yet." Such a response implies that he is not significant enough to be found but, also, that Amy will be ready for him later and that there is some kind of future relationship. Ironically it is Mels, as their daughter, who finally prompts the relationship between Amy and Rory, knowing that they will become a couple in order for her to exist.

Love in the TARDIS

Although he was not always consciously waiting for Amy, as he was initially unaware that she was time-travelling, Rory subsequently discovers that Amy left Leadworth on the eve of their wedding to travel with the Doctor. His underlying distrust of the Doctor and the TARDIS, leads Rory to accompany Amy on her travels. Once in the TARDIS, Rory's main concern is for Amy so this spurs him to fight and do battle to save her. There are echoes of Rory within previous male companions in terms of his knowledge, skeptical attitude, and emotions, and it is their relationship that becomes established in the eleventh Doctor's arc. This is mainly because Rory and Amy spent so much time together on the TARDIS and conceived their daughter, River, whilst on board. According to Steven Moffat the conception occurred during the episode the "Big Bang" episode: "My favorite dirty joke in *Doctor Who* is the title of Episode 13 in Series 5, 'The Big Bang,' the night when River began."[4] As with so many male companions who become involved with the Doctor's adventures and the female companions, the potential for jealousy, rivalry, and competitiveness can exist between them as each may feel threatened in some way. This dislike may often be a form of defense that can also disappear with time and develop into friendliness, camaraderie, and mutual respect.

From classic to new *Who*, the male characters often compensate for the Doctor's personality and may clash with him. The first Doctor, in his cantankerous manner, initially found Ian Chesterton quite opinionated and referred to him patronizingly as "young man" extensively when they first met. Ian was in many ways similar to Rory in that he was interested in science and was a science teacher who eventually married his fellow companion, Barbara Wright, after they had finally left the TARDIS. Barbara was a history teacher, somewhat echoing Amy's interest in history, and Ian and Barbara's relationship was the first of a number of burgeoning romantic pairings of companions and companion/Doctor relationships, often ending in the couple leaving the Doctor or living separately from him: these include Leela and Andred, or Jo Grant's attraction to Captain Mike Yates and her eventual departure to marry Professor Clifford Jones and go with him to explore the Amazon. Other relationships include the romance depicted between a Doctor and his companion, beginning with the eighth Doctor and Grace Holloway in the television movie *Doctor Who* (1996) and followed by the romance between the tenth Doctor and Rose. Their relationship finally develops with the meta-crisis regeneration of a half-human version of the tenth Doctor, who goes to live with Rose in the alternative universe or Pete's world in "Journey's End" (4.13). We also see Mickey Smith and Martha Jones eventually get together and, more recently, the established relationship between the Paternoster Gang favorites, Vastra and Jenny.

As part of their attempt to live their everyday lives together, Rory and Amy eventually return to live at their home in Leadworth in order to be away from the Doctor for longer periods of time as depicted in "Pond Life." After the birth of Melody Pond, Amy discovers that she is unable to have another baby. The five "Pond Life" mini-episodes depict Rory and Amy's domestic life and the issue of having children culminates in an argument, as Amy knows that Rory has always wanted children. It is not until later that that we learn that Rory and Amy adopted a child after they were sent back in time in New York. It is assumed that Amy and Rory's parental urge is fulfilled.[5] The pull between everyday life and the TARDIS adventures are also depicted in the relationship between Clara Oswald, now an English teacher, with Danny Pink who teaches maths, echoing Barbara and Ian's relationship. Both Clara and Danny teach at Coal Hill School where Ian and Barbara originally taught before entering the TARDIS. Clara increasingly becomes caught between two worlds as she teaches and goes on adventures with the Doctor at the same time. As Samuel Anderson explains about his character, Danny: "He's a 'straight man' to Capaldi's Doctor and a 'companion for the companion.'" But there is tension between him and the Doctor. "There's a bit of friction that arises between Danny and the Doctor midway through the season," he reveals. "And [Danny's knowledge of math] is a tool for that friction."[6]

Danny is also a former soldier and military warfare is a contentious issue for the twelfth Doctor, as it has been for some of his previous incarnations. Like many other prospective male companions, Danny's resolve is tested. The desire for the Doctor to test the male companions is compounded when there is a potential romance, as with Rory and Amy or Danny and Clara. Taking on the role of a stern father figure, the twelfth Doctor tries to intimidate Danny and push him to determine if he is "worthy" of Clara, as illustrated in "The Caretaker" (8.6). This attempt to test the suitability of the companion's love interest is initially echoed in the eleventh Doctor's attitude to Rory although eventually he overcomes his misgivings and realizes Rory's devotion and determination.

The Man Who Dies and Dies Again

Out of all the male companions, Rory is the one who seems to endure the most testing experiences across his story arc. One of the most contentious issues about Rory's character in *Doctor Who* is the number of times he has died, or experienced versions of dying such as being erased or "replaced." In "The Wedding of River Song" (6.13) one of the Silence exclaims, "Rory Williams: The man who dies and dies again. Die one last time and know she will never come back for you." Rory dies and returns so many times that many fans believe it to have happened rather too often and been over relied upon as a plot device. In many ways this process of "returning" to life is similar to the Doctor's regenerations.

Rory is reborn in a number of ways. For example, he is lost in the time rift and forgotten by Amy, then cloned as a weapon to kill her, only to return in human form after the Big Bang. The last time Rory leaves the series he faces his own timeline after he has sees a gravestone in a cemetery with his name carved on it. Just after he realizes the grave is there, the one remaining Weeping Angel sends him into 1930's New York ("The Angels Take Manhattan" 7.05). He is soon followed by Amy, who decides to be touched by the Weeping Angel so she will be sent back into the past to be with him. Although the couple lives for many years, as can be seen on the gravestone, they leave the program somewhat abruptly in this final scene. Rory is missed as a character by audiences because he is also a treasured companion. Many fans demanded a more fitting ending for the beloved pair when Rory and Amy left the show. The un-filmed but storyboarded postscript "Doctor Who: P.S." was released with a voice-over by Rory to show what happened to Rory's father, Brian, who was still waiting for his son and daughter-in-law to return. As Brian reads his son's letter, we learn from Rory's voice-over that the couple lived a long and happy life and that they adopted a child named Anthony.

Although a major concern in calling for the un-filmed ending was to find out what happens to Rory's father, there is also a sense that, in showing Brian's emotional response to seeing his grandson Anthony, we can all share in mourning Rory's demise as well as engaging in a celebration of his life. Such a postscript compensates for the lack of an opportunity to contemplate Rory and Amy's departure into the past, as it was denied in the original ending of this episode due to the rapid disappearance of both characters following the Weeping Angel's touch.

In her account of the caring approach of Rose Tyler's character, and her willingness to risk sacrificing herself, Amy-Chinn argues that there is a need, "to take issue with the consequences that arise from care in the universe of new Who and in particular the way in which it all too often requires sacrifice of the self—a familiar female trope."[7] Within Rory and Amy's story arc it is often Rory who is sacrificed or sacrifices himself for the story and whose various "deaths" challenge the definition of such sacrifice as a female trope. Equally his role as a nurse and his love for Amy, illustrated in his waiting for her both as a child and an adult, represent traditionally feminine qualities. Amy-Chinn also argues, as in the case of Rose Tyler, that caring for the Doctor is a form of self-sacrifice that should be countered because, to a degree, it made Rose vulnerable as a type of victim. Furthermore, Amy-Chinn sees that Rose's caring is based on a "relational" as opposed to a "rational" model where she will champion humanity and those she knows and loves. This account of Rose seems flawed as she is extremely brave and seeks to understand the universe. It is her compassion that is her strength and she often acts against type throughout her story arc.

In comparison to Rose, Rory, as Mr. Pond, displays similar feats of bravery and strength within a caring goal. However, although the Doctor benefits from his actions, Rory's sacrifice is ultimately for Amy. The extent to which self-sacrifice is constituted as a negative act may be viewed as a gendered distinction in Amy-Chinn's account as Rose's potential sacrifice for her family or the Doctor could be viewed as less heroic than a similar decision made by Rory. Clearly Rose displays her bravery when she looks into the heart of the TARDIS in an attempt to save the Doctor, even if it might lead to her own death, in "The Parting of the Ways" (1.13). This act is heroic, even though it does lead to Rose becoming Bad Wolf and also to the Doctor's next regeneration, when he takes the time vortex energy from her body to save her. But are Rory's actions any less self-sacrificing than those of Rose, as they concern who he loves, as well as for the wider universe?

Rory's "deaths" are only challenged in number by the Doctor's regenerations and the infinite resurrections of Captain Jack Harkness. As a companion, Jack is attracted to the Doctor but, as with Martha Jones, the feelings are not reciprocated. Captain Jack is also technically adept as he runs the rejuvenated Torchwood Institute and is familiar with alien technology. The ninth Doctor initially appears jealous of Jack but, by the tenth Doctor's regeneration, Jack has established himself with his abilities and his loyalty. The apparent regenerations, near deaths, and resurrections of characters such as Rose, Jack, Rory and Clara, provide a sense of mystery and fascination as they seem to be able to "cheat" death somehow in order to survive.

One of the most notable aspects of the number of times Rory "dies" is that these "deaths" have reinforced the emotional bond in his relationship with Amy.

One of Rory's "dying" episodes occurs in a psychic dream constructed by the Dream Lord in "Amy's Choice" (5.07) where Amy realizes what it would mean to lose him. In an interview with James Busch, Arthur Darvill, who plays Rory, has commented that "as much as Rory can be a bumbling idiot at times I think he's proved to the Doctor and to, you know, to everyone else around that, you know, when everything starts kicking off you can really step up to the plate and deliver. And, you know, and be of use and—because I think fundamentally he's a good person." Busch concludes that, due to becoming a centurion for two millennia, he has "manned up" somewhat although he is also more world weary. Darvill also expressed the hope that Rory's "deaths" do not continue: "I personally hope that Rory just stops dying."[8]

However, Rory's various "deaths" within *Doctor Who* have also provoked some criticism, as responses to his loss have moved from poignant concern to a feeling that these deaths are becoming a running joke. One review comments on Rory's simulated death by the entity known as House ("The Doctor's Wife" 6.04), "At this point, we're all privy to the "Rory's dead!" psych-outs, so we suspect this one was thrown in purely to add to the reoccurring joke."[9] Before their final encounter with the Weeping Angel, Rory and Amy have a shared "almost death" experience when they decide to sacrifice themselves by jumping off the Statue of Liberty, potentially the largest and most intimidating Weeping Angel of all. When Rory finally faces the Weeping Angels in "The Angels Take Manhattan," Amy says of her impending loss: 'You think you'll just come back to life?' and Rory replies, "When don't I!" It is likely that Amy and Rory establish a more stable life together when they are estranged from the Doctor so, although their eventual exit from the series is sad, as a couple they have many years together.

Killing with Kindness

In the later episodes featuring the eleventh Doctor, the Doctor's circle is once again widened. Madame Vastra, Jenny Flint, and Strax have formed the Paternoster Gang, which often helps the Doctor and Clara. Commander

Strax is a Sontaran who has been demoted from warrior to nurse. The Sontarans would appear to be the antithesis of Rory's character as they are a warrior race that believes fighting and dying in battle are noble and desirable, similar to the Viking belief that dying in battle is the greatest honor. Although their approach to war would seem to be a traditionally masculine trait, the Sontarans are clones without gendered distinctions. It is in Strax' nature to fight; even though his new role is a nurturing one, he takes pride in his nursing skills whilst still exhibiting the urge to fight. As Strax proudly declares when Rory and Amy's daughter is born: "Rory, I'm a nurse! I have gene-spliced myself for all nursing duties, I can produce magnificent quantities of lactic fluid" ("A Good Man Goes to War" 6.07). Strax is an alternative version of Rory, as he too is a nurse and thus technically a nurturer, although his opinion of humans is very poor and he is prone to aggression and general annoyance. The comparison between the two characters highlights the extent to which being a nurse does not necessarily involve a lot of compassion and understanding as the caring nurse is a stereotype as much as the impatient one. Rory has a strong desire to care; this perhaps illustrates a sensitive trait.

One of the most notable aspects of Amy and Rory's relationship occurs in "The Girl Who Waited" (6.10) on Apalapachia when Amy is left behind at Two Streams, a kindness facility that effectively imprisons her because she is deemed to be infectious. Rory and the Doctor enter the green side of the facility and are deemed to be uninfected. Amy instead goes into the Red Waterfall and is assumed to have the plague so she has to live out her time imprisoned in a series of entertainment zones. Within the Red Waterfall, Amy is imprisoned in a different time period where time is accelerated so that the families of those who are infected can see them live out their lives. By the time Rory and the Doctor return to rescue Amy she has aged thirty years. Only Rory can go out into the Red zone as the plague is deadly to the Doctor. The handbots who roam the Red zone seek to anesthetize or "kill with kindness," although Amy has to stop them from injecting her as she is not really ill. Older Amy is very bitter and has been alone for many years. She has had to learn to survive on her own. Her one "companion" is a handbot that has had its arms removed so it is no longer harmful and thus can keep her company. Amy has drawn a smiling face on the handbot and calls it Rory. Initially Rory is rather alarmed at his docile replacement but we can see that the person Amy has missed is Rory and not the Doctor, because she has not constructed a version of her "raggedy man" to keep her company but a version of Rory instead.

Although Amy is an adult, her reconfiguration of the handbot into a replacement for Rory echoes the function of the transitional object, a psychological stage where a child begins to identify the caregiver as a separate entity, different from it. In this phase the child begins to recognize the caregiver's face and uses a transitional object "to which to devote its attention in the absence of the caregiver."[10] The transitional object also enables the child to cope with separation from the caregiver. In using the transitional object, "the infant has begun to realize that the caregiver is not just a dimension of the infant's own experience but rather is a being that can be absent as well as present and therefore other as well as self."[11] But whether Amy uses the Rorybot as a transitional object to cope with Rory's absence or merely to replace him, she eventually begins to identify with Rory as an individual in his own right through her relationship with the bot. When older Amy sacrifices herself she knows that her younger self has the capacity to mature and finally decides to let Rory and her younger self have their time together. Nevertheless, the Rorybot facsimile is mute and subservient and when Amy has to confront the real-life Rory she is angry and confused because he is a separate individual and because there still might be some mutual attraction. The fact that Rory tries to save her and does not seem to distinguish between the older and younger versions of Amy indicates that his love for her is very deep and not superficial. The Doctor knows that both Amys cannot survive, and Rory feels a great loss at older Amy's death. In this episode it is Amy who sacrifices herself so her younger version can live out her life with Rory. It seems to mark a transition point in the Pond's story arc whereby a more experienced and mature Amy sacrifices herself. We know that this character is a part of the younger Amy, particularly as they are both played by Karen Gillan. Amy is also replaced by a duplicate from the Nestene consciousness whilst she was pregnant with Melody/River Song and echoes the forms of "deaths" we see in Rory's timeline. But Rory's reincarnations are the most distinctive recurring motifs in addition to the Doctor's regenerations within new *Who*.

Conclusion

Beginning as a companion's companion to Amy Pond, Rory proves himself throughout his time on the TARDIS by his love for Amy. His strengths lie in a sense of responsibility and purpose, driven by his emotional and caring perspective. His attraction lies in his geek chic appearance, self-effacing manner, and dry sense of humor. Audiences can identify with his responses to the events around him as he often responds as someone who is new to a situation but who is trying to figure it out. He also often uses comedy as a way to handle a situation. Rory is a well-loved and popular character because, in his own quirky way, he has established himself both as a "perfect," and loyal, boyfriend and an ideal, if skeptical, companion. Rory Williams is the boy who waited until, we assume, he finally got what he wanted.

NOTES

1. McApline, "Doctor Who Cosplay."
2. Williams, "Desiring the Doctor," 139.
3. Feasey, *Masculinity and Popular Television*, 60.
4. Nguyen, "*Doctor Who* Boss and Karen Gillan."
5. "Doctor Who: P.S." Season 7, webisode.
6. East, "Samuel Anderson Speaks on Doctor/Danny."
7. Amy-Chinn, "Rose Tyler: The Ethics of Care and the Limit of Agency," 245.
8. Busch, "DOCTOR WHO's Arthur Darvill Talks Repeatedly Dying, More."
9. Ho, "Five Memorable Rory Deaths on Doctor Who."
10. Washburn, *Transpersonal Psychology in Psychoanalytic Perspective*, 48.
11. Ibid.

A Muted Melody
The (Dis)Empowerment of River Song

TOM POWERS

Ever since the televised saga of *Doctor Who* began in 1963 and continued its long-running narrative to the present through the media of television, audio, and print, the Doctor has been depicted as a character possessing both an extraordinary intelligence and an uncanny knowledge of future events due to his Time Lord life style and abilities. When River Song first enters the tenth Doctor's life in the Fourth Series episode "Silence in the Library" (4.08), however, she enacts a potent hold over the enigmatic time traveler with her locus of knowledge concerning his future self. This appearance, of course, coincides with a period of the show's history where a growing number of fans of both sexes have embraced the show's positive depiction of the female companion as near-equal to the Doctor, whereas, in the past, she was relegated to a secondary "assistant" status.[1] In River's subsequent nonlinear appearances during the eleventh Doctor's era, moreover, her agency as an independent, empowered woman is continually reinforced although she is correspondingly devalued or disempowered. Hence, one must consider the complex and problematic elements typifying Steven Moffat's masculine authorship of River Song as he writes her as an altruistic, flirtatious, and sacrificial heroine.

Feminine Songs of Power and Blue-Box Diaries

As a male academic, this author is often reminded how patriarchy has a totalizing effect upon all elements of Western society, luring and ensnaring both females and males in its gaze of masculine oppression, especially in regard to gendered expectations for both sexes. Resistance to patriarchy naturally occurs in art and politics. To view the character of River Song as a form of "writing back" against tradition notions of oppressed, secondary female characters, still, is problematic since River, via Moffat's authorship, navigates between the binaries of liberated and oppressed. Thankfully, when French feminist Hélène Cixous, in her classic piece, "The Laugh of the Medusa," writes about the inherent power of all women, she offers a better understanding of River Song's name and agency. Cixous declares, "In women's speech, as in their writing, that element which never stops resonating, which, once we've been permeated by it, profoundly and imperceptibly touched by it, retains the power of moving us—that element is the song; first music from the first voice of love which is alive in every woman."[2]

In applying Cixous' words to River, one can comment that she indeed is a character full of love—for life and the Doctor—when he first meets his future wife in "Silence in the Library." As this mysterious character interacts with the Doctor in the planet-sized book repository known as the Library, moreover, she is relating to him as if he is a dear old friend or possible lover. Telling him she cannot reveal anything to him of his future as that action would constitute her providing "spoilers," River gives credence to the oft-cited expression that knowledge is power. Although this is her first appearance, chronologically speaking, this is the oldest living chronological version of River the show will present.[3] More importantly, she interacts with the youngest version of the Doctor she has ever known. Nonetheless, via the Doctor's psychic paper, she has utilized the power of writing to enact a sense of control over the Doctor as she has successfully summoned him to the Library. Language thus works for River not only as a means to communicate with the Doctor but as a way of manipulating him to assist her in her adventures as well.

The Doctor skeptically accepts River's claim that she is someone of importance to his future self, but he does not fully believe her until this moment between them occurs:

> River: Doctor, one day I'm going to be someone that you trust completely, but I can't wait for you to find that out. So I'm going to prove it to you, and I'm sorry. I'm really very sorry. (She whispers something in the Doctor's ear.) Are we good? Doctor, are we good?
> The Doctor: Yeah, we're good.

Whether these unheard words reveal River's knowledge of the Doctor's true name or some equally intimate secret, they possess a truth that convinces him she knows his future self. At the same time, a dualistic feeling of unease and comfort has been provided in this exchange as River's apology for knowing the Doctor's secret uncomfortably hints of some traumatic event that has occurred during his long existence, but then the exchange of *good* in the aftermath of this shared knowledge reassures viewers that, regardless of his potential sins or regrets, he can carry on behaving heroically in front of his twin watchers: both River and the audience. Therefore, as much as River enacts power over the Doctor in this moment, she empowers him by bearing witness to his heroically masculine composure.

At the conclusion of the second episode of River's debut, "Forest of the Dead" (4.09), she has sacrificed herself to prevent the Doctor from burning out his own mind in ensuring the 4,022 corporal forms of the people "saved" by CAL, the Library's computer, are restored. Although her physical body has perished, River's essence is uploaded into a virtual reality via CAL, where she can live forever, thanks to the Doctor's present and future selves' efforts. She has also empowered him once again via her earlier taunt that the older, future version of the Doctor she knew could open his TARDIS with the snap of his fingers. Subsequently, the Doctor discovers that he is capable of opening his beloved TARDIS by snapping his fingers in one of the closing scenes of the episode, granting him a stronger affinity with the feminized, maternal time machine.[4]

River also leaves behind her diary, whose cover resembles the London-police-box outer shell of the TARDIS, but the Doctor respects its contents by not opening the book, choosing instead to leave it behind in the Library. Interestingly, as the outside blue-box appearance of the Doctor's Type-40 TARDIS obscures the wonders of Gallifreyan time-travel technology and transdimensional engineering found inside of it, River's diary's similar TARDIS-exterior wrapping contains the off-limits-to-the-Doctor narrative of the Time Lord's future adventures with her. Cixous' thoughts on a woman's inner strength as a person and writer is key to comprehending the power of River's cryptic diary: "Even if phallic mystification has generally contaminated good relationships, a woman is never far from 'mother' (I mean outside her role functions: the 'mother' as nonname and as source of goods). There is always within her at least a little of that good mother's milk. She writes in white ink."[5] For River, her feminine narrating of her chronologically-inverted travels with the Doctor, which he will never read, functions as her "white ink,"[6] whose present—or *invisible*—writing will resonate as the diary reappears many times accompanying Doctor Song when she meets up with the Doctor.[7] In short, River's diary exists as an extension of the "mother" within her, and its unread pages resist and complement any of the "phallic mystification" embodied and created by the Doctor.

When the Doctor next encounters River in the Fifth Series two-part story, "The Time of Angels"/"Flesh and Stone" (5.04 & 5.05), he is in his eleventh incarnation.[8] River, however, who is meeting up with him at an earlier part of his timeline since she already knows his future self, has been imprisoned at the Stormcage Containment Facility for the murder of a man whose identity is not divulged in these episodes (but will later be revealed in the following series as the Doctor himself). As a means of reducing her sentence, she is working with an order of militarized clerics to investigate the crash of the Galaxy-Class starship Byzantium on the planet Alfava Metraxis.

In order to involve the Doctor in this mission, River utilizes the twin powers of gender and language. For the former, she uses hallucinogenic lipstick on a Byzantium soldier to make the seduced man believe he is standing in a beautiful outdoors setting. As River confidently walks toward the ship's room holding the Home Box (the futuristic equivalent of an airplane's black box), a close-up shot of her high-heeled red shoes is offered to viewers followed by close-up shots showing her holding a gun in her right hand and a purse in her left, which symbolize her complementary masculine-feminine traits.

Regarding River's application of language in order to contact the Doctor, once she shoots her way into the room holding the Home Box, she proceeds to burn a message onto the device. 12,000 years later, as a screen caption informs viewers, the Doctor finds the aged box in the Delirium Archive and proudly tells Amy that the graffiti on the box had been composed in Old High Gallifreyan, upon which he also comments, "There were days; there were many days when these words could burn stars, and raise up empires, and topple gods." But when Amy asks him what is written on the Home Box, he is dismayed to reveal that River's application of the venerable language of the ancient Time Lords translates into her catchphrase greeting, "Hello, Sweetie." When one considers that Time Lord society has predominately been depicted as a patriarchal affair in the classic and modern series,[9] River's good-humoredly emasculating application of their ancient language with her flirty, feminine salutation destabilizes any reverential feelings the Doctor may possess for his ancestors. He, nevertheless, reviews the Home Box's video recording to receive the necessary coordinates from River in order to rescue her from her predicament, literally catching her flying figure in his arms in his TARDIS after she triggers an airlock to escape the Byzantium. With this sequence of events, River's mastery of a language known only to the Doctor combined with her intimate knowledge of his penchant for rescuing damsels-in-distress thus works as the means for her to once more achieve a position of mastery over the Time Lord.

After defeating a swarm of Weeping Angels with River, the Doctor later interacts with a past version of her in the two-part season five finale, "The Pandorica Opens"/"The Big Bang" (5.12 & 5.13). At the conclusion of this adventure, River shows up during Amy and Rory's wedding reception to retrieve her diary, and she and the Doctor share this conversation:

River: Did you dance? Well, you always dance at weddings. Don't you?
The Doctor: You tell me?
River: Spoilers.

> The Doctor: (He hands River's diary back to her.) The writing's all back, but I didn't peek.

Although this scene demonstrates the Doctor's acknowledgement that River's unread words have achieved a form of power over him, in the following moment, his equal control of her, in an emotional sense, is confirmed through a playful exchange of language:

> The Doctor: Are you married, River?
> River: Are you asking?
> The Doctor: Yes.
> River: Yes.
> The Doctor: No, hang on: Did you think I was asking you to marry me, or, or, or asking if you were married?
> River: Yes.
> The Doctor: No, but was that yes or yes?
> River: Yes.

For River, the power she holds over the Doctor is concerned with his marital status. Since viewers later find out that the Doctor indeed married River's younger self—all part of Moffat's master plan for her character—one can state that River controls the Doctor through this foreknowledge. At the same time, she needs to put the thought of marrying her in the Doctor's mind before the events of "The Wedding of River Song" (6.14), which, by default, puts her heart—her inner power—into his hands.

A Regenerating Pond or a River Sue?

In the following series, the audience, not the Doctor, is first privy to learning about River's genesis when they view her original incarnation, a child, begin to regenerate at the end of the two-part story, "The Impossible Astronaut"/"Day of the Moon" (6.01 & 6.02). The audience later learns in the episode "A Good Man Goes to War" (6.07) that this girl is the daughter of Amy and Rory, her birth name being Melody Pond, a variation of the nomenclature River Song. As for River's ability to regenerate, it is also revealed that this gift is the result of Amy and Rory conceiving her in the TARDIS while it was traveling in the Time Vortex, an event which fused Time Lord DNA into River's human physiology. River's later comment that she is the "Child of the TARDIS" in "The Wedding of River Song" then accounts for her ability to fly the time craft in a more accomplished manner than the Doctor himself. From a gendered perspective, consequently, the matriarchal TARDIS has bestowed its exclusive powers of flight upon its humanoid female progeny—River.

Moffat, at this point in his River Song narrative, or story arc, has significantly developed the character to the extent that her abilities rival or challenge the Doctor's, who, of course, is the nominative lead of the series. However, of importance to the process of weighing whether or not Moffat has crafted a strong or weak character in the form of River Song, one must consider the most obvious question of them all: Why did he create the character in the first place? In regard to any economic incentive Moffat may have considered in nurturing this character, one must consider that, yes, he stands to gain financially from any spin-off media or merchandise featuring her. Unlike his predecessor, Russell T. Davies, who created Captain Jack Harkness, a major addition to the *Doctor Who* mythos, for the arguable primary reason of launching a spin-off series, *Torchwood*, Moffat, to date, has not attempted to launch a separate show around River's solo adventures. Why, then, has he chosen to make River Song a stand-out character during his tenure as the steward of *Doctor Who*?

A potential answer is that River represents Moffat's "Mary Sue" character, a term originating from a 1974 short story composed by Paula Smith for issue #2 of the *Star Trek* fanzine, *Menagerie*. In this brief eight-paragraph parody of *Star Trek* fan-fiction, Smith delineates the tongue-in-cheek tale of Mary Sue, fifteen-and-a-half-years old and the youngest lieutenant in Starfleet, who quickly wins the attention of Captain Kirk, Mr. Spock, and Dr. McCoy. Through a rapid succession of events, Mary Sue, Kirk, Spock, and McCoy, along with Mr. Scott, are imprisoned on Rigel XXXVII, where she reveals to Mr. Spock that she too is half-Vulcan and helps them escape with the use of a hairpin. After they return to the Enterprise, those four officers fall ill, and Mary Sue runs the ship in their stead, earning her numerous prizes including the Nobel Peace Prize. Tragedy strikes in the eighth paragraph of Smith's story, however, as Mary Sue fatally succumbs to the disease and is deeply mourned by Kirk, Spock, McCoy, and Scott. In the years since this story initially resonated throughout *Star Trek* fandom, the term Mary Sue has been applied to not only fan-composed wish-fulfillment characters but also legitimate characters (e.g., *Star Trek: The Next Generation*'s Wesley Crusher and *Twilight*'s Bella Swan), who have been accused of being "Canon Sues."

While one can argue that River serves as a Mary Sue in "Silence in the Library"/"Forest of the Dead," her various subsequent appearances in *Doctor Who* during the Moffat era negate this assumption as she has not remained a one-off character. Simultaneously, she could be perceived as a Canon Sue in the sense that she serves as Moffat's fantasy of the perfect woman who will sacrifice everything for her man. Arguably, for Moffat to do anything less than create a worthy female counterpart to stand up against the strong-willed Doctor would be to ignore this positive literary/cinematic zeitgeist and disappoint women viewers who expect to identify with strong female characters on *Doctor Who*. From another perspective, since so many of River's stories show her relinquishing, in chronological order (for her), her regenerative abilities, her freedom, and her very life, she serves as a Canon Sue by way of constantly having to reaffirm her sacrificial agency to the Doctor.

The X- and Y-Crescents of Two Time-Crossed Lovers

The next episode in Moffat's River Song narrative, "Let's Kill Hitler" (6.08), reveals that the Caucasian Melody Pond regenerated into a black girl in 1969 New York City. The significance of this regeneration for the show as a whole should not be downplayed since, with this second incarnation of Melody Pond, the audience is presented with a character who can switch skin color, thus transcending barriers of race to present a richer, multicultural vision regarding the power of regeneration. At the same time, this incarnation of Melody Pond has been secretly tracking down the Doctor, living near Amy and Rory in the hope that the Time Lord will show up, so she can assassinate him according to her mental programming initiated by the Silence. When she regenerates in 1936 Berlin after being shot by a Nazi, her third incarnation is revealed to be the form of the character as traditionally embodied by the actress Alex Kingston. Moreover, although the new Melody Pond poisons the Doctor via a kiss from her deadly Judas-tree fruit-covered lips,[10] he still believes in her eventual redemption—that she will evolve into the heroic River Song.

With his characteristically heroic mindset to save others, the Doctor, nonetheless, is functioning in a patriarchal manner towards a younger female character, River, as he has numerous times throughout the show's history. However, this enactment of patriarchy is balanced out by a later penitent Melody, who, by the end of "Let's Kill Hitler," has sacrificed her remaining regenerations in order to restore the nearly dead Doctor to life. One can code this sacrificial moment either as that of the maternal Melody bestowing life to the weakened Time Lord or as River Song's first act in a series of heroic self-sacrifices for her savior-figure, the Doctor. Regardless of how one views Melody's choice in this moment, the fact remains that it is the patriarchal, nameless Doctor who chronologically supplies her with the inherent power of her new feminine name—River Song. By the episode's end, he is also the person who grants her power over him through the medium of writing by leaving her convalescing figure with the gift of a TARDIS-shaped diary, which she will use to keep track of her adventures with him as she encounters earlier, nonlinear versions of the Time Lord. In other words, the Doctor never needs to peek at the contents of River's journal as he confidently knows he has shaped her writing productions through a paper receptacle, one that visually echoes the exterior of his own box and thereby serves as his repository of creation and control over his wife.

During River's time away from the Doctor, however, she best experiences her sense of agency and independence. In her influential essay, "Feminist Criticism in the Wilderness," Elaine Showalter synthesizes Oxford anthropologist Edwin Ardener's diagram expressing the relationship between what he posits as the muted group, *women*, and the dominant group, *men*. The diagram constitutes two circles, the Y circle representing women and the X circle for men; unfortunately, the Y circle showing the muted group that is women is mostly dominated by the X circle of men. Yet there exists a crescent for the Y circle that fall outside the boundaries of the X, which Ardener deems as "wild."[11]

Showalter then augments this concept by claiming, "We can think of the 'wild zone' of women's culture, spatially, experimentally, or metaphysically."[12] In terms of this wild zone's spatial aspect, which can be applied to River Song, Showalter writes, "It stands for an area which is literally a no-man's land, a place forbidden to men, which corresponds to the zone in X which is off limits to women."[13] River's "wild zone," then, is her life away from the Doctor. At this point, a visualization of this *Doctor-Who*-themed appropriation of Showalter's application of Ardener's diagram is necessary:

With this model in place, River's archaeological education at Luna University, culminating in her achievement of a doctorate, works as her first successful foray into this wild zone of empowerment, visualized as her Y-crescent. And her subsequent career as an academic and time-and-space traveling archaeologist, later leading to her promotion to the rank of professor, serves as a testament to her achieving a title of power akin to the Doctor's own moniker.

One can also extend River's Y-crescent wild zone to her TARDIS-shaped journal, which contains her secreted knowledge of

River Song's Wild-Zone (created by the author).

the tenth and eleventh Doctor's future actions. Conversely, since she encounters the Doctor out of chronological sequence, his corresponding X-crescent, which is equally off-limits to River, comes into focus. In other words, this X-crescent is the eleventh Doctor's knowledge of River's inevitable fate in the Library. At other times, the Doctor draws from this X-zone, especially in "Let's Kill Hitler," when, as discussed, he applies his foreknowledge of the future heroic River Song to the newly regenerated Melody Pond in order to help her begin to break the Silence's programming. As the Doctor's X-crescent grows, however, he gains a sense of emotional and chronological supremacy over River, which, in turn, diminishes the former omnipotent power of River's Y-crescent wild zone.

Perhaps the ultimate manifestation of the Doctor colonizing River's Y-zone occurs when she marries the Time Lord in the Sixth Series finale, "The Wedding of River Song." In terms of a positive reading of the Doctor agreeing to marry River, one can argue that she is a true equal, a worthy mate, for this genius alien. Can the same be said for River by the time they exchange wedding vows?

Before that problematic moment, the Doctor, Amy, Rory, and River have been existing in an alternate reality where all times exist at once. This situation is a result of River creating a divergent reality in her attempt to undo the Silence-engineered assassination of the Doctor at a fixed point in time at Lake Silencio, Utah, on April 22, 2011. After fleeing the attacking Silence by going to the top of the United States governmental pyramid located in the American Southwest, the Doctor and River have the following emotional exchange after River reveals she has been sending out a distress beacon—"The Doctor is dying. Please, please help."—to the future and the past. The Doctor replies, "River, River, this is ridiculous. That would mean nothing to anyone. It's insane. Worse—it's stupid. You embarrass me."

One can attempt to explain away the Doctor's angry, condescending tone to River in the scene as the words of a man who has the fate of the universe on his shoulders, a stressful responsibility exacerbated by the ostensible fact that he must die at a fixed point in time. Otherwise, all of reality is in danger of collapsing due to the time paradox River has created in her attempt to save him. At the same time, one can contend that the Doctor, despite his stressful predicament, should never take this tone with anyone, least of all, River Song—the ultimate companion who has repeatedly proven her worth to him.

Regardless of my aca-fan-hued investment[14] in River Song's state of happiness, the fact that the Doctor has disrespected this strong, selfless character who has devoted her life to him is readily apparent to any viewer. Considering that River has sacrificed her future lives and her one remaining life for this man, is it too hard to conceive of him being more graceful and appreciative of this woman when she reveals that she has stopped time to prevent her Silence-brainwashed self from carrying out an appointed execution of the man? Perhaps her love for the Doctor is too pure, or just utterly obsessive. After all, when the Doctor subsequently asks her in this episode if she is willing to sacrifice billions of lives to save his own, she honestly answers yes. In order to mute her protests to assassinating him, he agrees to marry her, and, in his best patriarchal way, initiates the wedding ceremony himself. This action, of course, is designed so that he can reveal to River that she will only be destroying a Teselecta, which is an android-ship, version of him in the true reality. When they return to "reality," an argument could then be made that the Doctor's marriage to River, precipitated out of necessity, possesses neither emotional validity for the Doctor nor any legal weight whatsoever since the ceremony was initiated outside of time and space, where such conventionally binding social contracts leave no legitimate record.

Depowered Like the Best of Genre Heroines

As mentioned in this chapter's title, River is gradually being disempowered throughout her chronologically-warped appearances on *Doctor Who*. The term disempowerment is similar to the comic-book narrative concept of "depowerment," in which a superhero is stripped of his or her extraordinary abilities. Unfortunately, in comparison to their male counterparts, female superheroes often lose their powers in a disproportionate manner. When veteran comic-book writer Gail Simone became sensitive to this issue, she coined the term "Women in Refrigerators" for a website dealing with this problem. The title refers to the death of Alexandra DeWitt, Green Lantern Kyle Rayner's girlfriend during issue #54 from the third volume of *Green Lantern*. In this issue, Kyle comes home to his apartment to find Alex's corpse infamously stuffed inside his refrigerator by his nemesis, Major Force, a deplorable act that had inspired the title of Simone's website, which, through professional and fan participation, has amassed a damning list of women in comics who have been raped, killed, mutilated, or have lost their powers. Granted, one can argue that numerous male characters have also been killed off or depowered throughout the history of comics, and another argument can be made that, oftentimes, supporting characters, whether they are male or female, are a lazy writer's fodder for the Grim Reaper. However, when one compares the total number of female superhero deaths, dismemberments, and depowerments for both main and supporting characters and weighs it against the corresponding number for their male counterparts, the results show that the women suffer the most.

Can the same be said for *Doctor Who*? In terms of the three companions who have died on the show, two of them, Katarina and Sara Kingdom, who perished in "The Daleks' Master Plan" (#21), were females. A possessed Peri was even killed at the end of episode eight of "The Trial of a Time Lord" ("Mindwarp" #145) but this story point was later rescinded as a fabrication on the Valeyard's part. Nonetheless, by adding River Song to this list, considering her physical body expires in "Forest of the Dead," one has three[15] female companion deaths weighed against one male's, Adric's, in "Earthshock" (#122). In the world of *Doctor Who*, this number may not appear to be too noticeable when one considers that the majority of the Doctor's companions have been women. However, in comparison to the disproportionate number of female superheroes written into a depowered or deceased state by a male comic book, science fiction, or fantasy writer looking for a supporting character to make an ultimate sacrifice for the heroic male lead, River joins a continually disproportionate list of marginalized, fictitious casualties.

Although this chapter's weighing of the pros and cons of Steven Moffat's characterization of River Song may be leaning toward positing her as a weak female character, one must also point out that she possesses many admirable virtues necessary for a strong hero. She is fearless, resourceful, and self-sacrificing, just like the Doctor has been on many occasions throughout the five-decade history of the franchise. In the Seventh Series episode, "The Angels Take Manhattan" (7.5), written by Moffat, River is portrayed in this ideal heroic mode. This episode delineates her parents Amy and Rory Williams' last appearance on the show as they travel to New York and face the life-stealing threat of the Weeping Angels. Since Rory is propelled into 1938 Manhattan by a Weeping Angel, the only clue the Doctor and Amy have to finding him rests with the novel the Doctor has been reading titled, "The Angel's Kiss: A Melody Malone Story." The author of this pulp detective novel, which, in actuality, is a memoir, or narrative blueprint revealing the fate of Rory and eventually Amy as well, is one Melody Malone, an old New York town private investigator who serves as an alter ego and pen name for River Song. Although the version of River present in the episode has yet to compose this work as it will be written by her future self, who has already experienced the events she is presently living out, the work, like her TARDIS-shaped diary, which contains stories of the Doctor's future life, places her in an omnipotent position.

Moffat also reveals in the episode, via exposition between River and the Doctor, that she is now a full professor of archaeology and that the Doctor has helped to ensure that she has been pardoned from her prison sentence as she can no longer be incarcerated for the murder of a man who does not exist, as the Time Lord has been erasing all records of his existence from universal data banks. On the one hand, from the confines of *Doctor Who*'s fictitious world, this action on the Doctor's part helps him in his quest to regain his anonymity, and it absolves him of any guilt he feels toward River suffering in jail on his behalf for a period of approximately five years. On the other hand, could this plot development serve as Moffat's way of ameliorating one of the horrendous fates he had written for River? In other words, has he chosen to back himself out of a complicated writing situation in which he has locked his favorite heroine in jail to serve out an unjust murder sentence for a man who is not even dead, a man who has been traveling freely across the cosmos?

Regardless of Moffat's intentions, he does redeem River significantly in this episode as she proves herself to be even stronger than the Doctor. In one scene, the Doctor discovers she has covered up the fact she had broken her wrist to escape from the stony grasp of a Weeping Angel. As the Doctor sits with River to inspect the damage to her wrist, they share an honest discussion:

> The Doctor: Why did you lie to me?
> River: When one's in love with an ageless god who insists on the face of a twelve-year old, one does one's best to hide the damage.
> The Doctor: It must hurt. Come here.
> River: Yes, the wrist is pretty bad too.

Although a reading could be made that the damage River alludes to is concerned with her lingering psychological issues that may stem from having a much older appearance in comparison with the eleventh Doctor's, one does have to remember that she is aging backwards, as revealed in "Let's Kill Hitler." In the next moment of this revealing scene, the Doctor grabs River's wrist and, against her protests, heals it with a portion of his regenerative energy. Her wrist now healed, she slaps his face, scolding him for his sentimentally "stupid waste of regeneration energy" and adding "You embarrass me!"

This line clearly shows River paying the Doctor back with his disdainful words of "You embarrass me" from "The Wedding of River Song." River continues to remain strong when she soon informs Amy about the Doctor's weakness towards the ravages of time upon his companions by telling her mother, "Never let him see the damage. And never, ever, let him see you age. He doesn't like endings." Tellingly, River's insistence to Amy that she never let the Doctor see her age may have been anticipated by Professor Song herself with her decision at the beginning of her current incarnation to make herself age backwards.

By showing River as someone who is in control of the situation and the characters around her, Moffat's positive development of her character, nonetheless, situates her narrative progression as being on the upswing. More importantly, at the end of the episode, after her parents have been torn away into the past of New York City and the ages of their deaths have been revealed on a tombstone, River remains resilient, as seen in this scene:

> The Doctor: River, they were your parents. Sorry, I didn't even think.
> River: Doesn't matter.
> The Doctor: Of course it matters.
> River: What matters is this, Doctor: Don't travel alone.
> The Doctor: Travel with me then.
> River: Wherever and whenever you want. But not all the time. One psy-

chopath per TARDIS, don't you think? (pause) Okay this book I've got to write—"Melody Malone"—I presume I sent it to Amy to get it published?

When River tells the Doctor that the death of her parents "doesn't matter," her words reveal a conflicted inner truth. What she may actually be saying is that her true emotions toward this situation *cannot* matter as she must subsume her feelings of grief in order to remain strong enough to comfort the child-like Doctor in his heartache for his companions' deaths. Regardless of her maternal comforting of her husband, she cultivates a sense of self-preservation by telling the Doctor she cannot always travel with him. In the same vein, she reaffirms her agency to compose a text that enacts power over him by agreeing to become the author of "Melody Malone," which assures the future for all of them. She likewise extends this ability to assume control over the Doctor's words, actions, and feelings to her mother, Amy, who writes an afterword that inspires the Doctor, at the close of the episode, to race frantically across Central Park in order to retrieve the ripped-out final page that is the afterword from a basket, so he can read Amy's final wishes for him.

At the same time, since both River and Amy must both write in "Melody Malone" to ensure the Doctor's continual existence and happiness, their words are proscribed by the patriarchal Time Lord's chronologically-convoluted lifestyle. Returning to Showalter, one can now appropriately include another of her comments: "The concept of a woman's text in the wild zone is a playful abstraction: in the reality to which we must address ourselves as critics, women's writing is 'double-voiced discourse' that always embodies the social, literary, and cultural hierarchy of both the muted and the dominant."[16] In the case of the mother-daughter authorship of "Melody Malone," the "double-voiced discourse" of the writing not only reflects their dominant literary position over the Doctor but also their "muted" resignation in adhering to the "timey-wimey" dictates of predestination as frequently defined by the Time Lord himself.

River: Loyal Ghost or Feminine Archetype?

As much as "The Angels Take Manhattan" works toward strengthening River Song's tarnished image as an autonomous, self-respecting character, Moffat's depiction of her in the Seventh Series finale, "The Name of the Doctor" (7.13), reverses this positive progression of her character. The River the audience sees in this episode, moreover, is the version of her the Doctor had uploaded into the Library during the conclusion of "Forest of the Dead." One explanation for River's weakened characterization in this episode could be attributed to the fact that Moffat was aware (or considering the possibility) that Matt Smith was soon to depart the role of the eleventh Doctor when he was writing this story. Consequently, he may have wished to provide the audience with a sense of closure for River's long-running story arc by composing a proper farewell scene between her and the Doctor.[17]

In "The Name of the Doctor," on the mass cemetery battlefield of Trenzalore, River once more rescues her husband when she saves him from the trouble of revealing his name to the Great Intelligence by silently speaking the unrevealed word(s) to the future TARDIS in order to open one of its size-leak-generated[18] massively enlarged doors. Inside this TARDIS-tomb, after the Doctor plans on sacrificing himself in order to save Clara, who is lost in his time stream, the voiceless, intangible River shouts at him to seek alternatives. As she goes to slap the Doctor, however, he stops her hand, triggering this cathartic discussion:

> River: How are you even doing that? I'm not really here.
> The Doctor: You're always here to me, and I've always listened, and I can always see you.
> River: Then, why didn't you speak to me?
> The Doctor: Because I thought it would hurt too much.

The question as to who endures more pain in this situation is a problematic one, but the fact that the Doctor has consciously ignored the seemingly incorporeal River's voice firmly places the blame for both their sufferings on him. Although he next goes on to passionately kiss River, one could label his act as the kiss of death since he is soon telling her, "There is a time to live and a time to sleep. You are an echo, River. Like Clara, like all of us. In the end, my fault, I know. But you should have faded by now." As a result, the Doctor has reduced this sentient, caring version of River to a spectral fraction of her former organic self, and so Cixous' thoughts on a woman who does not write can now likewise be applied to her: "A woman without a body, dumb, blind, can't possibly be a good fighter. She is reduced to being the servant of the militant male, his shadow."[19]

More troubling, this electronic-River, who has long pined away in the Doctor's ear, only agrees to go to "sleep" once she receives his permission to do so through a proper farewell. When the Doctor then begs River to tell him how to say goodbye to her, she prompts his dialogue by saying, "There's only one way I'd accept. If you ever loved me, say it like you're going to come back," to which he performatively responds, "Well, then, see you around, Professor River Song." In other words, this continuously muted woman has to supply the language for her own final demise to the very person who tuned her out for an untold period of time. From a classically romantic viewpoint, River's poignant farewell to the Doctor is the stuff that satiates viewers seeking well-written melodrama occurring between the couple. At the same time, for female viewers seeking a strong, empowered role model in the form of River

Song, with this bittersweet farewell they may be disappointed as the character literally fades away, arguably forming one last sacrifice to a Doctor who cannot effectively continue to communicate with what, in essence, amounts to be her eternally loving ghost.

On a closing note, Christine Cornea's article, "British Science Fiction Television in the Discursive Context of Second Wave Feminism," can perhaps offer a more comprehensive lens in which to view River's complex characterization. In this piece, Cornea traces how "powerful feminine archetypes like the hag, the witch, the female warrior, and the ice goddess" are performed in the 1970s permutation of *Doctor Who*, which coincides with the second-wave feminism movement.[20] Representing the hag and the witch archetypes, in Cornea's view, are the female guardians of the "elixir of life," the Sisterhood of Karn, who are featured in "The Brain of Morbius" (#84). Two of the fourth Doctor's companions, Leela, a savage warrior from the Sevateem tribe, and Romana, a fellow Time Lord, respectively embody the *female warrior* and *ice goddess* archetypes. One can thus cite them as the narrative progenitors of River Song, who, in many ways, serves as an amalgamation of all four archetypes. Since she is physically older than Amy and Rory when she first meets them and more well-traveled and educated than they are, River functions as the wise witch who imparts her knowledge to her younger, naïve parents.

Furthermore, although the eleventh Doctor is chronologically several hundred years older than River, physically, to an outside observer, she looks old enough to be his mother. She also initially holds knowledge of his future actions and secrets about his TARDIS, further cementing her role as the guide-like *witch* or *hag*. Admittedly, calling River a hag may be viewed as somewhat of an insult to the character. However, if one considers the term to be synonymous with *crone*, which better suggests the empowerment of an older woman, then it serves as a chronological reference point for River's years of experience, which could number in the centuries if her aging process has been slowed down like the Doctor's.

As for her prowess as a *warrior woman*, this is boisterously exemplified several time by River. While the Doctor has traditionally shunned using a gun, River exuberantly wields a handheld weapon. Moreover, in "The Big Bang," she point-blank shoots the stone Dalek, and, in "Day of the Moon," she offers a cascading array of firepower to protect the Doctor and company from the attacking Silence. Through this gun-toting behavior, River more or less functions as the Doctor's muscle, using a weapon in an aggressively masculine manner to save the day and/or carry out his ostensibly pacifist agenda.

The *ice goddess* archetype is rarely demonstrated by River as she often displays her emotional state. However, a newly regenerated Melody Pond in "Let's Kill Hitler" evinces a cold reaction to the Doctor being on the verge of death as a result of receiving a quick kiss from her Judas-tree poisoned lips.

This attitude, of course, is a result of the Silences' programming, and one which she gradually eliminates with the help of the Doctor and her imploring mother. Thus, the sacrificial heat of her remaining regeneration energy being poured into the dying Doctor to restore his life eliminates the ice-goddess aspect of her personality.

* * *

Ultimately, Steven Moffat's characterization of River Song, a brilliant female match for the Doctor—the best the show has seen to date—can be subject to both praise and criticism. She is paradoxically strong and weak, independent and subservient, empowered and disempowered, but her evolution as a bicultural, multitalented individual works as a finer paradigm for the feminine hero on *Doctor Who*, who, despite her myriad flaws, sets the template for an inevitably future female incarnation of the Doctor.

NOTES

1. Although River may not strictly be considered a companion since she does not consistently travel with the Doctor, she nonetheless meets many of the criteria for this role. During the conclusion to the documentary, "The Ultimate Companion," presenter Peter Davison summarizes what he views to be the essential characteristics of a *Doctor Who* companion: "[T]hey're adventurous, heroic individuals who adapt to their Doctors and manage to keep them in check. More importantly, they're our way into the TARDIS, our way of traveling with the Doctor." Applied to River, these traits ring true, especially when one considers how she quickly adapts to the tenth and eleventh Doctors and reveals new aspects of their complex personalities to the audience.

2. See Cixous, "Laugh," 881.

3. There is the exception of the "ghost" River who appears in "The Name of the Doctor" (7.13).

4. One can naturally posit the TARDIS as a *she* during the eleventh Doctor's tenure as he refers to her as "sexy" in "The Eleventh Hour" (5.1). This argument is given further weight when the TARDIS's essence, or consciousness, is poured into a female vessel, Idris, in "The Doctor's Wife" (6.4).

5. See Cixous, "Laugh," 881.

6. Cixous leaves the exact nature of this white ink up to reader interpretation. From a biological standpoint, it could possibly refer to a woman's lactations when she is nursing a child. Conversely, a psychoanalytical reading could transform the milk into a form of feminine semen.

7. In the "The Time of Angels" (5.4), Amy asks the Doctor about the blue book River is flipping through and referencing, and he replies, "Her diary." River then corrects him with, "*Our* diary," succinctly summarizing their co-authorship of the tome via their chronologically-inverted relationship.

8. Thirteenth, actually, when one both considers Moffat's later retcon revelation in "The Day of the Doctor" (2013) that there had been a "forgotten" incarnation of the Time Lord, the War Doctor, who existed between the eighth and ninth Doctors, and the eleventh Doctor's confession to Clara in "The Time of the Doctor" that his predecessor had vainly used up a regeneration.

9. Then again, although there has not yet been a televised female Lord Presi-

dent, classic *Doctor Who* had presented strong Time Lord women in the form of such characters as Romana, the Rani, and the Inquisitor. Recently, in the Eighth Series, the Master has been regendered as the female villain Missy, who dresses like Mary Poppins and possesses a complex hold on the twelfth Doctor's hearts.

    10. She also claims the poison had disabled the Doctor's ability to regenerate. Yet, in light of the Doctor's revelation in "The Time of the Doctor" (Christmas 2013) that he is in his last incarnation, one can wonder how honest the significantly younger River is being at this moment.

    11. See Showalter, "Feminist Criticism," 262.

    12. *Ibid.*

    13. *Ibid.*

    14. "Aca fan," a term coined by media theorist Henry Jenkins, easily defines a *Doctor Who* aficionado such as myself, especially when my obsessive love for the show potentially intersects, overlaps, and contradicts my critical analysis of River Song.

    15. One could pose the argument that Donna Noble belongs to this list of the deceased as the version of her who traveled with the tenth Doctor and bettered herself is euthanized by him to save her life in the conclusion to "Journey's End" (4.13).

    16. See Showalter, "Feminist Criticism," 263.

    17. Moffat may have also chosen to write River out of the show altogether as he wished to provide a fresh start for the twelfth Doctor, who would later be announced as being played by Peter Capaldi. Moreover, she did not appear in the Eighth Series.

    18. According to the Doctor, a size leak occurs when a dying TARDIS's dimension dam starts breaking down, and, in his words, "[A]ll the bigger-on-the-inside starts leaking to the outside."

    19. See Cixous, "Laugh," 880.

    20. See Cornea's online article about "British Science Fiction Television" at: http://www.genders.org/g54/g54_cornea.html

Companions Who Weren't
The Pompadour and the Pauper

Pamela Achenbach

The first question a Whovian asks another Whovian is "Who was your first Doctor?" The second question is often dependent on the answer to the first: "Which companion is your favorite?" Sometimes the second question might be more specific and name the possible companions. These two questions almost always go hand in hand because the show would not be the same without the lucky sidekicks who get to travel the stars with the Doctor each week. For many fans, the companions are just as important as the Doctor himself. Especially in the revival, the episodes are directed through the eyes of the companion, creating an instant connection with the viewer.

In the more recent years of *Doctor Who*, the companions seem to be the focus of the storyline, and the audience watches as the Doctor changes their lives. It is an honor to be asked to venture forth in the brilliant blue box with the Doctor. This privilege is extended to only a few and rarely is the Doctor's invitation turned down. But life happens while the Doctor is chronologically displaced, and the Doctor is notoriously late. Sometimes, the companions the Doctor chooses never step into the TARDIS, but these companions can leave a lasting impression on the Doctor. Reinette, or Madame de Pompadour, from "The Girl in the Fireplace" (2.4) and Astrid Peth from "Voyage of the Damned" (4.1) are examples of this illusive type of companion who is not able to accept the Doctor's invitation to "see those stars a little closer."[1]

Viewers love the companions because they want to be them. They identify with them, finding something in their personalities and quirks to latch onto that connects them with the companion of the hour. During each episode, the viewer becomes one with the companion, joining the Doctor on his adventures. Captivated by the story unfolding on the screen, the viewer waits with bated breath, not blinking, not turning around to see the thing in the dark, and always counting the shadows. When the hour ends, the viewers are once again separated from the companion, free (or forced) to go about their lives until the next episode airs ... or until they begin yet another *Doctor Who* binge.

What does it take for an ordinary person to be invited into the TARDIS? Every Whovian knows that the ultimate honor a fan can receive is to be invited into the TARDIS for an adventure. According to Courtney Lewis and Paula Smithka, editors of *Doctor Who and Philosophy*, "It's a sign that [the Doctor] thinks you're capable of considering the abstract, being adventurous, daring, as well as understanding and compassionate toward strange aliens."[2] The Doctor surely cannot choose a companion who would be anything other than diplomatic in their encounters with alien races. And the Doctor is notorious for choosing companions who need him, like Ace[3] in classic *Who*, who was a runaway, stranded on a foreign planet until the Doctor whisked her away and gave her a place to belong with a sense of purpose.

Likewise, Rose Tyler was a drifter of sorts, a shop girl with little prospects for the future, when she met the Doctor. For Rose, the Doctor changed everything: her views on life and even her perception of herself. "The Doctor showed me a better way of living your life. You don't just give up. You don't just let things happen. You make a stand. You say no. You have the guts to do what's right when everyone runs away."[4] It is little wonder that Rose fell in love with the Doctor, the one man who could bring out who she really was and complete her. Rose was always ready for the adventure, a clean slate onto which the Doctor could impress his world.

Martha Jones also had a sense of adventure, but her adventure began before she met the Doctor. As a medical student, her goal was to save lives, something that she did repeatedly while with the Doctor. Martha was able to see everything the Doctor was and was willing to do whatever it took to save mankind, including trekking all over the world to spread word of the Doctor in his fight against the Master. Martha endured more than other companions and still she was able to venture forth and see the world around her as miraculous.

But certainly there is more than just personality involved with the decision to invite a stranger into the TARDIS. Although the Doctor often seems to choose a companion based on who is nearest to him at the time, he always ends up with someone who can teach him something about humanity, life or himself, indicating that either he has quite an amazing knack for serendipitous moments, or he actually is very careful about choosing his companions, perhaps because he is able to see all of time and space. He can see all of the possible outcomes with each companion, and perhaps his curiosity about which possibility will become reality is what helps him make his decision.

The Doctor has travelled the universe for the better part of a thousand years. He has seen countless pasts and futures, a variety of worlds and beings, and has experienced every state of existence possible. The very thing that the viewer deems outstanding is a part of the everyday mundane for the Doctor. The Doctor needs his companions to have some sense of astonishment and wonder when they see the universe for the first time, in order to experience it for the first time again himself. Although he has seen all these places and events before, he is experiencing it for the first time with this specific companion and sharing their wonder.

Laura Geuy Akers suggests that the companions' reactions impact their relationship with the Doctor. For example, although the Doctor has experienced the universe many times, the very act of "re-experiencing time is source of wonder, and this wonder infuses [the companion's] relationship with the Doctor."[5] The Doctor needs his companions to marvel at what they see and experience so he can vicariously experience it through them. With a companion in tow, everything is new again begging to be explored and re-experienced for the first time.

Whereas Rose needed the adventure to find out who she was, Martha was already on the path to her future when she met the Doctor. Studying to be a doctor herself, Martha didn't need the Doctor in order to grow up; she was well on her way to establishing her career and had a strong sense of family, whereas Rose only had her mother. According to Akers Martha "doesn't need wonder to inspire her to act. The Doctor values Martha's enthusiasm, skills, and dedication, but he can't make the empathic connection with her that he had with Rose, probably in part because Martha doesn't find wonder energizing in the way that Rose did."[6] Martha, however, becomes enthralled with the Doctor, and it is unclear whether the Doctor keeps her around because he enjoys the way she sees the universe or if he just likes the way she looks at him. However, she quickly proves herself a valuable companion who is willing to make the ultimate sacrifice for her vision of what the Doctor represents.

Why Her?

"Why her?" Rose asks the clockwork man, repair droid seven. "You've got all of history to choose from. Why specifically her?"[7] In this scene, Rose is being slightly upstaged by Reinette Poisson, who is standing close to her "imaginary friend," the Doctor. Rose, who in earlier episodes began to show her attachment and affections for the Doctor, is at this point becoming increasingly jealous of the Doctor's sudden relationship with the Madame de Pompadour, who the Doctor describes as "one of the most accomplished women who ever lived." Rose and Reinette are almost on the same visual plane, but Rose, who is holding a futuristic fire extinguisher that looks like a large gun, is half a step behind Reinette. Throughout the scene, Rose, who was a cashier prior to meeting the Doctor, throws glances toward Reinette, not necessarily accusing her but certainly suspicious. When she addresses the clockwork man, who refuses to answer anyone unless Reinette orders him to, her tone is quiet, almost like she does not want anyone to hear her ask the question that is going to reveal her jealousy. Her question is not only out of jealousy; she is asking the same question that the Doctor asked in the scene before and the one that the audience has been asking since the opening sequence: Why her?

The tenth Doctor "inherited" Rose from the Ninth, and Rose insists on bringing Mickey with her. However, Reinette is the first person the tenth Doctor specifically asks into the TARDIS. The 18th-century aristocrat is surprisingly open-minded to the concept of the Doctor stepping through time, like the pages of a book. The Doctor is fascinated by Madame de Pompadour from the moment he meets her as a child, through the fireplace. He is intrigued by the looming question: how can Revolutionary France be found on a 51st-century spaceship? When he meets her moments later, she is a grown woman who promptly begins to "snog" him. After she leaves the room, the Doctor discovers who she is and will be, and he is hooked, his curiosity quickly replaced with stronger emotions, enamored by her passion for life.

Madame de Pompadour never questions the Doctor's validity. She never considers how absurd the wibbly-wobbly, timey-wimey[8] concept is. Instead, she treasures the moments when she is with the Doctor and eagerly waits for him to return. When she sees the spaceship, she is startled, but not by disbelief. She accepts the premises proposed to her by the Doctor and by Rose. Her sense of wonder is solely for the Doctor rather than the adventure, although she is not quick to shy away from danger. While she dreams of the stars, the Doctor is the one who makes her eyes sparkle, and he loves every moment that she looks at him.

The Doctor admires the way Reinette looks at him; however, he is equally intrigued by the way Astrid looks at everything else. Astrid is the first non-human companion in the revival series. While it has never been determined why so many of the Doctor's companions are humans, the Doctor seems to adore the human race, possibly because he is able to show them things that they never even imagined, unlike races on alien planets where space travel is common. Astrid, however, is a perfect companion. Although her home planet is familiar with Earth and its people and was often fascinated by Earth's culture, Astrid was only able to dream of the stars, as the closest she was able to get to them was securing a job as a waitress on an intergalactic cruise ship. When she meets the Doctor, he invites her to join him on a sojourn to Earth. When they and their tour guide are transported there, her reaction makes the Doctor pause. "It's beautiful," she exclaims. "Really? Do you think so? It's just a street," the Doctor retorts.[9] She draws excitement from the smell of the air, the little "alien" shops, and the "concrete" (it is actually asphalt) under her feet. She sees beauty where the Doctor only sees the mundane. And Astrid never expects anything more; for her, that one tiny journey was the highlight of her life. But, of course, the Doctor offers her the entire universe.

Astrid's very name provides a new look for an old concept: Astrid is an anagram of TARDIS, although Neil Wilkes, co-founder of *Digital Spy*, cautions fans to not read too much into her name.[10] Surely, Wilkes cannot expect fans to do anything but speculate about her name! With the writers of the show also being fans who watched *Doctor Who* as children, every aspect of each episode is undoubtedly planned, especially when a name also spells out one of the key "characters" in the show. Astrid's fate is similar to that of the TARDIS: forever flying through the stars.

Looks Are Everything

Jean-Paul Sartre suggests that the presence of another person causes a person to look at him or herself with objectivity. The process of this enables the self to view the world as it appears to the Other.[11] "By the mere appearance of the Other, I am put in the position of passing judgment on myself as on an object, for it is as an object that I appear to the Other."[12] For the Doctor, this gaze enables him to see the universe with fresh eyes, the eyes of his companion. For the companions, this gaze opens a new world, the Doctor's world. Rose, for example, cannot see anything beyond this gaze. Without the Other looking at her, she no longer exists. She cannot find a way to live without the Doctor, so she continually tries to get back to him. This is reinforced in the show by having Rose trapped in a parallel world, completely erasing her existence from "our" world. She only reappears when she meets up again with the Doctor, and when she returns to the parallel world, she once again ceases to exist. Without the Doctor in her life, she makes no progress, no personal growth, which makes the Doctor's gift of the Metacrisis even more precious.[13]

Unlike Rose, Reinette offers the Doctor a look at himself. Where Rose was the one objectified, Reinette is able to return the Doctor's gaze, objectifying him. The Doctor scans Reinette's brain, telling her that she can close any door in her mind, and he won't look. However, instead of closing doors, she passes through them, entering the Doctor's own mind and revealing his secrets. Startled, the Doctor asks her how she did that, to which Reinette replies, "A door once opened may be stepped through in either direction."[14] In this moment, Reinette is able to offer the Doctor the one thing that Rose cannot: reciprocity. Whereas the Doctor can see the universe through Rose's gaze, it is Madame de Pompadour's gaze that allows him to view himself in a new way.

In "The Girl in the Fireplace," Reinette's gaze is the first we see. Her gaze is focused directly into the camera as she looks for the Doctor in her fireplace. Her eyes are not necessarily scared, but they are urgent as she demands the Doctor to come to her. This is not the typical gaze we see directed toward the Doctor, and it is certainly not the gaze we get from Rose's eyes. Within the first 50 seconds of the episode, we know that this relationship is much different than any we have previously encountered.

The first time the Doctor looks at Reinette, she is a little girl, someone defenseless who needs to be saved from the monsters in her dreams. Perhaps this encounter left an impression on the child, because moments later, the Doctor is met with a much different gaze.[15] The grown Reinette gazes upon the Doctor with slight disbelief at first, but almost instantly her gaze melts into one of familiarity. To the Doctor, Reinette is still a stranger, but for her, she has known the Doctor, dreamed of the Doctor since she was seven.[16] Clearly, she had the advantage, and she quickly dominates the conversation, her gaze unwavering until she pins the Doctor against the fireplace, kissing him.[17]

Reinette gazes upon the Doctor and claims him as her imaginary friend.[18] This is a new experience for the Doctor. Instead of him gaining a new perspective of the universe through the eyes of his companion, Reinette offers him only a new view of himself. Through her gaze, he encounters only himself, or rather, who she perceives him to be. Through her gaze, the Doctor sees himself as a hero, the "nightmare" monsters dream of, her companion and consort.

Reinette's gaze is not only reserved for the Doctor. During her encounter with Rose, Reinette's gaze reveals two key components that would make her a terrific companion. Much to Rose's dismay, she is both open-minded and understanding, possibly even more so than Rose herself. Her conversation with Reinette begins with Reinette standing by a clock on a mantle and Rose sitting on an ottoman. Reinette, who has control over the conversation, shows dominance by standing, her eyes never moving off of Rose, but she also shows the temperance for which Madame de Pompadour was adored.[19] Rose's gaze, however, wavers as she tells Reinette that she was not supposed to have any of this, neither the Doctor nor the clockworks, and that the droids were messing with history. Reinette snaps politely, putting Rose in her place by saying: "Supposed to happen—what does that mean? It happened, child. And I wouldn't have it any other way. One may tolerate a world of demons for the sake of an angel." During the conversation, Rose's gaze continually darts between Reinette and the entrance to the spaceship. Against Rose's protests, Reinette crosses times and enters the spaceship where she hears the screams of her future. Before she heads back to her own time to "take the slower path," she tells Rose "you and I both know, don't we, Rose? The Doctor is worth the monsters." She gives Rose a knowing smile before going back through the portal, and Rose stands for a moment, her gaze on Madame de Pompadour, the candlelight from Versailles highlighting the contemplating look on her face, before turning and running into the darkness to help the Doctor.

This scene reveals Reinette's gaze to be superior to Rose's. Reinette has the advantage of being older, more mature, and more confident than Rose, and for Reinette at least, she has known the Doctor longer than Rose. To Reinette, Rose is not competition any more than the King of France is competition to the Doctor (although the Doctor has his moment of jealousy in the next scene). Instead, Rose's gaze gives Reinette another view of the Doctor, a view that she missed by the Doctor stepping through her life like the pages of a book. For Rose, however, Reinette offers the Doctor something she is not capable of: Reinette is independent of the Doctor and sees the Doctor as her friend and equal.

Reinette's final gaze at the Doctor lasts well after the Doctor has disappeared from view. She watches him as he passes through the fireplace and gazes at him through the flames. The Doctor turns away, breaking his gaze from her only for a moment in his time. However, as she must stay on the slower path, her return gaze can only be in her memory as her life fades. Despite never getting to join him, her gaze remains on the stars, waiting for the Doctor to return to her. But the Doctor is once again too late, and his final look can only be at her handwriting in her final letter to him. Tears in his eyes, he turns off the fireplace, his gaze frozen on *her* fireplace for a moment before his gaze focuses on the emptiness around him.

The first time the Doctor "sees" Astrid, he barely notices her as he scans the room in an attempt to figure out where he has landed the TARDIS. Likewise, Astrid barely notices him as she scans the room at the same time, looking for an empty glass to fill. For both Astrid and the Doctor, everyone and everything in the room is nothing more than one of Sartre's objects. The Doctor first takes a long look at Astrid when a first class passenger bumps into her, causing her to drop glasses. He stands by watching as Rickston Slade yells at Astrid, treating her as if she were nothing more than a mere object. Astrid barely looks at Rickston except for a brief moment when she apologizes. Her gaze darts to anything other than him. Her gaze continues to dart around as the Doctor interacts with her as he helps her to pick up the broken glass. Her gaze finally locks on the Doctor when he tells her "Merry Christmas." With a smile, she looks upon him and begins to see him for the first time.

After a brief interaction, both characters look out the window of the ship, and their gaze falls upon Earth. As Astrid gazes longingly at Earth, the Doctor looks at her and tells her what she has always dreamed of: "You dreamt of an open sky. New sun, new air, new life. A whole universe teeming with life. Why stand still when there's all that life out there?"[20] The Doctor continues to look at her as her gaze is fixed on the view outside the window, her eyes transfixed on everything that could possibly be out there. In this moment, the Doctor sees the possibility of re-seeing the universe again through Astrid's experience; Astrid, on the other hand, has more to gain. For Astrid, the possibility of all her dreams coming true stands before her. But Astrid, as we find out, will also have more to lose.

Astrid's gaze upon the Doctor soon changes. When she asks to go with the Doctor, she offers to take care of him when things get dangerous. Her gaze now is on the Doctor and the adventures ahead of them. For Astrid, the Doctor is not the savior he will turn out to be for the survivors, but rather a possible companion for her. She offers to be a stowaway on the TARDIS, much like the Doctor, who is a stowaway on the Titanic. This statement reverses the roles: Astrid wants to be to the Doctor what the Doctor has been to the Titanic. She proves this when she goes to Deck 31 to find the Doctor.

Astrid and the Doctor share a final look before Astrid lifts Max Capricorn into the air and drives over the edge. Tears welling up in her eyes, she locks eyes with the Doctor as the overt, non-diegetic music fades into soft vocals. The Doctor calls her name, but it is almost inaudible as Astrid presses down on the gas pedal and, wincing, pushes forward, plunging into the whirling inferno below. The Doctor can only watch, his stare full of anguish; anguish at the loss and at his inability to save her. The scene cuts, and non-diegetic music overwhelms the diegetic sounds that would be made by Slade and Mr. Copper's shouts and then cuts again to Alonso's silent scream. When it cuts back again to the Doctor, he is walking away from the explosion, his eyes hard and determined, the eyes of a man who has seen too much loss and refuses to endure any more. This is not the same Doctor who began the episode. This Doctor has changed into a desperate man who has nothing to lose and who will do whatever it takes to set things right, even if it means violating the very laws of time and space. Mr. Copper, at the end of this episode tells the Doctor that he cannot choose who lives and who dies. "If you could, you would be a monster."[21] The tenth Doctor will very soon decide who will live and who will die, and once he crosses that line, he will not be able to turn back.[22]

We Kant Be Together After All

Despite what they can offer as companions, neither Reinette nor Astrid actually step foot on the TARDIS, but they leave a lasting impression on the Doctor that is felt repeatedly for years. At the start of the revival series, the ninth Doctor arrives shortly after making possibly the most difficult decision of his life, and we only learn about the Time War through snippets.[23] What we do know is that he had to choose between killing off his own people or allowing the Daleks to destroy all of creation. He sacrificed his people in order to save the universe. Since this event, the ninth, tenth, eleventh, and twelfth Doctors repeatedly face conflicts which each must endure both physically and morally.

Donna Smith suggests that the Doctor's actions are a combination of his knowledge of history and his experiences during the Last Great Time War, as well as the lessons his companions have taught him. When Smith applied Immanuel Kant's theories to the relationships the tenth Doctor had with his companions, she discovered that "…while their love helps to inform the Doctor's and Rose's individual sense of moral responsibility, it's their love that ironically causes their eventual separation. The Doctor and Rose ultimately act out of their own sense of justice and not specifically out of their feelings for each other."[24] This is similarly true for both Reinette and Astrid.

Kant states: "Act always in accordance with that maxim whose universality as law you can at the same time will."[25] Kant's moral theory implies that morality is not an inherent part of one's personality, and good cannot be done by inclination alone. Instead, moral worth is only achieved when a person does "good" because it is his or her duty to do so despite his or her personal interests. Rose repeatedly sacrifices herself for the Doctor, as in "The Parting of Ways" (1.13). After the Doctor sends her home in the TARDIS, she looks into the heart of the TARDIS in order to go back and help the Doctor. She never considers what might happen to her, but instead she acts without concern for her personal wellbeing.

Martha also makes the ultimate sacrifice when she leaves the Doctor, Jack, and her family in the hands of the Master in order to travel the world to tell people about the Doctor. Ultimately, her sacrifice enables her to save her family as well as the Doctor; however, when she acts, she has no idea what the outcome will be. She only knows that she will go to the ends of the earth to save the Doctor.[26]

Reinette also sacrifices for the Doctor. When the Doctor jumps through the mirror on horseback, he breaks the connection to the ship, stranding himself in the 18th century. Reinette could have him at her side for the rest of her life, but her love for her "lonely angel" trumps her desire to be with him. She leads him to the fireplace retained from her childhood bedroom, which is still intact. The Doctor fixes the connection and disappears from her life. She never considers another path, and it never occurs to her to keep him in her world. Without any consideration, she acts, contrary to her own desires, because she knows it is the right course of action. "From her actions, the Doctor learns about love and personal sacrifice. Madame de Pompadour teaches him how to love selflessly and to be a better person because of this love."²⁷ The Doctor will use this lesson in "Journey's End" when he tells Rose that she made him a better man.

Astrid also sacrifices herself for the Doctor. She arrives in the Doctor's life after he has lost Reinette, Rose, and Martha. He has hardened, once again alone. Despite his losses, he is willing once again to open his heart to Astrid, allowing her into his life and inviting her into the TARDIS. After only one small sojourn to Earth, Astrid sacrifices herself to save the Doctor. In this act, she truly becomes his caretaker, just as she suggested she could be when she asked to join him.²⁸

Astrid's death deals a devastating blow to the Doctor. At the end of the episode, the Doctor is not the same, and Astrid lingers in his mind. Astrid returns as a vision in "Journey's End" (4.13) when Davros asks "how many more have died in your name?" Both Reinette and Astrid are referenced in "Journey's End," and this will not be the last time the Doctor remembers his would-be companions. Madame de Pompadour is referred to as recently as in "Deep Breath" (8.1). When her sister ship, the SS Marie Antoinette, brings the return of the clockworks, the twelfth Doctor remarks that they are "out of control repair droids cannibalizing human beings. I know that this is familiar, but I just can't seem to place it." This rather vague reference shows that Reinette has not been completely forgotten through the two regenerations and proves that she did impact the Doctor in subtle ways.

The Doctor continually surrounds himself with companions who are willing to make sacrifices for him and what he stands for without him ever asking—or perhaps he only chooses those he foresees will have the best possibility of making those sacrifices. The companions take on the Doctor's moral code without thought and without discussion, but most often, the companions share the Doctor's morality as an inherent part of who they are both before they met the Doctor and because of him. It is no wonder that the Doctor leaves a lasting impression on the lives of those he chooses to be around, and his companions always affect the Doctor as well.

Lasting Impressions

Reinette was most recently referenced by the twelfth Doctor in "Deep Breath." When the Doctor and Clara encounter the SS Marie Antoinette, the sister ship of the SS Madame de Pompadour, and the Clockwork Repair Droids, the Doctor insists that he has met them before, but his memory fails him. Perhaps the memory of Madame de Pompadour is too painful for him to recall. Whatever the reason for his memory lapse, this episode is full of references to "The Girl in the Fireplace."

In the David Tennant years, Reinette's influence on the Doctor created the opportunity for the Doctor to fall in love with Rose, an event that would not have been possible if Reinette had not first taught the Doctor how to love selflessly and without hesitation. Without Reinette, the Doctor would have merely loved Rose from afar, but he would never have been capable of letting her into his hearts. That love would have been self-serving and co-dependent and neither character would have been able to make the sacrifices necessary to save the world or each other.

Astrid served as a bridge between Martha and Donna Noble. With Martha, the Doctor was distant. He was still pining after Rose when he met Martha, and he was not capable of another co-dependent relationship. He had to keep Martha at arm's length simply because she loved him. Astrid, however, offered something different. One moment, she is getting engaged to Bannakaffalatta, and the next she is kissing the Doctor. Astrid lives in the moment and never expects anything beyond it. For the Doctor, she offers love at a distance. She can be a companion and possibly be close to him without strings attached. For Astrid, one trip with the Doctor is just as grand as 50, and that is exactly what the Doctor needs at the moment: a rebound companion.

Rose offered the Doctor true love; Reinette revealed a deeper love for the Doctor to experience; Martha loved unconditionally; and Astrid's love was safe from emotional pain, or so the Doctor thought. This progression led the way for Donna to return. Donna offered the Doctor a companion who did not love him, which is quite a change from the previous companions.

But Donna offered more than that. While the others drew motivation from experiencing the Doctor's world for the first time, Donna became a companion with the knowledge of the possibilities that travelling with the Doctor offered. Because she had encountered him before, she knew to expect the unexpected. Instead of the companion experiencing a sense of wonder and astonishment, "Donna's deepest motivation is to be able to believe that others might feel wonder in their encounters with *her*."[29] However, Donna could have easily been cast off as a companion; if she were the perfect companion to begin with, why didn't the Doctor take her with him after their first encounter? Neither the Doctor nor Donna was ready for the kind of relationship that would develop between them. The Doctor needed time to mourn the loss of Rose, and Donna needed to recover from the loss of her fiancé, who died on their wedding day. Donna refused the Doctor's offer to take her along because she knew the Doctor was not ready for her, that he needed time.[30] He needed Martha and Astrid to pave the way for Donna Noble.

The Doctor may be the central character of the story, but it is often the companions who steal the show. Sometimes we love the companions, and sometimes we love to hate them. And sometimes, if we are very lucky, we meet a would-be companion who is so special that even the briefest encounter can create change. Every companion the Doctor chooses impacts him in some way, and the Doctor often needs his companions as much as they need him. Sometimes, the Doctor's choice of companion is so perfectly timed that it only takes a moment for them to change his life. Both Reinette and Astrid are this type of companion. They are the type of companion who comes into the Doctor's life right when he needs them most, and they help him just as much, if not more, than he helps them. And in the process, they reveal to him a truth about himself and about a new way to live. These companions never have the honor of stepping into the TARDIS because the honor is not in being invited; for these companions, it is the Doctor's honor for having met them in the first place.

Notes

1. "The Girl in the Fireplace."
2. Lewis and Smithka, "We've Been Abducted By the Doctor, and We Love it!," 35.
3. Dorothy Gale "Ace" McShane was the companion of the seventh Doctor.
4. "The Parting of the Ways."
5. Akers, "Empathy, Ethics, and Wonder," 177.
6. *Ibid.*, 178.
7. "The Girl in the Fireplace."
8. "Blink."
9. "Voyage of the Damned."
10. Wilkes, "I'm 903 Years Old."
11. Sartre, *Being and Nothingness*, 269.
12. *Ibid.*, 222.
13. "Journey's End."
14. "The Girl in the Fireplace."
15. This is a look that the Doctor will later receive from Amy Pond when he meets her as an adult.
16. Again, just like Amy Pond will do with the eleventh Doctor.
17. Amy Pond will also kiss the Doctor in a similar way.
18. Another similarity between Reinette and Amy Pond.
19. Madame de Pompadour's popularity was also due in part to her being born in a lower, poorer class, which helped her to relate to the King's subjects.
20. "Voyage of the Damned."
21. *Ibid.*
22. In "The Waters of Mars," the Doctor will save Adelaide Brooke, altering a fixed point in time.
23. This changes in the 50th Anniversary episode when viewers are introduced to the War Doctor and are shown what he does to end the Time War.
24. Smith, "Why the Doctor and Rose," 196.
25. Kant, *Groundwork for the Metaphysics of Morals*, 55.
26. "The Last of the Time Lords."
27. Smith, "Why the Doctor and Rose," 195
28. "Voyage of the Damned."
29. Akers, "Empathy, Ethics, and Wonder," 128.
30. "The Runaway Bride."

When No One Can Hear You Scream
Doctor Who Companions on the Printed Page

Aaron John Gulyas

Viewers of *Doctor Who*, whether they watch the show with the passion of a fan or merely as an innocent bystander, often believe they have a good handle on the "companion" character. She (and it is often a "she," at least in the conventional wisdom) exists to ask the Doctor what's going on, to get captured, to escape capture, and—particularly in the classic, cliffhanger-dependent iteration of the show—scream every 25 minutes or so to keep viewers on the edges of their seats for seven days. This is, of course, a broad stereotype of the program, what Lance Parkin has referred to a "consensus" *Doctor Who*.[1] Larger ensemble casts were the norm in the show's early years until the arrival of Liz Shaw in 1970.[2] With few exceptions, *Doctor Who* would maintain the convention of the Doctor being accompanied by a single female companion until the dawn of the 1980s.

The role of the companion characters within the televisual world of *Doctor Who* often moves beyond these boundaries. The role has, additionally, changed over the years. This is, of course, unsurprising given the 50–plus year history of the show. There are, however, bits of consistency over this time. One of the common threads that runs through the decades is the companion characters' particular relationship to the show's viewers. Sometimes this role was unique and unrepeated (and unrepeatable), such as Ian Chesterton and Barbara Wright being created, cast, and directed as main protagonists at the very dawn of the series. More commonly, the companions have functioned as generic viewer identification figures. They exist to ask questions, get captured, and befriend whatever beleaguered populations they may find.

Occasionally, the series producers created a companion that moved the plot forward in more concrete ways. Examples from the series' 1963–1989 run include the first Romana, initially foisted on the Doctor against his will for a specific mission, and Turlough the untrustworthy servant of the Black Guardian or Kameleon who was actually under the control of the Master. During this phase of *Doctor Who*, the depth of the companions' characterization varied wildly with companions such as Sarah Jane Smith being well-defined and revered enough to be resurrected for the first *Doctor Who* spinoff (*K-9 and Company*, which filmed and broadcast only a pilot episode), the 20th anniversary special, "The Five Doctors" (129), as well as being the first original series companion to appear in twenty-first century *Doctor Who* and receiving her own spinoff, *The Sarah Jane Adventures*. Only Jo Grant and Captain Jack Harkness have joined Sarah Jane as companions who have developed lives of their own.[3]

Over the course of the revitalized series, launched in 2005, the companions' roles have often been more complex than in the earlier run. The same basic roles for companions still exist. They ask questions and move the plot forward while serving as an identifiable figure to whom viewers can relate. While it sounds obvious to say, in both the classic series and the 2005 relaunch, the companions' roles have been created and developed within the context of television. Producers developed roles that appealed to specific segments of a broad audience. The performers cast as companions brought their own talents and interpretations to the roles as well. As is often the case, performances matured, improved, or otherwise changed as a result of production demands or on-screen chemistry.

But *Doctor Who*—particularly during its lengthy off-air period of the 1990s—has not always been a strictly televisual phenomenon. Beginning in 1991, original, full-length novels continued the seventh Doctor's and Ace's adventures beyond the end of the show's 26th season. Liberated from the confines of a 25–minute per week serial format, freed from budget constraints and with a mandate to be "too broad and deep for the small screen," these novels transformed the traditional companion role.

This transformation took place within several contexts. One context was the two and a half decades of existing *Doctor Who*. The show had provided both a template for the companion role and also served as an example of something to move beyond in very specific ways. Another context was that of the novel format itself. The ability to provide characters' internal monologues as well as the more basic fact that—ideally—a full-length novel is structured differently than a 100-minute television serial required authors to use the companions differently than they had on television. A final context to consider is the direction in which the television series took the character of Ace during the final season of *Doctor Who*'s original incarnation. Three of the four stories in the twenty-sixth season—"Ghost Light" (153), "The Curse of Fenric" (154), and "Survival" (155)—revolved around Ace's childhood, family, or both. Several writers would continue this trend.

Another aspect of the transformation of the companion role from screen to page arose when publishers and writers undertook to create new companions for the original novels. Beginning with Bernice Summerfield and continuing through Trix MacMillan new, never-to-be-seen-on-television companions appeared, building on, and occasionally subverting, the established paradigm of the character type.

In addition to the continuations of the current Doctor and companion, original novels slotted in between the extant canon of televised stories. One manifestation of the shift in companion characterization was the transformation of already familiar television companions when they appeared in print. Readers may have been familiar with Sarah Jane, Jo Grant, Tegan Jovanka, or Ace (Dorothy Gale McShane) but the novels would often push these characters in new directions. This was even more prevalent for more obscure companion characters. Even the most dedicated *Doctor Who* fans (especially in an age before routine video or DVD releases) would have less knowledge or experience of a character such as Dodo (Dorothea Chaplet), Vicki Pallister, Polly Wright, or Ben Jackson. These characterizations could be much more safely shifted. In both cases, authors (and the editors who guided the publishing lines) sought to balance the need (or perceived need) for a traditional companion role with the desire to expand the scope of characterization to fit long-form prose works. These shifted characterizations sometimes went beyond the bounds of what fans had long accepted as the "place" of the companion. In the cases of companions who had originated on television, there existed the additional burden of remaining faithful to a particular portrayal and performance as well as a familiar characterization.

When discussing *Doctor Who*'s shift to print fiction it is important to define some boundaries. The focus of this study is on the book-length original fiction published by Virgin Books and BBC Books. Specifically, this includes the New Adventures and the Missing Adventures from Virgin (1991–1997) as well as the Eighth Doctor Adventures and Past Doctor Adventures from BBC books (1997–2005). The short stories or comics that appeared in *Doctor Who Magazine* or works that appeared in the various Annual volumes (such as those published by World Distributors) or various fan publications, while certainly part of the broad universe of *Doctor Who*, are beyond the scope of this chapter.

In a world where *Doctor Who* has returned to airing on our television screens to great popular and critical acclaim, it may seem odd to return to these tie-in novels. Such items are often written for (and marketed to) the hardest of hard-core fans. There are good reasons, however, for examining these stories and the changing roles of the companion character they presented.

One compelling reason to examine the novel length adventures of the 1990s and the early 21st century is that the place of the continuation novels (the Virgin New Adventures and BBC Books Eighth Doctor Adventures) is slightly different than that of most licensed media spinoff books. In 2007, New Adventures author (and writer for the revived *Doctor Who*) Paul Cornell discussed the thorny topic of canonicity in *Doctor Who* and directly addressed the position of the New Adventures:

> The closest we ever got to a BBC pronouncement on canonicity was a couple of years after the end of the original series of *Doctor Who*. The show's last production team declared that Virgin's *Doctor Who* novels, the New Adventures, were an official continuation of the series, overseen by the last producer, John Nathan-Turner, with the last writing team onboard, heading towards the aims that that team had put in place.[4]

Andrew Cartmel, the show's script editor from 1987–1989, Marc Platt, the writer of "Ghost Light," and Ben Aaronovich, writer of "Remembrance of the Daleks" (148) and "Battlefield" (152) all contributed to the first ten New Adventures novels. Whether or not fans considered the New Adventures to be the official continuation of the Doctor's adventures beyond the confines of television, it is clear that many of those involved in writing, editing, and approving the novels did.

Apart from this pronouncement of their official status, the New Adventures would exist in an intertwined relationship with the televised series. The final Seventh Doctor New Adventure, Marc Platt's *Lungbarrow*, led directly into the 1996 Fox television movie, and Lance Parkin's *The Dying Days* featured the eighth Doctor, as played by Paul McGann. The 2005 relaunch of the series included a reference to the planet Lucifer in "Bad Wolf," (1.12), the setting of the New Adventure novel *Lucifer Rising* by Jim Mortimore and Andy Lane. "The Pandorica Opens" (5.12) made reference to the Chelonians, a race created by New Adventures author Gareth Roberts in *The Highest Science*. During the third season, Paul Cornell's novel *Human Nature* was adapted into the two-part story comprised of "Human Nature" and "The Family of Blood" (3.08 and 3.09).

The stories produced as part of the New Adventures, Missing Adventures, and their BBC Books successors as well as their authors' characterizations of the companions emerged and existed in a world without new, televised *Doctor Who*. Occasional television specials, such as *Dimensions in Time* (1993), the Fox *Doctor Who* television movie (1996), or *The Curse of Fatal Death* (1999), did appear. Two radio specials aired as well during this period, "Paradise of Death" (1993) and "The Ghosts of N-Space" (1996). It was, however, with good reason that fans referred to 1989 to 1996 as the "Wilderness Years." With no new, regularly produced television series, the line of ongoing novels was—for a time—the closest thing to "official" *Doctor Who*. The New Adventures, as well as later series of novels featuring both current and past Doctors and companions, filled an important gap in the ongoing story of *Doctor Who* at a time when there were few options for fans.

Just as several of *Doctor Who*'s writers from the original series contributed to the New Adventures, several New Adventures authors would contribute to the revitalized series that began in 2005. Chief among these was Executive Producer and head writer Russell T. Davies (*Damaged Goods*). Paul Cornell (*Timewyrm: Revelation, Love and War, No Future, Human Nature,* and *Happy Endings*), Mark Gatiss (*Nightshade* and *St. Anthony's Fire*), Gareth Roberts (*The Highest Science, Tragedy Day,* and *Zamper*), and Matt Jones (*Bad Therapy*) would also write episodes for the new series.

Virgin Books' New Adventures series of novels began in 1991 with the four-book *Timewyrm* arc. These books featured the seventh Doctor and Ace, who had carried the television series through its final two seasons in 1988 and 1989. The seventh Doctor/Ace tandem was particularly suited to the transition from screen to page. The stories of seasons 25 and 26 had been, in general, more complex than those of previous seasons. In particular, the characterization of Ace throughout seasons 25 and 26 of the series had shown an atypical amount of growth and development.

Beginning with Paul Cornell's *Timewyrm: Revelation*, a new generation of fans emerged. Cornell and others such as Marc Platt and Andrew Cartmel took full advantage of the opportunity to stretch both the characters and the format of *Doctor Who*. *Timewyrm: Revelation* breaks new ground in the role a companion could play within the confines of *Doctor Who*. Cornell expands upon Ace's childhood and relationship with her peers and mother—already referenced on screen more than most companions'—and weaves it into the incredibly intricate story. The story takes place within the Doctor's psyche, allowing the companion to get inside the Doctor's head in a manner that, up to this point, had been impossible; impossible because of the series' traditional conception of the companion as an "assistant" to the Doctor rather than a partner.

Paul Cornell was also the first of the New Adventures writers to create and introduce a new, ongoing companion, 26th-century archaeologist Bernice (Benny) Summerfield in *Love and War*. Bernice's introduction followed the culmination of the relationship breakdown between the seventh Doctor and Ace. The Doctor's manipulation of the situation and people around him, culminating in the death of the man with whom Ace had fallen in love, results in Ace leaving the Doctor. Bernice's entry into the ranks of companions begins with her warning the Doctor against manipulating her as he had Ace. Bernice, thus, demonstrates an awareness of the Doctor and his actions both within the context of the story as well as within the larger context of illustrating that the changes in the relationship between the Doctor and his companions have continued to evolve beyond the end of the televised series. Paul Cornell, in a 1992 interview with New Zealand fanzine *Time Space Visualizer*, said "Bernice Summerfield, the Doctor's new companion, is someone he can feel comfortable with because she's not part of his plans, she's a sort of healing thing for him because they can just be friends. He doesn't have to include her in any grand schemes."[5]

Bernice, as a professional woman in her thirties, was a different sort of companion: not girlish, not needing the Doctor to act as a paternal figure. She was also remarkably free from the teenage angst that had become a hallmark of the novels' treatment of Ace. According to the June 1995 version of the New/Missing Adventures Writers' Guide from Virgin, "Bernice is travelling with the Doctor because she likes travelling. And because, at times, she thinks the Doctor needs her. He's so indecisive sometimes, and rather sad—let's face it, he needs looking after." This is a shift from the more familiar ideal of the Doctor being a guide and protector as established in the television series. As the Doctor's character changes, so must the companions'. The Writers' Guide describes the new character as being "like a female Indiana Jones with a Home Counties accent. But she's no superhero; in fact, she's one of the most human souls ever to walk the TARDIS corridors. She doesn't suffer fools gladly, and her quick wit can get her into trouble. She's a cynic, but only because she has ideals that the universe can't live up to."[6] But, at the same time, "inside, Benny sometimes thinks of herself as a fake, keeping up appearances and not quite, well, whole. Maybe one day the military will catch up with her, or some leading academic will question the fact that her school records were lost in the war." While it may seem too obvious to state, one of the key differences in developing a *Doctor Who* companion for the printed page as opposed to a television series is that writers have the opportunity to explore the inner monologue of these characters. The writers are able to provide insight into companions' motivations in ways that were not possible in the television program. Bernice, being a new character, created for the books, is the first ongoing companion who authors were able to develop in this manner.

If most companions in the televised series were designed to be audience identification figures, then Bernice was also a writer's identification figure. As many of the writers of the New Adventures were fans coming up through the "New Fandom" of 1980s Britain, which was increasingly focused on writing, creation, and analysis than the "fact collecting" of previous decades, the fan and writer demographics overlapped to a much greater degree than within the universe of writers who worked on the classic television series. Cornell, in 1996, expressed surprise that other New Adventures authors had written Bernice well, and claimed that Bernice was "part of me, a voice that I use very often, and that people are starting to spot in everything I write. I didn't expect her to get a mind of her own."[7]

When Ace returned in Peter Darvill-Evans's *Deceit*, she was in many ways a different character than the one who had left the Doctor and certainly different from the character who had appeared in the television series. Due to the vagaries of time travel, Ace was several years older than when she had left the Doctor and in her journey through space had served as a soldier in numerous battles against the Daleks. This Ace was more violent and cynical than she had been before her exit in *Love and War*. Upon returning to the TARDIS, Ace explains her desire to rejoin the Doctor in very practical terms, "The war's over.... The Corporations haven't got the cash to hire night-club bouncers. They certainly can't afford me.... The TARDIS looks like the best bet."[8] Throughout the remaining New Adventures that featured Ace there would be a recurring theme of her character being fairly far removed from the recognizable teenage girl of the television series and first nine New Adventures.

The TARDIS crew of Ace, Bernice, and the seventh Doctor is a tense one, with a great deal of conflict. The nature of prose allows for greater flexibility in how to portray and illustrate this conflict. The televised series had attempted, in the 1980s, to present a spikier, more conflict-ridden relationship. During the Peter Davison years, first with Adric and again with Vislor Turlough, there was an atmosphere of irritation or distrust. The creative staff raised the stakes with Colin Baker's sixth Doctor, creating a situation in which the tension was between the Doctor and his companion. The nature of television and especially the weekly, serial nature of *Doctor Who* at the time meant that these conflicts were very much out in the open, dominating entire scenes with bickering often overshadowing other aspects of the plot and characterization.

Within the confines of a novel however, internal dialogue could convey much more multi-dimensional conflict than dialogue or acting could. This conflict could also be portrayed in a much more subtle manner. The nature of prose over televised drama allows for a much more nuanced approach to characterization and conflict within the relationships between characters. In *Deceit*, upon Ace's return to the TARDIS, Bernice contemplates Ace's motivations, thinking "I could leave now and let these two fight it out. If I could be sure that the Doctor would win. Ace must have some ulterior motive for wanting to come back."[9] The tension between Ace, Bernice and—often—the Doctor would continue throughout the remaining New Adventures with that version of the TARDIS crew.

Later companions Chris Cwej and Roz Forrester expand the TARDIS crew as well as the types of companions that could be part of *Doctor Who*. As police officers, they bring an authoritarian edge to the cast of characters that did not previously exist. As a result, authors could create a wider variety of dramatic scenarios for the Doctor's companions. Chris and Roz, were very specifically defined by their occupations: "We want them to function like TV cops, with a Hill Street Blues–type rapport—maybe even the odd 'nice & nasty' routine. Their Academy training will prove difficult to shake off; they have a police mentality, and will tend to see everything in terms of the law, infringements of rules, criminals, witnesses and so on."[10]

This was entirely in keeping with the ongoing development of the seventh Doctor's "manipulative" characteristics. Roz, Chris, and Bernice could carry out a broad array of assignments for the Doctor, who would control things behind the scenes. Lance Parkin's World War II-based novel *Just War* operates within this paradigm of the companions carrying out specific, specialized, and crucial missions at the Doctor's direction. The "missions" in *Just War* are harrowing and critical, placing the Doctor's companions in considerably more visceral danger than the television show could convey. Bernice, for example, working undercover in Nazi-occupied Guernsey, is captured by the Nazis and brutally interrogated in a manner that would not be considered appropriate for the televisions series. Roz is stationed in London with British Intelligence, dodging German bombs, while Chris is behind enemy lines in the French countryside. This "team" approach surfaced several times during the Russell T. Davies era of the revived *Doctor Who*. "Boom Town" (1.11) and, particularly "The Stolen Earth" / "Journey's End" (4.12 & 4.13) all show the Doctor and his companions functioning as an organized unit utilizing their specific skill sets.

Steve Lyons' 1995 New Adventures novel *Head Games* represents a turning point—not necessarily in how the companion characters are used in the New Adventures but, rather, in the open and slightly metatextual manner in which it addresses the use of these characters and compares it to the original series. A key theme in *Head Games* is the Doctor using his companions (Benny, Chris, Roz, and a briefly returning Ace) as pawns and soldiers in wars and battles that none of them comprehend. Despite moments of doubt and reluctance, they carry out his instructions. They trust that the Doctor is undertaking his plans for morally justified reasons, even if the means are sometimes questionable and even violent.

Near the conclusion of the story, Mel Bush confronts Ace. Ace has, by this point in the New Adventures, left Bernice and the Doctor for good, barring occasional guest appearances. She travels through the cosmos as "Time's Vigilante," righting temporal wrongs with a vengeance that the Doctor cannot match. Mel's one encounter with Ace was when Mel left and Ace first joined the Doctor on his journeys. Shocked and dismayed by the transformation in Ace, Mel tells her, "I don't know you. I knew a nice little girl called Dorothy." To which Ace replies that she "was never a 'nice little girl'!" Mel continues her assessment of Ace, declaring "Now what have you turned into? A hardened space bitch!"[11]

This exchange between Mel and Ace mirrors notions some critics held about the New Adventures novels existing on a different moral plane than the original series; seeing those novels as less moral, altruistic approach to the *Doctor Who* mythos, not at all in keeping with the television show they loved. *Transit*, for example, famously featured profanity and sexual references far beyond any *Doctor Who* fiction before or since. One letter writer to *Doctor Who Magazine* considered it "a cheapening and lessening of all that makes *Doctor Who* unique" and found that the use of "four-lettered words" including "the F-word" had "dirtied the name of *Doctor Who*." While *Transit*, perhaps, saw the greatest volume of complaints about the un–*Doctor Who*–like content of the New Adventures, it was not the only novel subject to scrutiny from fans concerned with "real" *Doctor Who*.[12] Lyons is using these diametrically opposed companion characters not only to illustrate the differences between the old series and the new adventures but also to illustrate to fans that the original series wasn't necessarily what they remembered it being. The "Mature Ace" of the New Adventures is, to a significant degree, television Ace with the volume turned up. She had been, in many ways, the Doctor's soldier since season 25 of the original series. Mel, however, was a companion about as reviled by organized fandom as ever existed. One fan opined that the "concept" of Mel was "a washout and un-believable."[13] Another, before the character had even appeared on screen, that the character (and particularly Bonnie Langford's casting) would "drive the final nail in the coffin and seal the fate of the good Doctor's future forever."[14] Gary Levy, editor of *DWB*, a *Doctor Who* fanzine, proclaimed it to be an example of producer John Nathan-Turner "tailor[ing]" the show "around his own theatrical image of a pantomime come [*sic*] circus!"[15] Lyons was able to effectively highlight the differences between the classic television series and the New Adventures in a way that privileges the changes made by the novels toward a more complex and, frankly, violent direction.

Much like earlier iterations of the television show, the move to a four-person was, in some ways, a call-back to the original four-person crew during the show's first and second seasons or the similar situation during season 19. The Virgin Books Writers' Guide explicitly asserts this: "We're hoping to recreate the balance in the TARDIS that was achieved with Susan, Ian and Barbara: Bernice will be closer to the Doctor, while Cwej and Forrester will work with each other." One parallel between the structure of the earliest 1960s *Doctor Who* and the New Adventures is that the longer duration of the 1960s serials (with the majority of the serials during the Hartnell and Troughton eras comprised of at least six 25-minute episodes) as well as the novels of the 1990s provided more space to use a larger regular cast. This additional breathing room allows writers the opportunity to stretch the characterizations and the relationships the companions had with the Doctor, with each other, and with other supporting characters in a way that shorter stories made difficult.

By changing the nature and role of the companion characters—both through their relationship to the narrative and their relationship to the Doctor—the New Adventures provided a template for changing several aspects of televised *Doctor Who*. Just as the use of the companions—or the structure of the cast of characters—sometimes hearkened back to the original series, the revitalized series that began in 2005 sometimes hearkened back to the New Adventures. The concept of well-rounded supporting characters such as Rose Tyler, Martha Jones, or Captain Jack Harkness is mostly the result of modern television viewers' sensibilities likely not tolerating the one- to two-dimensional companions of years past. Yet it is not difficult to see the influence of the New Adventures on some aspect of the companion/Doctor relationships in the new series. Other familiar tropes from the twenty-first century incarnation of *Doctor Who* include the companion figure that appears only once, rather than as an ongoing character, such as Lady Christina de Souza from "Planet of the Dead" (4.15) or Adelaide Brooke from "The Waters of Mars" (4.16). The New Adventures pioneered this through the use of characters like Ruby Duvall, who served in the companion role in *Iceberg*. Ace, after leaving the Doctor's company for the final time in *Set Piece*, returns occasionally as an associate of the Doctor. The ninth Doctor's literary companion Anji Kapoor, also, abandons constant travel in the TARDIS while maintaining contact with the Doctor and his companions. Much like Martha Jones or Captain Jack Harkness, these companions develop a life outside of the Doctor. Apart from the recurring presence of UNIT personnel during the early 1970s, this "occasional companion" status was a novelty when the New Adventures attempted it.

These character developments among the companions, including Ace's maturation into a character distinct from that which had been shown on television, and the expansion of the TARDIS crew to a size and complexity which would have been dramatically unwieldy in the series' 25-minute per week serial format, were part of the broad spectrum of changes that fulfilled the New Adventures' back-cover copy promise to present "stories too broad and deep for the small screen." One interpretation of "too broad and deep" is that it refers primarily to the subject matter of the stories—space operas and bizarre alien creations which could never be presented on a BBC television budget. Another could refer to a journey inside the Doctor's very mind in which Ace would meet and interact with his previous incarnations. However, an important aspect of the breadth and depth of the New Adventures lay in using the characters of the Doctor's companions in ways that the televised series could not. The continued development of the seventh Doctor as a cosmic-level conductor of events allowed the development of the companion figures as the players who followed the conductor's lead and suffered through the psychological and physical effects of doing so.

In 1997, after the BBC failed to renew Virgin's license to publish original *Doctor Who* fiction, BBC Books launched their own line of continuing *Doctor Who* adventures featuring the eighth Doctor, as played by Paul McGann in the 1996 Fox *Doctor Who* television movie. BBC Books was unable to use Doctor Grace Holloway—the companion figure in the movie—in the books so a new companion, Samantha "Sam" Jones filled that role.

Sam Jones was, in many ways, a throwback to the manner in which companions had been presented in the original series. She was introduced with a remarkable amount of superficial back story (she hates drugs, she's socially-conscious and ecology-minded) but beyond that, she served the typical *Doctor Who* companion role of asking the Doctor questions, getting captured, and making contact with friendly aliens. Sam's character would change however over the course of the eighth Doctor novels, not the least of which was the creation of an alternate universe version of Sam known as "Dark Sam." The "Dark Sam" character, introduced by Jonathan Blum and Kate Orman in *Unnatural History*, can be read as an attempt to make the quite bland Sam something more interesting. Like many characters in the Virgin New Adventures, Sam's alternative self is suffused with sex, IV drug use, and angst. She is everything the wholesome Sam Jones is not.

Fitz Kreiner, introduced in Michael Collier's *The Taint*, hailed from 1963, serving as the first "historical" companion to debut since the 1960s. Like Sam, Fitz seemed to be a "high concept" companion; a character that writers and editors could summarize in a sentence or two. If Sam was a modern, socially-conscious young woman, Fitz was a moody, early 1960s man who longed to be significant, leading to him ending up on the wrong side of the Doctor several times. In *Revolution Man*, he leaves the Doctor's company for two years, becoming an agent of the Communist Chinese, following brainwashing. In the *Interference* novels, written by Lawrence Miles, he becomes an agent of the evil Paradox organization. Fitz will remain with the eighth Doctor through the end of the novel series in 2005, taking numerous roles, chameleon-like, to fulfill the needs of various stories.

Anji Kapoor, introduced in Colin Brake's *Escape Velocity*, was a return to a more traditional modern day, British companion. Much was made, when the character and her South Asian heritage was announced, of the book series attempting to be more relevant to the changing demographics of the UK. Series editor Justin Richards described Anji as "someone very professional, very good at the job she does ... something [financial] in the City and absolutely the tops at what she does."[16] Anji was an example of a return to the companion character serving as an audience identification figure; a contemporary, middle-class, Briton. One of the most striking attempts to make Anji more than a cardboard-cutout, "contemporary-Earth" companion comes in Lance Parkin's *Trading Futures*. Anji, as a financial analyst, takes a keen interest in the economy of the near-future setting of the novel, to the point of considering meddling in established history through a few well-placed investments in her own time.

The companion characters introduced in the BBC Eighth Doctor Adventures all conform to a fairly strict set of character guidelines. The characters all have personalities and traits that are easily summarized and rarely stray beyond that. This was especially true during the early days of the Eighth Doctor Adventures as Samantha Jones served in a traditional companion role.

The New Adventures and the Eighth Doctor Adventures, as a semi-official continuation of *Doctor Who*, represent only one strand of development of the companion characters in print. The other strand was the addition of stories about past Doctors and TARDIS crews, the series of Missing Adventures (from Virgin Books), and Past Doctor Adventures (BBC Books). These series feature the first six (or in the BBC Books series, seven) Doctors and their companions. Virgin did not launch the Missing Adventures until 1994, three years after the New Adventures. Virgin (and later, BBC Books) intended each of the Missing Adventures or Past Doctor Adventures to slot seamlessly between extant television serials.

Virgin's goal for the New Adventures included pushing the boundaries of what *Doctor Who* and, thus, the companions could be. The Missing Adventures—for the most part—had the goal of remaining true to the characterizations and story styles of the televised series. This was also true of the BBC Past Doctor Adventures. As these novel lines developed, there were several examples of the companions from the television series being subject to character development. In some cases this development was far afield from what the Missing Adventures/Past Doctor Adventures existed to provide.

These novels demonstrate the ways in which these new literary approaches to *Doctor Who* (both the New Adventures/Eighth Doctor Adventures and the Missing Adventures/Past Doctor Adventures) served to expand the *Doctor Who* Universe. From their beginnings, the novels had pushed the boundaries of the types of stories and characters addressed within *Doctor Who*. They also accomplished the very fan-oriented goal of filling in supposed voids in the original series continuity. The Doctor's original companion, his granddaughter Susan Foreman, saw substantial character development, particularly in the BBC Eighth Doctor Adventures and Past Doctor Adventures ranges of novels. In Steve Lyons' *The Witch Hunters*, Susan is embroiled in the Salem witch-hunts as a result of her telepathic skills (briefly mentioned in the television serial "The Sensorites" [6]). John Peel's *Legacy of the Daleks* reunited the eighth Doctor with Susan in the aftermath of "The Dalek Invasion of

Earth" (10). Both of these novels highlighted Susan's alien and Gallifreyan heritage in a manner distinct from what the television series had done.

Perhaps no companion character from the original series underwent more alteration, abuse, or distortion than Dorothea "Dodo" Chaplet. Dodo debuted at the very end of the 1966 story "The Massacre of St. Bartholomew's Eve" (22) with very little back story (she dashed into the TARDIS thinking it was a real police box), and little detail about her was revealed over the course of the five subsequent television serials in which she appeared. She left the Doctor in the middle of "The War Machines" (27) after being hypnotized by the evil computer that was the villain of the serial. Her exit was off-screen, with no actual interaction between her and the Doctor. Despite her being one of the most forgettable companions of the television series, two novels that feature Dodo provide a comprehensive view of the various ways authors changed her character and used it to comment on the series.

The Man in the Velvet Mask by Daniel O'Mahony was a tale of the first Doctor and Dodo's visit to a planet modeled on Revolutionary France. The novel is heavily focused on Dodo, providing the bulk of the characterization she would ever receive. Interviewed in 2004, O'Mahony recalled: "I picked up on her purely because I wanted to do a first Doctor story with one companion and she just happened to be around at the point in the series' history that I wanted to write for … the fact that she was so obscure was quite appealing. I felt like I had more freedom to explore her as a character than someone more visible and popular."[17] Companions such as Dodo (along with Vicki, Ben, and Polly) were a prime target for Missing Adventures and Past Doctor Adventures' authors for this very reason. Critics (and commissioning editors) were likely to be much more forgiving or even enthusiastic for stories which added layers to characters about whom readers knew little, unlike Sarah Jane Smith, Romana, Tegan, or other companions viewed as having at least a degree of "iconic" status. *The Man in the Velvet Mask*, quickly became an object of fascination and—in some cases—revulsion. It represented perhaps the limits of what could be done to a companion in the original fiction series. Over the course of the novel, Dodo loses her virginity to the character Dalville. As a result she is infected with a virus developed by the villain Minski. In effect, this novel has one of the innocent young girls of *Doctor Who's* black and white years pick up an alternate-reality sexually-transmitted disease. Not officially a New Adventure or a Missing Adventure, *Who Killed Kennedy* is an anomaly among Virgin's *Doctor Who* output. Wholly written by David Bishop, the book's "co-author" James Stevens is the book's main character and narrator. An investigative reporter, Stevens' narrative follows the "real" world consequences of the Doctor fictional narrative in the early 1970s. The book is written in an *All the President's Men* style conspiracy investigation, examining the hidden truths of alien invasions and the shadowy role of UNIT.

Who Killed Kennedy, like *The Man in the Velvet Mask*, features Dodo. While *The Man in the Velvet Mask* saw her infected with an otherworldly STD, *Who Killed Kennedy* picks up Dodo's story after her departure from the Doctor in "The War Machines." Amnesiac and disoriented after the events of that story, she ends up in The Glasshouse, a secret military mental hospital administered by the Master. During her time there, she kills a fellow patient who attempts to rape her. She and Stevens fall in love and move in together. She gets pregnant but, as a result of evil and mysterious forces warning Stevens off the trail of his journalistic investigations of UNIT, Dodo is shot to death.

Who Killed Kennedy pushes the boundaries of the original show through its use of the companion characters. The narrative of the show, as a serial television series, was constrained in how much attention it could pay to the aftermath of companions' adventures with the Doctor. This was especially the case as the companions became increasingly designed to serve as question-asking devices and foils for the increasingly central and heroic character of the Doctor. The original novels did not only explore time and space but also the consequences of being a part of that adventure.

The development of the companion characters in the lines of original novels illustrates the degree to which these spin-off media continued the process of developing the overall narrative of *Doctor Who* beyond the confines of the television series which, after all, was no longer being produced at the time, with the exception of the 1996 Fox television movie. If *Doctor Who* is, as John Tulloch and Manuel Alvarado called it, an "unfolding text,"[18] the novels' treatments of television companions and the creation of new companions are certainly worth examining. The development of the companion role in the New Adventures was one factor that informed the development of the characters in the revived series beginning in 2005. Similarly, the Missing Adventures and Past Doctor Adventures, in their handling of previously undeveloped companions, illustrated that *Doctor Who*'s past was not a static document. Rather, like the continuing adventures of the Time Lord and his friends, the past could be the future.

NOTES

1. Parkin, *Time, Unincorporated*, 31.
2. "Spearhead From Space."
3. Sherry Ginn has extensively explored Sarah Jane's life beyond the TARDIS. See the bibliography for the complete reference.
4. Paul Cornell, "Canonicity in Doctor Who."
5. David Bishop, "A Conversation with Paul Cornell."
6. "Writers' Guide: The New Adventures," *Broadsword*, April 12, 2001.
7. Paul Scoones. "Paul Cornell Interview."
8. Darvill-Evans, *Deceit*, 302.
9. *Ibid.*, 302–303.
10. "Writers' Guide: The New Adventures."

11. Lyons, *Head Games*, 210.
12. Walter, "Virgin Territory," 16.
13. Cotton, "Victorian Attitudes," 4.
14. Roberts, "Bonnie Langford Doubts," 5.
15. "Letters," 3.
16. Barnes, "Set the Controls for the Heart of the Sun," 12.
17. "Interview: Daniel O'Mahony."
18. Tulloch and Alvarado, *Doctor Who: The Unfolding Text*.

Selected Filmography

"The Almost People." Season 6, episode 6. Written by Matthew Graham. Directed by Julian Simpson. First broadcast May 28, 2011.
"Amy's Choice." Season 5, episode 7. Written by Simon Nye. Directed by Catherine Morshead. First broadcast May 15, 2010.
"The Angels Take Manhattan." Season 7, episode 5. Written by Steven Moffat. Directed by Nick Hurran. First broadcast September 29, 2012.
"The Ark in Space." Story #76. Written by Robert Holmes. Directed by Rodney Bennett. First broadcast January 23–February 15, 1975.
"The Asylum of the Daleks." Season 7, episode 1. Written by Steven Moffat. Directed by Nick Hurran. First broadcast September 1, 2012.
Back to the Future. Written by Robert Zemeckis and Bob Gale. Directed by Robert Zemeckis. Universal Pictures, 1985.
"Bad Wolf." Season 1, episode 12. Written by Russell T. Davies. Directed by Joe Ahearne. First broadcast June 11, 2005.
"Battlefield." Story #152. Written by Ben Aaronovitch. Directed by Michael Kerrigan. First broadcast September 6–27, 1989.
"The Beast Below." Season 5, episode 2. Written by Steven Moffat. Directed by Andrew Gunn. First broadcast April 10, 2010.
"Beginning the End." DVD special feature. *Doctor Who: The Time Warrior*. London: BBC Home Entertainment, 2008.
"The Bells of Saint John's." Season 7, episode 6. Written by Steven Moffat. Directed by Colm McCarthy. First broadcast March 30, 2013.
"The Big Bang." Season 5, episode 13. Written by Steven Moffat. Directed by Toby Haynes. First broadcast June 26, 2010.
"Blink." Season 3, episode 10. Written by Steven Moffat. Directed by Hettie MacDonald. First broadcast June 9, 2007.
"Boom Town." Season 1, episode 11. Written by Russell T. Davies. Directed by Joe Ahearne. First broadcast June 4, 2005.
"The Brain of Morbius." Story #84. Written by Robin Bland. Directed by Christopher Barry. First broadcast December 3–24, 1975.
Buffy, the Vampire Slayer. Created by Joss Whedon. WB & UPN, 1997–2003.
"The Caretaker." Season 8, episode 6. Written by Gareth Roberts and Steven Moffat. Directed by Paul Murphy. First broadcast September 27, 2014.
"Castrovalva." Story #116. Written by Christopher H. Bidmead. Directed by Fiona Cumming. First broadcast January 4–12 1982.

152   Selected Filmography

"Children of Earth." *Torchwood*. Written by Russell T. Davies. Directed by Euros Lyn. First broadcast July 6–10, 2009.
"The Claws of Axos." Story #57. Written by Bob Baker and Dave Martin. Directed by Michael Ferguson. First broadcast March 13–April 3, 1971.
"Cold Blood." Season 5, episode 9. Written by Chris Chibnall. Directed by Ashley Way. First broadcast May 29, 2010.
"Colony in Space." Story #58. Written by Malcolm Hulke. Directed by Michael Briant. First broadcast April 10–May 15, 1971.
"The Curse of Fenric." Story #154. Written by Nicholas Mallett. Directed by Ian Briggs. First broadcast October 25–November 15, 1989.
"The Curse of the Fatal Death." [Comic Relief]. Written by Steven Moffat. Directed by John Henderson. First broadcast March 12, 1999.
"The Dæmons." Story #59. Written by Guy Leopold. Directed by Christopher Barry. First broadcast May 22–June 19, 1971.
"Dalek." Series 1, episode 6. Written by Robert Shearman. Directed by Joe Ahearne. First broadcast April 30, 2005.
"The Dalek Invasion of Earth." Story #10. Written by Terry Nation. Directed by Richard Martin. First broadcast November 21–December 26, 1964.
"The Daleks' Master Plan." Story #21. Written by Terry Nation and Dennis Spooner. Directed by Douglas Camfield. First broadcast November 13, 1965–January 29, 1966.
"Dark Water." Series 8, episode 11. Written by Steven Moffat. Directed by Rachel Talalay. First broadcast November 1, 2014.
Davison, Peter, and Janet Fielding. [Audio Commentary]. *Doctor Who: Resurrection of the Daleks*. London: BBC Home Entertainment, 2012.
"The Day of the Doctor." Season 7, episode 14. Written by Steven Moffat. Directed by Nick Hurran. First broadcast November 23, 2013.
"Day of the Moon." Season 6, episode 2. Written by Steven Moffat. Directed by Toby Haynes. First broadcast April 30, 2011.
"The Deadly Assassin." Story #88. Written by Robert Holmes. Directed by David Maloney. First broadcast October 30–November 20, 1976.
"Death of the Doctor." *The Sarah Jane Adventures*. Season 4, episode 3. Written by Russell T. Davies. Directed by Ashley Way. First broadcast October 25 & 26, 2010.
"Deep Breath." Season 8, episode 1. Written by Steven Moffat. Directed by Ben Wheatley. First broadcast August 23, 2014.
"Dimensions in Time." [Children in Need]. Written by John-Nathan Turner and David Roden. Directed by Stuart McDonald. First broadcast November 26 & 27, 1993.
"Dinosaurs on a Spaceship." Series 7, episode 2. Written by Chris Chibnall. Directed by Saul Metzstein. First broadcast September 8, 2012.
"The Doctor Dances." Series 1, episode 10. Written by Steven Moffat. Directed by James Hawes. First broadcast May 28, 2005.
Doctor Who. Created by Sydney Newman, C. E. Webber, and Donald Wilson. BBC, 1963–1989; 2005–present.
Doctor Who (telefilm). Written by Matthew Jacobs. Directed by Geoffrey Sax. Universal TV & BBC Worldwide, 1996.
"Doctor Who: Pond Life." Season 7 (webcast). Written by Chris Chibnall. Directed by Saul Metzstein. First broadcast August 27–31, 2012.
"Doctor Who: P.S." Season 7 (webcast). Written by Chris Chibnall. First broadcast October 12, 2012.

Selected Filmography

"Doctor Who Stories: Elisabeth Sladen Part 1." [DVD special feature]. *Doctor Who: Invasion of the Dinosaurs*. London: BBC Home Entertainment, 2012.

"The Doctor's Wife." Season 6, episode 4. Written by Neil Gaiman. Directed by Richard Clark. First broadcast May 14, 2011.

"The Doll of Death." [Audio Story]. Written by Marc Platt. Directed by Lisa Bowerman. Berkshire, UK: Big Finish Productions, 2008.

"Doomsday." Series 2, episode 13. Written by Russell T. Davies. Directed by Graeme Harper. First broadcast July 8, 2006.

"Earthshock." Story #121. Written by Eric Saward. Directed by Peter Grimwade. First broadcast March 8–16, 1982.

"The Eleventh Hour." Season 5, episode 1. Written by Steven Moffat. Directed by Adam Smith. First broadcast April 3, 2010.

"The Empty Child." Series 1, episode 9. Written by Steven Moffat. Directed by James Hawes. First broadcast May 21, 2005.

"End of the World." Series 1, episode 2. Written by Russell T. Davies. Directed by Euros Lyn. First broadcast April 2, 2005.

"The Face of Evil." Story #89. Written by Chris Boucher. Directed by Pennant Roberts. First broadcast January 1–22, 1977.

"Family of Blood." Season 3, episode 9. Written by Paul Cornell. Directed by Charles Palmer. First broadcast June 2, 2007.

"The Five Doctors." Story #129. Written by Terrance Dicks. Directed by Peter Moffatt. First broadcast November 23, 1983.

"Flesh and Stone." Season 5, episode 5. Written by Steven Moffat. Directed by Adam Smith. First broadcast May 1, 2010.

"Forest of the Dead." Season 4, episode 9. Written by Steven Moffat. Directed by Euros Lyn. First broadcast June 7, 2008.

"The Girl in the Fireplace." Season 2, episode 4. Written by Steven Moffat. Directed by Euros Lyn. First broadcast October 20, 2006.

"The Girl Who Waited." Season 6, episode 10. Written by Tom MacRae. Directed by Nick Hurran. First broadcast September 10, 2011.

"Ghost Light." Story #153. Written by Marc Platt. Directed by Alan Wareing. First broadcast October 4–18, 1989.

"Ghosts of N-Space" [Audio Story]. Written by Barry Letts. Directed by Phil Clarke. First broadcast January 20–February 24, 1996.

"Girls! Girls! Girls! The 1970s." [DVD special feature]. *Doctor Who: Revisitations 3*. London: BBC Home Entertainment, 2012.

"Girls! Girls! Girls! The 1980s." [DVD special feature]. *Doctor Who: Paradise Towers*. London: BBC Home Entertainment, 2011.

"A Good Man Goes to War." Season 6, episode 7. Written by Steven Moffat. Directed by Peter Hoar. First broadcast June 4, 2011.

"The Green Death." Story #69. Written by Robert Sloman. Directed by Michael Briant. First broadcast May 19—June 23, 1973.

"Human Nature." Season 3, episode 8. Written by Paul Cornell. Directed by Charles Palmer. First broadcast May 26, 2007.

"The Hungry Earth." Season 5, episode 8. Written by Chris Chibnall. Directed by Ashley Way. First broadcast May 22, 2010.

"The Impossible Astronaut." Season 6, episode 1. Written by Steven Moffat. Directed by Toby Haynes. First broadcast April 23, 2011.

"Into the Dalek." Season 8, episode 2. Written by Phil Ford and Steven Moffat. Directed by Ben Wheatley. First broadcast August 30, 2014.

154   Selected Filmography

"Journey's End." Season 4, episode 13. Written by Russell T. Davies. Directed by Graeme Harper. First broadcast July 5, 2008.

"The Keeper of Traken." Story #114. Written by Johnny Byrne. Directed by John Black. First broadcast January 31–February 21, 1981.

"K-9 and Company: A Girl's Best Friend." Written by Terence Dudley. Directed by John Black. First broadcast December 28, 1981.

"The Last of the Time Lords." Season 3, episode 13. Written by Russell T. Davies. Directed by Colin Teague. First broadcast June 30, 2007.

"Let's Kill Hitler." Season 6, episode 8. Written by Steven Moffat. Directed by Richard Senior. First broadcast August 7, 2011.

"Logopolis." Story #115. Written by Christopher H. Bidmead. Directed by Peter Grimwade. First broadcast February 28–March 21, 1981.

"The Massacre of St. Bartholomew's Eve." Story #22. Written by John Lucarotti and Donald Tosh. Directed by Paddy Russell. First broadcast February 5–26, 1966.

"Midnight." Series 4, episode 10. Written by Russell T. Davies. Directed by Alice Troughton. First broadcast June 14, 2008.

"The Mind of Evil." Story #56. Written by Doug Houghton. Directed by Timothy Combe. First broadcast January 20–March 6, 1971.

"The Monster of Peladon." Story #73. Written by Brian Hayles. Directed by Lennie Mayne. First broadcast March 23–April 27, 1974.

"The Name of the Doctor." Season 7, episode 13. Written by Steven Moffat. Directed by Saul Metzstein. First broadcast May 18, 2013.

"The Pandorica Opens." Season 5, episode 12. Written by Steven Moffat. Directed by Toby Haynes. First broadcast June 19, 2010.

"Paradise of Death" [Audio Drama]. Written by Barry Letts. Directed by Phil Clarke. First broadcast August 27–September 24, 1993.

"Paradise Towers." Story #145. Written by Stephen Wyatt. Directed by Nicholas Mallett. First broadcast October 5–26, 1987.

"The Parting of the Ways." Season 1, episode 13. Written by Russell T. Davies. Directed by Joe Ahearne. First broadcast June 18, 2005.

"The Pirate Planet." Story #99. Written by Douglas Adams. Directed by Pennant Roberts. First broadcast September 30–October 21, 1978.

"The Planet of the Dead." [Easter Special]. Written by Russell T. Davies and Gareth Roberts. Directed by James Strong. First broadcast April 11, 2009.

"Pond Life." Season 7, Prequel. Written by Chris Chibnall. Directed by Saul Metzstein. First broadcast August 27–31, 2012.

"Pyramids of Mars." Story #82. Written by Stephen Harris. Directed by Paddy Russell. First broadcast October 25–November 15, 1975.

"Rebel Flesh." Season 6, episode 5. Written by Matthew Graham. Directed by Julian Simpson. First broadcast May 21, 2011.

"Remembrance of the Daleks." Story #148. Written by Ben Aaronovitch. Directed by Andrew Morgan. First broadcast October 5–26, 1988.

"The Rescue." Story #11. Written by David Whitaker. Directed by Christopher Barry. First broadcast January 2–9, 1965.

"Resurrection of the Daleks." Story #133. Written by Eric Saward. Directed by Matthew Robinson. First broadcast February 8–15, 1984.

"Robot of Sherwood." Season 8, episode 3. Written by Mark Gatiss. Directed by Paul Murphy. First broadcast September 6, 2014.

"Rose." Season 1, episode 1. Written by Russell T. Davies. Directed by Keith Boak. First broadcast March 26, 2005.

"The Runaway Bride." Written by Russell T. Davies. Directed by Euros Lyn. First broadcast December 25, 2006.
The Sarah Jane Adventures. Created by Russell T. Davies. CBBC, 2007–2011.
"The Satan Pit." Season 2, episode 9. Written by Matt Jones. Directed by James Strong. First broadcast June 10, 2006.
"School Reunion." Season 2, episode 3. Written by Toby Whithouse. Directed by James Hawes. First broadcast September 29, 2006.
"The Sensorites." Story #7. Written by Peter R. Newman. Directed by Mervyn Pinfield and Frank Cox. First broadcast June 20–August 1, 1964.
"Silence in the Library." Season 4, episode 8. Written by Steven Moffat. Directed by Euros Lyn. First broadcast May 31, 2008.
"Smith and Jones." Series 3, episode 1. Written by Russell T. Davies. Directed by Charles Palmer. First broadcast March 31, 2007.
"The Snowmen." Written by Steven Moffat. Directed by Saul Metzstein. First broadcast December 25, 2012.
"The Sontaran Experiment." Story #77. Written by Bob Baker and David Martin. Directed by Rodney Bennett. First broadcast February 22–March 1, 1975.
"Spearhead from Space." Story #51. Written by Robert Holmes. Directed by Derek Martinus. First broadcast January 3–24, 1970.
Star Trek: First Contact. Written by Brannon Braga and Ronald D. Moore. Directed by Jonathan Frakes. Paramount Pictures, 1996.
"The Stolen Earth." Season 4, episode 12. Written by Russell T. Davies. Directed by Graeme Harper. First broadcast June 28, 2008.
"Survival." Story #155. Written by Rona Munro. Directed by Alan Wareing. First broadcast November 22–December 6, 1989.
"Terror of the Autons." Story #55. Written by Robert Holmes. Directed by Barry Letts. First broadcast January 2–23, 1971.
"Terror of the Vervoids." Story #143c. Written by Pip Baker and Jane Baker. Directed by Chris Clough. First broadcast November 1–22, 1986.
"Time-Flight." Story #122. Written by Peter Grimwade. Directed by Ron Jones. First broadcast March 22–30, 1982.
"The Time of Angels." Season 5, episode 4. Written by Steven Moffat. Directed by Adam Smith. First broadcast April 24, 2010.
"The Time of the Doctor." Written by Steven Moffat. Directed by Jamie Payne. First broadcast December 25, 2013.
"The Time Warrior." Story #70. Written by Robert Holmes. Directed by Alan Bromly. First broadcast December 15, 1973–January 5, 1974.
Torchwood. Created by Russell T. Davies. BBC, 2006–2011.
Torchwood: Children of Earth. Written by Russell T. Davies, John Fay, and James Moran. Directed by Euros Lyn. First broadcast July 6–10, 2009.
"The Trial of a Time Lord" ["Mindwarp"]. Story #145. Written by Philip Martin. Directed by Ron Jones. First broadcast October 4–25, 1986.
"Turn Left." Season 4, episode 11. Written by Russell T. Davies. Directed by Graeme Harper. First broadcast June 21, 2008.
"The Twin Dilemma." Story #136. Written by Anthony Steven. Directed by Peter Moffatt. March 22–30, 1984.
"The Ultimate Companion." [DVD special feature]. *Doctor Who: The Complete Eighth Series*. BBC Home Entertainment, 2014.
"An Unearthly Child." Story #1. Written by Antony Coburn. Directed by Waris Hussein. First broadcast November 23–December 14, 1963.

Selected Filmography

"The Vampires of Venice." Season 5, episode 6. Written by Toby Whithouse. Directed by Jonny Campbell. First broadcast May 8, 2010.

"Vincent and the Doctor." Season 5, episode 10. Written by Richard Curtis. Directed by Jonny Campbell. First broadcast June 5, 2010.

"Voyage of the Damned." Written by Russell T. Davies. Directed by James Strong. First broadcast December 25, 2007.

"The War Machines." Story #27. Written by Ian Stuart Black. Directed by Michael Ferguson. First broadcast June 25–July 16, 1966.

"The Waters of Mars." Written by Russell T. Davies and Phil Ford. Directed by Graeme Harper. First broadcast November 15, 2009.

"The Wedding of River Song." Season 6, episode 13. Written by Steven Moffat. Directed by Jeremy Webb. First broadcast October 1, 2011.

Selected Bibliography

Aaronvich, Ben. *Transit*. London: Virgin Books, 1992.
Akers, Laura Geuy. "Empathy, Ethics, and Wonder." In *Doctor Who and Philosophy*, edited by Courtland Lewis and Paula Smithka, 145–156. Chicago: Open Court: 2011.
Allan, Nina. "Forever Playing Second Fiddle: How Sarah Jane and the Rest of Us are being Sold Short." In *Companion Piece: Women Celebrate the Humans, Aliens and Tin Dogs of* DOCTOR WHO, edited by L. M. Myles and Liz Barr. Des Moines, IA: Mad Norwegian Press, 2015.
Amy-Chinn, Dee. "Rose Tyler: The Ethics of Care and the Limits of Agency." *Science Fiction Film and Television* 1.2 (Autumn 2008): 231–47.
Anders, Charlie Jane. "Doctor Who Really Is a Love Story After All." May 14, 2011. i09.com. n.p.
Balstrup, Sarah. "*Doctor Who*: Christianity, Atheism, and the Source of Sacredness in the Davies Years." *Journal of Religion and Popular Culture* 26.2 (Summer 2014): 145–156.
Banks, David. *Iceberg*. London: Virgin Books, 1993.
Barnes, Alan. "Set the Controls for the Heart of the Sun." *Doctor Who Magazine*, Number 294 (August 23, 2000): 8–13.
Barrow, Becky. "Number of Stay-at-Home Mothers Hits Record Low and Is Falling by 500 a Day, Raising Fears that the Government Is Forcing Families to 'Outsource Childcare.'" *Daily Mail* (online), April 17, 2013.
Baumgardner, Jennifer, and Amy Richards. *Manifesta: Young Women, Feminism, and the Future*. New York: Farrar, Straus and Giroux, 2000.
Bechdel, Alison. *The Essential Dykes to Watch Out For*. Boston: Houghton Mifflin Harcourt, 2008.
Bignell, Jonathan. "The Child as Addressee, Viewer and Consumer in 1960s *Doctor Who*." In *Time and Relative Dissertations in Space: Critical Perspectives on Doctor Who*, edited by David Butler, 43–55. Manchester: Manchester University Press, 2007.
Bishop, David. "A Conversation with Paul Cornell," *The New Zealand Doctor Who Fan Club. TSV 28*, April 1992.
Blum, Jonathan, and Kate Orman. *Unnatural History*. London: BBC Books, 1999.
Booth, Paul, and Jef Burnham. "Who Are We? Re-Envisioning the Doctor in the 21st Century." In *Remake Television: Reboot, Re-use, Recycle*, edited by Carlen Lavigne, 203–220. Lanham, MD: Lexington Books, 2014.
Bouchier, David. *The Feminist Challenge: The Movement for Women's Liberation in Britain and the USA*. London: Macmillan, 1983.

Selected Bibliography

Brake, Colin. *Escape Velocity*. London: BBC Books, 2001.
Braybon, John, and Alice Frick. "BBC Survey Group: 'Report' to Donald Wilson, Head of Serial Dramas." July 25, 1962. BBC Archives.
Breines, Wini. *Young, White, and Miserable: Growing Up Female in the Fifties*. Boston: Beacon Press, 1992.
Britton, Piers D. *TARDISbound: Navigating the Universes of Doctor Who*. London: I. B. Tauris, 2011.
Busch, Jenna. "*Doctor Who*'s Arthur Darvill Talks Repeatedly Dying, More." www.Newsarama.com, September 10, 2011.
Chapman, James. *Inside the TARDIS: The Worlds of Doctor Who*. London: I. B. Tauris, 2013.
Cherry, Brigid. "'You're This Doctor's Companion. What Exactly Do You Do for Him? Why Does He Need You?': *Doctor Who*, Liminality and Martha the Apostle." In *Time and Relative Dimensions in Faith: Religion and Doctor Who*, edited by Andrew Crome and James McGrath, 79–93. London: Darton, Longman and Todd, 2013.
Cixous, Hélène. "The Laugh of the Medusa." Trans. Keith Cohen and Paula Cohen. *Signs* 1.4 (1976): 875–893.
Coile, Charlie. "More than a Companion: 'The Doctor's Wife' and Representations of Women in *Doctor Who*." *Studies in Popular Culture* 36.1 (2013): 83–103.
Collier, Michael. *Doctor Who and the Taint*. London: BBC Books, 1999.
Cornea, Christine. "British Science Fiction Television in the Discursive Context of Second Wave Feminism." *Genders* 54 (Summer 2011): n.p.
Cornell, Paul. "Canonicity in Doctor Who," February 10, 2007. http://www.paulcornell.com/2007/02/canonicity-in-doctor-who/.
_____. *Happy Endings*. London: Virgin Books, 1996.
_____. *Human Nature*. London: Virgin Books, 1995.
_____. *Love and War*. London: Virgin Books, 1992.
_____. *No Future*. London: Virgin Books, 1994.
_____. *Timewyrm: Revelation*. London: Virgin Books, 1991.
Cornell, Paul, Martin Day, and Keith Topping. *The Discontinuity Guide*. Austin, TX: MonkeyBrain Books, 2004.
Cotton, Kiv. "Victorian Attitudes." *Doctor Who Magazine*, Number 128 (September 1987): 4.
Danahay, Martin A. Introduction. *The War of the Worlds*. By H. G. Wells. Ed. Martin A. Danahay, 9–29. Ontario: Broadview, 2003.
Darvill-Evans, Peter. *Deceit*. London: Virgin Books, 1993.
Davies, Russell T. *Damaged Goods*. London: Virgin Books, 1996.
Decker, Kevin S. *Who Is Who? The Philosophy of Doctor Who*. New York: I. B. Tauris, 2013.
"The Den of Geek Interview: Sophie Aldred," *Den of Geek*, Interview by Simon Brew, February 14, 2008.
Dicker, Rory, and Alison Piepmeier. "Introduction." *Catching a Wave: Reclaiming Feminism for the 21st Century*, edited by Rory Dicker and Alison Piepmeier, 3–28. Boston: Northeastern University Press, 2003.
Dicks, Terrance, and Malcolm Hulke. *The Making of Doctor Who*. London: Pan Books, 1972.
East, Michael. "Samuel Anderson Speaks on Doctor/Danny, Getting the Role." *Doctor Who Worldwide*, n.p.
Erikson, Erik H. *Dimensions of a New Identity*. New York: W. W. Norton, 1974.
_____. *Identity and the Life Cycle*, 2nd ed. New York: W. W. Norton, 1980.

_____. *Identity: Youth and Crisis*. New York: W. W. Norton, 1968.
_____. *The Life Cycle Completed: A Review*. New York: W. W. Norton, 1982.
Faludi, Susan. *Backlash: The Undeclared War Against American Women*. New York: Crown, 1991.
Feasey, Rebecca. *Masculinity and Popular Television*, Edinburgh: Edinburgh University Press, 2008.
Forde, Teresa. "'You Anorak': The *Doctor Who* Experience and Experiencing *Doctor Who*." In *Doctor Who: Fan Phenomena*, edited by Paul Booth, 62–71. Bristol: Intellect, 2013.
Franke, Alyssa. "The Bechdel Test and Doctor Who: So What's the Big Deal?" February 10, 2013. *Whovian Feminism*, n.p.
_____. "Clara in Control." January 31, 2014. *Whovian Feminism*, n.p.
_____. "Their Stories." February 1, 2014. *Whovian Feminism*, n.p.
Frankham-Allen, Andy. *Companions: Fifty Years of Doctor Who Assistants*. Cardiff: Candy Jar Books, 2013.
Frye, Susan. *Elizabeth I: The Competition for Representation*. Oxford: Oxford University Press, 1993.
Gannon, Charles E. *Rumors of War and Infernal Machines: Technomilitary Agenda-Setting in American and British Speculative Fiction*. Lanham, MD: Rowman & Littlefield, 2005.
Garland-Thomson, Rosemarie. "Integrating Disability, Transforming Feminist Theory." *NWSA Journal* 14.3 (2002): 1–32.
Garner, Ross P. "Patrick Troughton." *Science Fiction Film and Television* 7.2 (Summer 2014): 223–225.
Gatiss, Mark. *Nightshade*. London: Virgin Books, 1992.
_____. *St. Anthony's Fire*. London: Virgin Books, 1994.
Gay, Peter. *The Freud Reader*. New York: W. W. Norton & Co., 1995.
Geertz, Clifford. *The Interpretation of Cultures*. New York: Basic Books, 1973.
Ginn, Sherry. "Spoiled for Another Life: Sarah Jane Smith's Adventures with and Without Doctor Who." In *Doctor Who in Time and Space: Essays on Themes, Characters, History and Fandom, 1963–2012*, edited by Gillian I. Leitch, 242–252. Jefferson, NC: McFarland, 2013.
Golder, Dave. "Russell T. Davies on Jo Grant's Return in *The Sarah Jane Adventures*." *SFX* (September 17, 2010): n.p.
Hammond, Michael, and Lucy Mazdon. *The Contemporary Television Series*. Edinburgh: Edinburgh University Press, 2005.
Hardy, Sarah, and Rebecca Kukla. "A Paramount Narrative: Exploring Space on the Starship Enterprise." *The Journal of Aesthetics and Art Criticism* 57.2 (Spring 1999): 177–191.
Hills, Matt. "The Dispersible Television Text: Theorising Moments of the New *Doctor Who*." *Science Fiction Film and Television* 1.1 (Spring 2008): 25–44.
_____. *Fan Cultures*. London: Routledge, 2002.
_____. *New Dimensions of Doctor Who: Adventures in Space, Time and Television*. London: I. B. Tauris, 2013.
_____. *Triumph of a Time Lord: Regenerating Doctor Who in the Twenty-First Century*. London: I. B. Tauris, 2010.
Ho, Karen. "Five Memorable 'Rory' Deaths on 'Doctor Who.'" September 27, 2012. n.p.
"How Sexist Is Doctor Who?: Part One." *Simon's Incoherent Blog: Random Writings on TV, Film, and Politics*. June 24, 2014.

Howe, David J., Stephen James Walker, and Mark Stammers. *The Handbook: The Unofficial and Unauthorised Guide to the Production of Doctor Who.* Tolworth, Surrey, England: Telos Publishing, 2005.

Hughes, David Y. "The Garden in Wells's Early Science Fiction." In *H. G. Wells and Modern Science Fiction*, edited by Darko Suvin with Robert M. Philmus, 48–69. London: Associated University Press, 1977.

Hulke, Malcolm, and Terrance Dicks. *The Making of Doctor Who.* London: Pan Books, 1972.

"Interview: Daniel O'Mahony." *BBC: Doctor Who News*, January 1, 2004. Available at Internet Archive Wayback Machine.

Itzkoff, Dave. "Doctor Who's Companion." March 22, 2012. *The New York Times.* August 28, 2014.

James, P. D. *Talking about Detective Fiction.* Toronto: Vintage, 2011.

Jones, Matthew. *Bad Therapy.* London: Virgin Books, 1996.

Jowett, Lorna. "The Girls who Waited? Female Companions and Gender in *Doctor Who.*" *Critical Studies in Television: the International Journal of Television Studies* 9.1 (2014): 77–94.

Jung, Carl. *Collected Works of C. G. Jung* (Vol. 9, Part 1), 2nd ed. Princeton: Princeton University Press, 1968.

Kant, Immanuel. *Groundwork for the Metaphysics of Morals.* Translated by Allen W. Wood. Yale University Press, 2002.

Lacob, Jace. "The New Doctor Who." *The Daily Beast.* March 31, 2010.

Leach, Jim. *Doctor Who.* Detroit: Wayne State University Press, 2009.

Leonardi, Matilde, Jerome Bickenbach, Tevfik Bedirhan Ustun, Nenad Kostanjsek, and Somnath Chatterji. "The Definition of Disability: What's in a Name?" *The Lancet* 368, 9543 (2006): 1219–1221.

Lem, Stanislaw. "On the Structural Analysis of Science Fiction." *Science Fiction Studies* 1.1 (Spring 1973): 26–33.

"Letters." *Doctor Who Bulletin.* Number 32 (March 1986): 3–4.

Levinson, Daniel J. *The Seasons of a Woman's Life.* New York: Ballantine Books, 1996.

Lewis, Courtland, and Paula Smithka. "We've Been Abducted By the Doctor, and We Love It!" In *Doctor Who and Philosophy*, edited by Courtland Lewis and Paula Smithka, ix–xviii. Chicago: Open Court: 2011.

Lyons, Steve. *Head Games.* London: Virgin Books, 1995.

_____. *The Witch Hunters.* London: BBC Books, 1998.

Martin, William. "Tegan Voted Best 'Doctor Who' Companion Ever." *Cultbox*, July 9, 2013.

Marz, Ron (w), Steve Carr, Derec Aucoin, Darryl Banks (p), and Romeo Tanghal (i). "Forced Entry!" *Green Lantern* #54 (Aug. 1994). New York: DC Comics.

Matlin, Margaret W. *The Psychology of Women*, 3rd ed. Ft. Worth, TX: Harcourt Brace, 1996.

McAlpine, Fraser. "'Doctor Who' Cosplay: How to Dress Like Rory Williams." *Anglophenia*, July 10, 2012.

McMahon-Coleman, Kimberley. "'I was hoping it would pass you by': Dis/Ability and Difference in Teen Wolf." In *Remake Television: Reboot, Re-use, Recycle*, edited by Carlen Lavigne, 141–153. Lanham, MD: Lexington Books, 2014.

Meehan, Elizabeth. "British Feminism from the 1960s to the 1980s." In *British Feminism in the Twentieth Century,* edited by Harold L. Smith, 189–204. Aldershot: Elgar, 1990.

Mendes, Kaitlynn. "'The Lady Is a Closet Feminist!' Discourses of Backlash and Postfeminism in British and American Newspapers." *International Journal of Cultural Studies* 14:6 (2011): 549–565.
Miles, Lawrence. *Interference Book One*. London: BBC Books, 1999.
_____. *Interference Book Two*. London: BBC Books, 1999.
Miles, Lawrence, and Tat Wood. *About Time: The Unauthorized Guide to* Doctor Who. *1975–1979. Seasons 12 to 17*. Des Moines, IA: Mad Norwegian Press, 2004.
Miller, Christina L. "The Monstrous and the Divine in *Doctor Who*: The Role of Christian Imagery in Russell T. Davies's *Doctor Who* Revival." In *Time and Relative Dimensions in Faith: Religion and Doctor Who*, edited by Andrew Crome and James McGrath, 106–117. London: Darton, Longman & Todd, 2013.
Moore, Rebecca. "University Study on Sexism in BBC's Doctor Who (Infographic)." 29 May 2014. *The Life and Times of an Exceptionally Tall Mormon*.
Mortimore, Jim, and Andy Lane. *Lucifer Rising*. London: Virgin Books, 1993.
Myles, L. M., and Liz Barr, eds. *Companion Piece: Women Celebrate the Humans, Aliens and Tin Dogs of* DOCTOR WHO. Des Moines, IA: Mad Norwegian Press, 2015.
Nathan-Turner, John. *Doctor Who: The Companions*. New York: Random House, 1986.
Nguyen, Hanh. "*Doctor Who* Boss and Karen Gillan on River Song, How Her Parents Met and Hitler." *TV Guide* (August 24, 2011): n.p.
O'Mahony, Daniel. *The Man in the Velvet Mask*. London: Virgin Books, 1996.
Orman, Kate. *Set Piece*. London: Virgin Books, 1995.
Ortner, Sherry B. *Making Gender: The Politics and Erotics of Culture*. Boston: Beacon Press, 1996.
Pantozzi, Jill. "Steven Moffat Tweets Against Accusations of Misogyny." November 3, 2011. *The Mary Sue*, n.p.
Parkin, Lance. *Doctor Who: Trading Futures*. London: BBC Books, 2002.
_____. *The Dying Days*. London: Virgin Books, 1997.
_____. *Just War*. London: Virgin Books, 1996.
_____. *Time, Unincorporated 1: The Doctor Who Fanzine Archives*. Des Moines, IA: Mad Norwegian Press, 2009.
Peel, John. *Legacy of the Daleks*. London: BBC Books, 1998.
Peters, Christine. "Gender, Sacrament and Ritual: The Making and Meaning of Marriage in Late Medieval and Early Modern England." *Past and Present* 169 (2000): 63–96.
Platt, Marc. *Lungbarrow*. London: Virgin Books, 1997.
Pless, Deborah. "The Decline and Fall of the British Empire, Sponsored by TARDIS." In *Doctor Who and Philosophy: Bigger on the Inside*, edited by Courtland Lewis and Paula Smithka, 351–359. Chicago: Open Court, 2010.
Porter, Lynnette. *Tarnished Heroes, Charming Villains, and Modern Monsters: Science Fiction in Shades of Gray on 21st Century Television*. Jefferson, NC: McFarland, 2010.
Roberts, Andrew. "Bonnie Langford Doubts." *Doctor Who Bulletin*, Number 31 (February 1986): 3–5.
Roberts, Gareth. *The Highest Science*. London: Virgin Books, 1993.
_____. *Tragedy Day*. London: Virgin Books, 1994.
_____. *Zamper*. London: Virgin Books, 1995.
St. John, Graham. "Aliens Are Us: Cosmic Liminality, Remixticism, and Alienation in Psytrance." *Journal of Religion and Popular Culture* 25.2 (Summer 2013): 186–204.

Sandifer, Philip. "Civilizations of Pure Thought (Planet of Evil)." October 17, 2011.
_____. *Tardis Eruditorum Volume 1: William Hartnell*. CreateSpace Independent Publishing Platform, 2011.
Sartre, Jean Paul. *Being and Nothingness*. Translated by Hazel E. Barnes. New York: Washington Square Press, 1943.
Scoones, Paul. "Paul Cornell Interview." *The New Zealand Doctor Who Fan Club. TSV 48*, August 1996.
Showalter, Elaine. "Feminist Criticism in the Wilderness." In *The New Feminist Criticism: Essays on Women, Literature, and Theory*, edited by Elaine Showalter, 243–270. New York: Pantheon, 1985.
Sladen, Elisabeth. *Elisabeth Sladen: The Autobiography*. London: Aurum Press, 2011.
Sleight, Graham. *The Doctor's Monsters: Meanings of the Monstrous in Doctor Who*. London: I. B. Taurus, 2012.
Smith, Donna Marie. "Why the Doctor and Rose Tyler Kant Be Together." In *Doctor Who and Philosophy*, edited by Courtland Lewis and Paula Smithka, 167–176. Chicago: Open Court, 2011.
Smith, Paula. "A Trekkie's Tale." Reprinted in "Mary Sue: A Short Compendium," in *Archives V*, edited by Johanna Cantor, 34. New York: Yeoman Press.
Staley, Lynn. *The Island Garden: England's Language of Nation from Gildas to Marvel*. Notre Dame: University of Notre Dame Press, 2012.
Steiger, Kay. "No Clean Slate: Unshakeable Race and Gender Politics in *The Walking Dead*." In *Triumph of The Walking Dead*, edited by James Lowder, 100–114. Dallas: BenBella Books, 2011.
Stevens, James, and David Bishop. *Who Killed Kennedy: The Shocking Secret Linking a Time Lord and a President*. London: Virgin Books, 1996.
Telotte, J. P. *Science Fiction TV*. New York: Routledge, 2014.
"Time Lad Scores with Sex and Daleks." *The Scotsman*. June 6, 2004, n.p.
Tong, Rosemarie. *Feminist Thought: A More Comprehensive Introduction*, 3rd ed. Boulder, CO: Westview Press, 2008.
Tribe, Steve. *Doctor Who Companions and Allies*. London: BBC Books, 2009.
Tulloch, John, and Manuel Alvarado. *Doctor Who: The Unfolding Text*. New York: St. Martin's Press, 1983.
Tulloch, John, and Henry Jenkins. *Science Fiction Audiences: Watching Doctor Who and Star Trek*. London: Routledge, 1995.
Turner, Joan Frances. "Where in Eternity ... is Josephine Grant Jones? In *Companion Piece: Women Celebrate the Humans, Aliens and Tin Dogs of DOCTOR WHO*, edited by L. M. Myles, and Liz Barr. Des Moines, IA: Mad Norwegian Press, 2015.
Turner, Victor. "The Center out There: Pilgrim's Goal." *History of Religions* 12.3 (Feb. 1973): 191–230.
Ulaby, Neda. "'The Bechdel Rule,' Defining Pop-Culture Character." 2 September 2008. *National Public Radio*. 25 September 2014.
Utichi, Joe. "BBC's 'Doctor Who' Showrunner Promises 'A Blockbuster Every Single Week.'" *The Deadline*, August 25, 2012.
van Gennep, Arnold. *Rites of Passage*. Translated by Monika B. Vizedom and Gabrielle L. Caffee. London: Psychology Press, 1960.
"Virgin Worlds Writer's Guidelines: The New Adventures," April 12, 2001.
"Vote for Your Favourite Companion." Candy Jar Books: Online Poll Results (ongoing).
Wadsworth, Barry J. *Piaget's Theory of Cognitive and Affective Development: Foundations of Constructivism* 5th ed. Needham Heights, MA: Allyn & Bacon, 2003.

Walter, Nick. "Virgin Territory." *Doctor Who Magazine*, Number 197 (March 17, 1993): 16–18.
Washburn, Michael. *Transpersonal Psychology in Psychoanalytic Perspective*. Albany: State University of New York Press, 1994.
Webber, C. E. "Science Fiction." Report to Donald Wilson, Head of Serial Drama, BBC. March 29, 1963. BBC Archives.
Wells, H. G. *The War of the Worlds*, edited by Martin A. Danahay. Ontario: Broadview, 2003.
Wilkes, Neil. "I'm 903 Years Old." *Digital Spy*. 21 December 2007.
Williams, Rebecca R. "Desiring the Doctor: Identity, Gender and Genre in Online Fandom." In *British Science Fiction Film and Television: Critical Essays,* edited by Tobias Hochscherf, James Leggott, Donald E. Palumbo, and C. W. Sullivan, 167–177. Jefferson, NC: McFarland, 2012.
Wolfe, Gary K. "Coming to Terms." In *Speculations on Speculation: Theories of Science Fiction,* edited by James Gunn and Matthew Candelaria, 13–22. Lanham, MD: Scarecrow Press, 2005.
Women in Refrigerators. N.p. n.d. 31 Dec. 2014.
Wood, Tat. *About Time: The Unauthorized Guide to* Doctor Who. *Expanded Second Edition. 1970–1974. Seasons 7 to 11.* Des Moines, IA: Mad Norwegian Press, 2009.

About the Contributors

Pamela **Achenbach** has published several short stories and essays as well as a novel. She is working on a dissertation on *Doctor Who* examining fandom in science fiction film. She contributed to another anthology on *Doctor Who* and has served as a judge for the Bi Writer's Association's Bisexual Book Awards. In addition to writing, she teaches literature and writing classes at a local community college.

Teresa **Forde** is a senior lecturer in film and media at the University of Derby. She is program leader for film and television studies and the MA humanities. Her research interests include film, television, science fiction, soundtrack, memory, time travel, and the posthuman. She is working on an article on time travel and a book on the body and technology on screen as well as a project on a local surrealist artist from Derby.

David Boarder **Giles** is a lecturer in interdisciplinary arts and sciences at the University of Washington, Bothell. He writes and teaches about food, waste, homelessness, globalization, popular culture, and the cultural politics of "global" cities. He has done extensive anthropological fieldwork in Seattle and other cities in the United States and Australasia with dumpster divers, grassroots activists, and homeless persons.

Sherry **Ginn** has published numerous research articles in the fields of neuroscience and psychology, but also writes about the intersection of popular culture with those fields. She is the author or editor of books on women in science fiction television, sex in science fiction, and *Farscape* and *Fringe*. She has written a book on the television series of Joss Whedon and co-edited a collection of essays on Whedon's *Dollhouse*. Forthcoming are books on time travel in SF television (co-edited with Gillian I. Leitch) and on Marvel's Black Widow.

Aaron John **Gulyas** teaches history at Mott Community College in Flint, Michigan. His writing and research has addressed such topics as television science fiction, paranormal and extraterrestrial belief, and the pedagogical uses of popular culture in the history classroom. Forthcoming are books on paranormal-themed television in the 1990s and the historical development of conspiracy theory in the twentieth century.

Craig Owen **Jones** is a cultural historian and musicologist at Prifysgol Bangor University, Wales. His areas of interest include science fiction, memory, fandom, and the history of popular music, particularly popular music in the Celtic languages. His articles have appeared in journals such as *Science Fiction Film and Television*, *Music and Politics*, and *Popular Music History*. He is editor, with Dr. Gwawr Ifan, of the journal *Hanes Cerddoriaeth Cymru/Welsh Music History*.

Gillian I. **Leitch** earned a Ph.D. in Canadian history, with post-doctoral work at the University of Edinburgh. She is a senior researcher/historian at CDCI Research in Ottawa. Along with Sherry Ginn, she serves as chair of the Science Fiction and Fantasy Area of the Popular Culture Association. She is the editor of the essay collection *Doctor Who in Time and Space* (McFarland, 2013). A collection about time travel television, co-edited with Sherry Ginn, is forthcoming.

Kimberley **McMahon-Coleman** teaches in learning development at the University of Wollongong. Her work has been published in *A History of Evil in Popular Culture* (2014), *Open Graves, Open Minds: Representations of Vampires and the Undead from the Enlightenment to the Present* (2013), and *Fanpires: Audience Consumption of the Modern Vampire* (2011). With Roslyn Weaver, she has written *Werewolves and Other Shapeshifters in Popular Culture* (McFarland, 2012).

Tanja **Nathanael** is pursuing a doctorate in English literature at the University of Southern Mississippi. Her research interests include nineteenth-century British literature, children's literature, world literature, science fiction and fantasy, and geocriticism. Her book reviews have been published in *Bookbird: A Journal of International Children's Literature*.

Amy **Peloff** is the assistant director of the Comparative History of Ideas Program and an affiliate assistant professor of gender, women, and sexuality studies at the University of Washington. Her work examines the role that popular culture has played in disseminating feminist ideas beyond organizations and activists that identify as feminist. She continually studies the ways in which ideas about identities are created, presented, and shared through media and popular culture.

Tom Powers is a college writing instructor. Along with Marc Schuster, he co-authored *The Greatest Show in the Galaxy: The Discerning Fan's Guide to Doctor Who* (McFarland, 2007). His writing has also appeared in *Illuminating Torchwood: Essays on Narrative, Character and Sexuality in the BBC Series* (edited by Andrew Ireland; McFarland, 2010) and *Back Issue*.

Index

Aaronovitch, Ben 138
Adric 14, 15, 21, 24, 64, 83, 92, 116, 141
Aldred, Sophie 64; *see also* McShane, "Ace" Dorothy Gale
authority 85
Autons 97

Back to the Future 29, 93
Baker, Colin 14, 24, 63, 141
Baker, Tom 38, 58, 85, 92
Barrowman, John 13; *see also* Harkness, Capt. Jack
Bechdel (-Wallace) Test 40, 47, 57
Benton, Sgt. John 10
Bishop, David 147
Britain 81, 86, 87
Brooke, Adelaide 144
Brown, Perpugilliam "Peri" 17, 115
Buffy the Vampire Slayer 56
Bush, Melanie 21, 24, 142, 143; *see also* Langford, Bonnie

Canon Sue character 111
canonicity 138
Capaldi, Peter 12, 14, 58, 100
Cartmel, Andrew 138, 139
Chaplet, Dorothea 'Dodo' 147
character development 91, 146
Chesterton, Ian 13, 15, 28, 99, 135; *see also* Russell, William
Cognitive Development Theory 70
Coleman, Jenna-Louise 48, 49, 58; *see also* Oswald, Clara Oswin
companions: antagonism towards 92, 98–99; as assistants 3, 58, 72, 139; as caregiver 3, 33, 91, 96, 97, 103; character type 137; characterization 144, 146; choosing 8, 123, 124, 132; conflict between 141; as everyday people 9, 83; everyday life 99, 145, 146; as family 19, 29, 85, 139; as follower 14; as gateway characters 2, 10; gaze 128; as geek 94, 104; gender 4, 13–14, 39, 91, 92, 106, 116, 135; humans 12, 38, 85, 94, 140; as pawns 142; perfect 126; price for travelling with the Doctor 50, 69; qualities of 125; role of 135, 136, 144, 145; romance 4, 17–19, 45, 47, 72, 91, 99, 100, 119, 124, 126, 131, 133; sacrifice 112, 115, 116, 120, 125, 131, 132; as sceptic 98; screamer 29, 61, 73, 135; teasing 93; tension between 98, 99; testing 100; ultimate 114; young 13, 29
Cornell, Paul 138, 139, 140
creative decision 64
creative process 57
The Curse of Fatal Death 138
Cwej, Chris 141, 142
Cybermen 42

Daleks 42, 46, 48
damsel in distress 47, 49, 53, 58, 79, 109
danger 83, 91
Dark Sam 145
Darvill, Arthur 94, 102; *see also* Williams, Rory
Davies, Russell T. 20, 34, 37, 56–57, 111, 139, 142
Davison, Peter 13, 20, 63, 65, 141
De Souza, Lady Christina 144
Dicks, Terrance 57, 61
Dimensions in Time 138
disability 41–50
disempowerment 115, 116
Doctor: Doctor-Donna metacrisis 87, 99, 127; as male 38; as manipulative 142
Doctor Who: changes over time 54
Doctor Who (audio): Doll of Death 73
Doctor Who (episodes): Angels Take Manhattan 100, 116, 118; Ark in Space 62; The Asylum of the Daleks 42, 46;

Index

Bad Wolf 17, 83, 84, 138; Battlefield 138; The Bells of St. John 49; The Big Bang 109, 120; Blink 56; Boom Town 142; Brain of Morbius 62, 120; Castrovalva 32; Claws of Axos 73; Cold Blood 96; Colony in Space 73, 74; The Curse of Fenric 15, 137; The Curse of Peladon 18; The Daemons 73; Dalek Invasion of Earth 146; Dalek Master Plan 11, 115; Day of the Doctor 13, 84; Day of the Moon 120; The Deadly Assassin 9; Deep Breath 54, 132; Dinosaurs on a Spaceship 35; The Doctor's Wife 11, 38, 42, 43; Doomsday 84; Earthshock 63, 116; The Eleventh Hour 17, 91, 92, 93; The End of the World 80, 86; The Face of Evil 16, 85; The Five Doctors 65, 71, 136; Forest of the Dead 108, 111, 116; Ghost Light 137, 138; The Girl in the Fireplace 128, 132; The Girl Who Waited 45, 103; The Green Death 18, 60, 76; Human Nature/Family of Blood 138; The Hungry Earth 95; Into the Dalek 66; The Invisible Enemy 16; Journey's End 9, 87, 99, 132, 142; The Keeper of Traken 92; The Krotons 15; Let's Kill Hitler 44, 97, 112, 114, 117, 120; Logopolis 31, 32, 63; The Massacre of St. Bartholomew's Eve 147; Mind of Evil 73, 74; Monster of Peladon 62; The Name of the Doctor 118, 119; The Next Doctor 10; The Pandorica Opens 97, 109; The Parting of the Ways 16, 84, 101, 131; The Pirate Planet 86; Planet of Fire 17; Planet of the Dead 144; Pond Life 99; Pyramid of Mars 62; Rebel Flesh/The Almost People 96; Remembrance of the Daleks 138; The Rescue 29; Resurrection of the Daleks 64, 65; Ribos Operation 16; Rose 33, 80; The Satan Pit 83; School Reunion 69, 71, 72; The Sensorites 146; Silence in the Library 19, 106, 111; Smith and Jones 30; The Snowmen 41, 49; The Sontaren Experiment 58; Stolen Earth 9, 142; Survival 137; Terror of the Autons 52, 72; The Time of Angels/Flesh and Stone 108; Time Warrior 61, 71; Timeflight 31, 64; Trial of a Time Lord 115; Twin Dilemma 63; An Unearthly Child 28, 30, 33, 43; The Vampires of Venice 95; Vincent and the Doctor 96; Voyage of the Damned 86; War Games 13; War Machines 147; Water of Mars 144; The Wedding of River Song 19, 100, 110, 114, 117

Doctor Who (novels): *All the President's Men* 147; *Deceit* 141; *Dying Days* 138; *Escape Velocity* 145; *Highest Science* 138; *Interference* 145; *Just War* 142; *Legacy of the Daleks* 146; *Love and War* 139, 141; *Lucifer Rising* 138; *Lungbarrow* 138; *The Man in the Velvet Mask* 147, 148; *Revolution Man* 145; *Set Piece* 144; *The Taint* 145; *Trading Futures* 146; *Transit* 143; *Tymeworm* 139; *Unnatural History* 145; *Who Killed Kennedy* 147, 148; *The Witch Hunters* 146

Doctor Who (radio): *The Ghosts of N-Space* 138; *Paradise of Death* 138
Doctor Who Experience 28
Doctor Who Magazine 137, 143
Doctor Who: The Movie 28, 138, 145
Duvall, Ruby 144

Eccleston, Christopher 102, 131
Eighth Doctor Adventures 137, 138, 146
emotional consequences 83
England 87; nationhood 79; under threat 85

fan collective memory 30
fantasy 97
female stereotype 39
feminine archetype 120
feminism 56, 61, 62, 77, 120
Fielding, Janet 13, 21, 31, 53, 55, 63, 64, 65, 66; see also Jovanka, Tegan
Flight of the Navigator 29
Flint, Jenny 102
Ford, Carole Ann 13, 29; see also Foreman, Susan
Foreman, Susan 13, 19, 29, 146; see also Ford, Carole Ann
Forrester, Roz 141, 142

Gaiman, Neil 39, 43
Gascoigne, George 80
Gatiss, Mark 139
gender 37–50, 80, 85, 108; roles 53, 56, 61, 65, 66, 95, 101; stereotypes 48, 49, 94
Gillan, Karen 104; see also Pond, Amy
Grant, Jo 16, 17, 60, 69–78, 99, 136, 137; see also Manning, Katy
The Great War in England in 1897 82
The Great War of 189- 82
Grimwade, Peter 65

Harkness, Capt. Jack 13, 14, 16, 17, 24, 101, 111; see also Barrowman, John
Hartnell, William 12, 13, 19
Heriot, Zoe 15, 19
heroism 80, 86, 92, 94, 101, 112, 116
Hill, Jacqueline 13; see also Wright, Barbara

Holloway, Dr. Grace 18, 145
Holmes, Sherlock 2
How John Bull Lost London 82
human 48, 96; body 44, 79, 82
hybridity 41, 87

Idris 38, 43
infantalization 43
insanity 48
internal monologue 136, 140
invasion anxiety 79–80
invasion narrative 81, 82, 83

John, Caroline 55, 60; see also Shaw, Dr. Liz
Jones, Dr. Martha 18, 30, 101, 124, 131
Jones, Matt 139
Jones, Samantha 145
Jovanka, Tegan 13, 14, 16, 31, 53, 63, 64, 66, 137; see also Fielding, Janet

K-9 15, 24
K-9 and Company 71, 136
Kamelion 24, 136
Kapoor, Anji 145
Katarina 83, 115
Kingdom, Sara 11, 83, 115; see also Marsh, Jean
Kingston, Alex 13, 112; see also Song, River
Knights of the Round Table 80
Kreiner, Fritz 145

Lambert, Verity 54, 57
Langford, Bonnie 143; see also Bush, Melanie
language 107, 108
Lee, Chang 28, 33
Leela 15, 16, 120
Lethbridge-Stewart, Brigadier Alistair Gordon 10, 13, 15, 53, 92
Letts, Barry 57, 60, 61
Life-Course Development Theory 70, 74
liminal experience 32, 33, 34
London 82, 83
Lyons, Steve 142, 143, 146

MacMillan, Trix 137
madness 42
Manning, Katy 16, 70, 73; see also Grant, Jo
marriage 44, 45, 46, 47, 74, 75, 93, 109, 110, 114
Marsh, Jean 11; see also Kingdom, Sara
Marter, Ian 21; see also Sullivan, Dr. Harry
Mary Sue character 111
masculinity 94

maternal 74, 75
The Matrix 29
McCoy, Sylvester 24, 136, 139, 142
McCrimmon, Jamie 24, 92
McFly, Marty 93–94
McGann, Paul 18, 138, 145
McShane, "Ace" Dorothy Gale 15, 19, 33, 63, 124, 136, 137, 139, 142, 143, 144; see also Aldred, Sophie
merchandise 111
misogyny 39, 40, 45, 47, 50, 57
Missing Adventures 137
Mitchell, Adam 14, 20
Moffatt, Steven 14, 21, 26, 35, 37, 39, 56–57, 69, 98, 106, 110, 111, 116, 117, 121
the moment 84
motherhood 72, 108
multi-camera format 59

Nathan-Turner, John 10, 12, 14, 15, 16, 17, 63, 64, 65, 138, 143
neophytism 28
New Adventures 137, 138, 139, 141, 144, 146
Newman, Sydney 28, 54
Noble, Donna 13, 20, 21, 40, 69, 133; see also Tate, Catherine
nurse stereotype 103
Nyssa of Traken 14, 64; see also Sutton, Sarah

O'Mahony, Daniel 147
Oswald, Clara Oswin 21, 34, 38, 46, 48, 49, 66, 97, 99, 119; see also Coleman, Jenna-Louise
other 44, 127

Pallister, Vicki 19, 29
Parkin, Lance 142, 146
Past Doctor Adventures 137, 146
Paternoster Gang 102–103
patriarchy 106
Pertwee, Jon 13, 18, 31, 37, 43, 58, 59, 61
Peth, Astrid 18, 123–134
Pink, Danny 99
Platt, Marc 138
Pompadour, Madame de (Reinette) 123–134
Pond, Amy 17, 20, 38, 41, 45, 91, 93, 95, 96, 103, 116; see also Gillan, Karen
poor writing 63
power 81, 86, 107, 110, 112, 115, 117, 120
pregnancy 46, 47
The Princely Pleasures 80
Psychological Development Theory 70–71
Psychosexual Development Theory 70

170   Index

Queen Elizabeth I 79, 80, 84

racial barrier 112
rapid speech 38, 49
redemption 112
regeneration 110, 112, 121
Roberts, Gareth 139
Romana 11, 12, 14, 16, 136
romance 96
Russell, William 13; see also Chesterton, Ian

The Sarah Jane Adventures 70, 77, 136; Death of the Doctor 70
sexism 53, 61, 62, 64
Shaw, Dr. Liz 15, 16, 31, 52, 55, 73, 135; see also John, Caroline
Sladen, Elisabeth 53, 55, 58, 66, 69; see also Smith, Sarah Jane
Smith, Matt 13, 43, 84, 108, 113, 119, 120
Smith, Mickey 14, 92
Smith, Sarah Jane 14, 20, 21, 31, 53, 60, 61, 69, 71–78, 136, 137; see also Sladen, Elisabeth
Song, Dr. River 13, 40, 46, 69, 97–98, 106–121; agency of 106; see also Kingston, Alex
sonic screwdriver 34, 58
spin-off 111
Star Trek: First Contact 30
Stargate 29
Stevens, James 147
Stewart, Kate 84
Strax 102–103
Subaltern Practice Theory 54–55,
Sullivan, Dr. Harry 13, 15; see also Marter, Ian
Summerfield, Bernice 137, 139, 142
Sutton, Sarah 21, 64; see also Nyssa of Traken

TARDIS 27, 31, 38, 42, 44, 49, 86, 91, 108, 119, 127; entry as transformation 34, 94; as female 108, 110; matrix 43; as portal 33
Tate, Catherine 13; see also Noble, Donna
Tennant, David 13, 18, 43, 71, 84, 92, 102, 113, 126, 130, 133
Time War 131
Torchwood 17, 111
transitional object 103–104,
Troughton, Patrick 12, 19, 92
Tudor Rose 78, 84
Turlough, Vislor 136, 141
Tyler, Jackie 10
Tyler, Rose 18, 20, 24, 33, 34, 40, 70, 79–88, 99, 101, 124, 125–126, 127, 128–129, 131

UNIT 13, 60, 61, 72, 76, 77, 84, 144, 147

Vastra, Madame 102
viewer's gaze 27, 30
violation 81, 82

War Doctor 84
War of the Worlds 82, 83
Whedon, Joss 56–57
wild zone 113, 118
wilderness years 139
Williams, Rory 14, 41, 46, 47, 91–104, 116; deaths 100–102; see also Darvill, Arthur
women in refrigerators 115
World War II 86
Wright, Barbara 13, 28, 52, 99, 135

Yates, Capt. Mike 11, 18, 74, 99